Women in the face of change

Much has been written in the past few years about political and economic changes in the Soviet Union, Eastern Europe and China. What is seldom mentioned in these accounts, however, is how change affects the millions of women who live in these societies. This book begins the process of redressing the imbalance by presenting original and up-to-date analyses of many of the de-socialising societies.

Three crucial sites for examination are identified. The first is a gendered analysis of the programmes of economic and political restructuring and the interaction between social policy and change. The second is the way in which images of women have been constructed, and the book examines whether these, and women's self-images, are changing as the paternalistic state is rolled back. The third area to be considered is women's experience of reform and whether this experience is developing into a 'women's consciousness'.

The contributors to *Women in the Face of Change* have considerable research experience in their chosen areas and their analyses are a timely contribution to the debate on the extraordinary changes that are taking place in what used to be called the 'communist bloc'. They reveal the separate and critical 'women's voice' which is re-emerging in these societies.

Shirin Rai is Lecturer in the Department of Politics, University of Warwick. **Hilary Pilkington** is Lecturer in the Centre for Russian and Eastern European Studies at the University of Birmingham. **Annie Phizacklea** is Lecturer in Sociology at the University of Warwick.

D1331744

Women in the face of change

The Soviet Union, Eastern Europe and China

Edited by Shirin Rai, Hilary Pilkington
and Annie Phizacklea

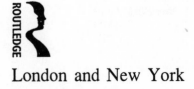

London and New York

First published in 1992
by Routledge
11 New Fetter Lane, London EC4P 4EE

Simultaneously published in the USA and Canada by Routledge
a division of Routledge, Chapman and Hall Inc.
29 West 35th Street, New York, NY 10001

Typeset in Times from the authors' wordprocessing disks by
NWL Editorial Services, Langport, Somerset

Printed in Great Britain by
Biddles Ltd, Guildford and King's Lynn

British Library Cataloguing in Publication Data
A catalogue record for this book is available from the British
Library.

Library of Congress Cataloging in Publication Data
Women in the face of change: The Soviet Union, Eastern
   Europe, and China
   edited by Shirin Rai, Hilary Pilkington and Annie Phizacklea.
   p. cm.
   Includes bibliographical references and index.
   1. Women – Communist countries – Social conditions.
   2. Women – Communist countries – Economic conditions.
   3. Communist countries – Politics and government.
   I. Rai, Shirin   II. Pilkington, Hilary.   III. Phizacklea, Annie.
   HQ1870.8.W66   1992   91–44517
   305.42.′09171′7 – dc20   CIP

ISBN 0–415–07540–8
       0–415–07541–6 (pbk)

Contents

Part III Towards a woman's consciousness?

Tables

Contributors

Chris Corrin lives in Glasgow and teaches politics. Since 1984 she has researched into women's situation in Hungarian society, and has been a regular visitor in Hungary and neighbouring countries for the last five years. Her current work includes a joint project on women's training needs in Hungary, and workshops in East-Central Europe on women's health and reproductive rights. Her published works include *Magyar Women: Hungarian Women's Experience of Change from the 1940s to the 1990s* (Macmillan 1992); and an edited collection *Women's Experience of Change in the Soviet Union and Eastern Europe* (Scarlet Press 1992), as well as numerous articles on women's politics.

Delia Davin is a senior lecturer in East Asian Studies at Leeds University. Her chief research interests are women, the family and population in Chinese society. She is the author of numerous articles, and of *Woman-work: Woman and the Party in Revolutionary China* (Oxford University Press 1976). She co-edited *China's One-child Family Policy* (Macmillan 1985), and with W.J.F. Jenner co-edited and translated Zhang Xinxin and Sang Ye's book, *Chinese Lives: an Oral History of Contemporary China* (Penguin 1989).

Harriet Evans is a senior lecturer and head of the Chinese Section at the Polytechnic of Central London. Her doctoral research considered the construction of female sexuality and gender in the People's Republic of China. She has written numerous articles covering areas of social history, marriage and the family.

Valentina Konstantinova is a senior research fellow at the Centre of Gender Studies in Moscow. She completed a doctoral dissertation on neo-feminism in Britain before turning her attention to the feminist movement in the Soviet Union. Her current research interests include women's political movements; the crisis of formal, and emergence of informal, movements; and women's participation in new political parties and organisations. She organised the first all-union independent women's forum in the town of Dubna in March 1991.

Marina Malysheva is a research fellow at the Institute of Sociology in Moscow. Her doctoral dissertation considered the problems of women's labour in the Soviet Union based on a comparative analysis of a number of countries. Her published work mainly concerns Soviet ideology on the family and the history of women's education in Russia and the Soviet Union. Her current research interest involves the use of social genealogies for understanding the position of women in Soviet social structure.

Annie Phizacklea is a lecturer in sociology at the University of Warwick. Her main research interest is in women's employment with particular reference to minority women. A long-term teaching interest in the Soviet Union and the dearth of material on women in the face of changes in that country led her to join forces with Shirin Rai and Hilary Pilkington in editing this book.

Hilary Pilkington is a lecturer in Soviet politics and society at the Centre for Russian and East European Studies, University of Birmingham. Her prime area of concern is changing social and cultural identities (gender, generation, class and ethnicity) in de-socialising countries. She is currently engaged in research on youth culture in contemporary Russia.

Frances Pine received her PhD in Social Anthropology from the University of London. She has conducted extensive research in the Polish Highlands and is currently working on the consequences of the austerity programme in Poland on rural women's work and lives. She is currently a Research Associate in the Anthropology Department at Cambridge University and at Corpus Christi College.

Shirin Rai is a lecturer in politics at the University of Warwick. She has researched into areas of university politics, higher education, and education and employment of women in contemporary China. She is particularly interested in the impact of the post-Mao reforms on state-civil society relations, especially as they effect the construction of the roles women play in society. She is the author of *Resistance and Reaction: University Politics in Post-Mao China* (Harvester-Wheatsheaf and St. Martin's Press 1991).

Natalia Rimashevskaia is Director of the Institute of Socioeconomic Problems of the Population in Moscow. She is a specialist in population studies, economic welfare and social demography. She has numerous academic publications to her name, including 12 monographs. She was the initiator of the first Moscow Centre for Gender Studies and headed the committee which drew up the draft State Programme for the Improvement of the Position of Women, the Family and the Protection of Mother and Child.

Rosamund Shreeves developed her interest in gender issues whilst living and studying in the Russian city of Voronezh. She went on to complete a postgraduate dissertation on women's participation in *perestroika* and has had articles published on this theme in Radio Liberty's Report on the Soviet Union. She is currently working as a translator with the Council of Europe in Strasbourg and retains a strong interest in the cultural construction of gender roles.

Zhang Junzuo is a staff member of the Commission of Integrated Survey of Natural Resources in the People's Republic of China at the Chinese Academy of Sciences. She has researched and written in the area of agriculture and rural development in contemporary China, especially on sustainable agriculture and rural industrialisation.

Introduction

Annie Phizacklea, Hilary Pilkington and Shirin Rai

The years 1989 and 1990 will probably be best remembered for the speed and breadth of political and economic change which swept through a large tranche of what Cold War rhetoric referred to as 'the Communist bloc'. With the disintegration of this 'bloc' there has been no shortage of western advice on how to 'democratise' economy and polity in these societies. Nevertheless little thought has been given to what political and economic change means for the millions of women in these societies who have toiled for decades alongside men in the factories and fields, as well as performing their 'womanly mission' in the home.

Some may feel it is still premature to pose questions about the impact of these changes for women in what we may tentatively call 'de-socialising'[1] societies. We think not, because we pose these questions as a contribution on the one hand to combating inertia and ethnocentrism in western feminism, and on the other to the separate and critical women's voice re-emerging in the Soviet Union, Eastern Europe and China. We retain the name 'Soviet Union' as the political and economic changes that we refer to in this volume were instituted by the Soviet state before its disintegration. That disintegration, we argue, does not alter the social and cultural relations which underpin gender relations.

It is our premise that a key component of the state-initiated project of economic and political restructuring is the enhancement of the role of the individual in society. The extent to which the initiative has been passed from the state to the individual has of course not been uniform. In China, the events of Tiananmen Square in June 1989 demonstrated the extent to which the state attempted to delimit increased individual activity to the economic sphere. In contrast, events in Eastern Europe later in 1989 emphasised the incapacity of the state to contain the role of the individual. In this collection we attempt to examine the extent to which the state concept of the re-structured individual is gender transparent. What we mean by this is the extent to which the state recognises that men and women currently occupy different positions in economic, political and social relations, whether this is reflected in the policies of restructuring and how they impact on women as compared to men.

Let us suppose for a moment that we are waiting in a bus queue in Moscow and that we strike up a conversation with the woman beside us. What, we ask her, does she think *Time* magazine's 'Man of the Decade', Mikhail Gorbachev has done for her? She will probably recount a grim tale of how she is now expected to do the work of five people for the same pay in the face of meteoric price rises for nearly non-existent food-stuffs for which she will queue for many hours. The same woman lives in a society which has witnessed the mass mobilisation of women as workers and as reproducers of the next generation of workers. But in a situation where her dual role as producer and reproducer has become increasingly onerous we should not be surprised if she regards the male leadership's current advice 'to return to the home' as a 'progressive' move.

In the chapters which follow we have identified three crucial sites for an examination of the position of women in the face of change in the Soviet Union, Eastern Europe and China. First, we attempt a gendered analysis of the programmes of economic and political restructuring and the interaction between social policy and change. Second, we consider the ways in which images of women have been constructed, self-images of women themselves, and whether either or both of these are changing as the paternalistic state is rolled back. Finally, we consider how women are experiencing these reforms, and how this might be developing into a 'women's conciousness'.

In order to understand better the dynamics of the current relation-ship between the state, the reform programme and the experience of women we need to consider the historical construction of the 'woman question' in what were generally referred to as state socialist societies. This will highlight divergent and common ground with western feminist views on the position of women which have come to dominate (though no longer without opposition) global debates.

THE CONSTRUCTION OF THE 'WOMAN QUESTION'

A number of different feminist analyses have emerged within western capitalist societies. All of these analyses share the view that women are systematically disadvantaged, but they vary in their explanations as to why this is so and the best means of overcoming these disadvantages. Here we will endeavour to define, briefly, three of these: the liberal, radical and socialist variants of feminist analyses. According to liberal feminism the establishment and practical enactment of equal rights and opportunities is the main route to sexual equality. Radical feminist theory views the relations between men and women as being determined by men's collective effort to assert and maintain power over women. Patriarchy, according to radical feminists, is an over-arching social system of male domination which constitutes the primary cause of women's subordination. In contrast, socialist feminism has attempted to reconcile the way in which two systems, one capitalist and the other patriarchal, combine to subordinate women. Thus a socialist feminist analysis suggests that while on the one hand it can be shown that capitalism profits from gender-based inequalities, it cannot fully explain those inequalities solely with reference to the benefits accrued by capital. One must also turn to patriarchy and the benefits which accrue to men. Belatedly, socialist feminism has recognised that capitalist societies are not just sexually stratified but racially stratified as well. This necessitates a consideration of how racial, gender and class hierarchies operate to produce different but related systems of domination and subordination.

Despite these theoretical differences there are a number of shared assumptions which guide western feminist analyses. Firstly, women's primary role has been defined as a wife and a mother, legally and economically dependent upon a male breadwinner, with women's waged work being cast as a secondary occupation. Secondly, women are deemed primarily responsible for the domestic sphere – including house-work and child-rearing – which is unpaid and therefore undervalued and trivialised. Thirdly, some would argue that this partly explains the undervaluation of women's work outside the home and sex segregation in the labour market. And finally, this has also been linked to a division between the private and the public domain with women being largely confined to the former and men monopolising the latter, particularly the political sphere.

The construction of the 'woman question' in 'state socialist societies' draws on both Marx's and Engels's view that the subordination of women is an aspect of class oppression. Engels maintained that monogamy allows the transfer of property from father to son, which strengthens the motive for capital accumulation. Thus women's subordination in his view is a natural consequence of private property and women's dependence within marriage. At this level there is much in common between Marx's and Engels's view of women's subordination and contemporary feminist theories, which point to the family as the primary site of women's oppression.

Where the two depart is with Engels's belief that with the abolition of private property and the integration of women into social production, women would gain economic independence and equality with men. Engels believed that once marriage was stripped of its relations of financial dependency it would become a union reflecting free choice between partners. In Engels there is no recognition that many aspects of women's subordination cannot be explained by reference to private property and the bourgeois family form. The bourgeois family form is neither culturally nor socially universal. Furthermore the control of women's sexuality and the inheritance of private property pre-date the bourgeois family. Thus most western feminists find Engels's analysis economically determinist since for him there is one over-arching source of women's oppression: private property relations.

Nevertheless despite significant economic and cultural differences between nations it was this explanation of women's subordination that was to form the basis of Marxist revolutionary strategy and subsequently state policy. Thus women's emancipation would result from their entry into the realms of waged labour, their proletarianisation and their participation in revolutionary struggle. There is little doubt that in the pre-revolutionary and immediate post-revolutionary period in Russia and in China feminist demands such as the vote and equal rights at work, which were in harmony with the objectives of the proletarian revolution, were acted upon. Women were active and enthusiastic protagonists in the revolutionary movement. For instance, in Russia on International Women's Day 1917 women textile workers went on strike, action which precipitated much more widespread industrial and popular unrest and culminating in the establishment of the provisional government. And in the immediate post-revolutionary period there is plenty of evidence of Russian women's active participation in demonstrations and conferences. Moreover in China as well as Russia women demonstrated their willingness to use and defend their newly acquired legal rights, such as divorcing their husbands and standing for public office.

Thus while women in Russia and China had made significant gains, these gains were limited to those acceptable to the proletarian revolutionary programmes and their realisation was constrained by them. Ultimately the male political leadership viewed women as another segment in society to be fully mobilised in realising the aims of a Marxist revolution. The pursuit of broader feminist objectives were regarded as a distraction from the furtherance of the main revolutionary goals.

In the 1920s women in the Soviet Union had the same rights as men before the law. In the public sphere women were deemed equally liable to be mobilised as workers while in the private sphere many of the reforms previously considered necessary for the liberation of women had either been jettisoned or drastically reduced, for instance communal living and socialised child-care. The Zhenotdel, a women's organisation set up within the Communist Party, had been given charge of organising such schemes. So it was women, not men who were expected to implement them. Even if much of the work of the Zhenotdel could be criticised for marginalising issues which were central to tackling gendered inequalities it came increasingly to be regarded as a threat to Party control and as divisive of working-class unity and was abolished in 1930. The notion of the socialist family with the mother of many children at its core was promoted, and legal abortion abolished in 1936. Thus women were encouraged by the state to remain primarily responsible for the private sphere in a political system where the pre-eminence of the public sphere was officially promoted. Even for those countries where Marxist states were established much later it was the Soviet model of women's dual role that was adopted as the basis of state policy. While there have been significant variations to this model however, what has not been questioned is the pre-eminence of the needs of the state over the individual. Delia Davin's chapter describes how in very different cultural and developmental contexts state socialist societies have persistently subordinated individual interests to national ones via interventionist population policies. A state-endorsed emphasis on women's 'natural propensity' for child-care and domestic labour, increased maternity leave, time off for children's sickness, the encouragement of part-time work, has all been premised on the assumption that child-care is women's responsibility.

REFORM: PROGRESSIVE OR REGRESSIVE?

With the reforms there has been an intensification of the ideological campaign to shift state responsibility for socialisation on to the family with the mother at its centre. Harriet Evans shows how in China the emphasis since 1978 has been to restore the family household as a key unit of economic, social and moral importance. A renewed emphasis on the monogamous relationship and the glorification of women's domestic role within it has particular consequences for the choices open to women. Harriet argues that at precisely the time when Chinese women would seem to be freer than ever before to embark on activities and experiences outside the domestic sphere they are being firmly reminded that that is where their primary societal responsibility lies.

In the Soviet Union, when social problems such as juvenile crime or alcoholism are identified it is apparently women's inability fully to carry out their 'womanly mission' because of their role as workers that provides an explanation for these problems. This has implications for women's identities and self-esteem an issue which is taken up by Chris Corrin in her chapter on Hungary.

Natalia Rimashevskaya evaluates recent radical measures on maternity leave, pay and child-care in the Soviet Union. She explains that given the renewed official position on women's 'rightful place', she cannot welcome these reforms as progressive. This is firstly because the function of parenthood continues to be encouraged only for women. Secondly, if women (as potential child-bearers and it would seem child-rearers) are eligible for what Rimashevskaya regards as a growing set of privileges, they will be increasingly displaced to the developing secondary labour market. The latter is one of the first outcomes of economic rationalisation.

In her examination of the relationship between market reform and education and employment in China, Shirin Rai points to a similar contradiction. The partial withdrawal of what she considers to be a paternalistic state allows the re-emergence of traditional values which embody patriarchal assumptions about women's rightful place. This assumption provides the justification for sexually discriminatory action ranging from the exclusion of girls from the educational process altogether to the experience of widespread employment discrimination by women graduates. Once more, we must question the 'progressive' nature of reform and change from a gendered perspective.

The introduction of market reforms also poses contradictions for women in rural areas. Zhang Junzuo considers the political implications of market reforms for women in rural areas where their role in pro-duction-related decision-making has been drastically reduced and with it their formal political representation. Frances Pine also addresses the position of rural women in her chapter on Poland, emphasising the gender-linked constraints under which rural women operate and which socialism did little to alleviate. There is in fact every reason to suppose that these constraints are likely to be carried over into the market economy.

Gendered identities were frozen and gendered inequalities remained a structural feature of post-revolutionary society and this has not been posed as a problem for de-socialising societies. There is therefore no reason to suppose that any democratisation of the public sphere will ameliorate male dominance and female subordination. Hilary Pilkington takes up this issue in her chapter on the gendered nature of relations in non-formal groups in the Soviet Union. Young people are officially being encouraged to become active citizens in the space between the individual and the state. This fails to recognise that the category of 'youth' is made up of gendered subjects whose identity is pre-determined by the social relations governing the space in which they are formed. Rosamund Shreeves's chapter draws out the implications of this for female sexual identity and its representation in contemporary Soviet culture. She argues that given the lack of understanding of female sexuality the new permissiveness in terms of the portrayal of sex is resulting in the sexual exploitation of women rather than the kind of sexual emancipation envisioned by the early revolutionary feminists.

A WOMAN'S VOICE?

The re-definition of the relationship between the state and the individual does in theory provide a space for a separate and critical voice to be heard. Marina Malysheva emphasises in her chapter that Russian feminism was incompatible with Bolshevism because of the latter's class reductionism and its negation of the rights of the individual. She argues that Bolshevism and patriarchy can only be fought by a feminism which places the woman's personality and individuality above the hierarchy of roles.

The process of de-socialising in these societies has thrown up a number of contradictions. The freezing of gendered identities in the post-revolutionary period has remained unchallenged and thus presents obstacles to a gendered re-thinking of the relationship between the state and the individual. To this extent class reductionism is being replaced by market reductionism.

Thus, while there is space now for a separate woman's voice, no single 'woman's consciousness' has emerged. Valentina Konstantinova's contribution highlights the fact that even without the ideological and political legacy of the post-revolutionary decades there is little reason to think that the millions of ethnically and regionally disparate women in a country such as the Soviet Union would identify with a single agenda. At the same time she is able to point to already identifiable groupings which purport to represent a 'woman's' voice. What is clear is that a space has been carved within the de-socialising state and women are to some extent using it for self-expression. This collection marks a contribution to current debates and we hope a continuing dialogue between women across national boundaries.

NOTE

1 By which we mean a retreat by the state from a commitment to socialised production and public activity and a prioritisation of collective over individual norms.

Part I

Swings and roundabouts

The political economy of reform

1 *Perestroika* and the status of women in the Soviet Union

Natalia Rimashevskaia

The radical changes which have occurred in all spheres of social life in the USSR as a result of the transition to a market economy raise a number of questions about their impact on women and their implications for social policy. This chapter addresses some of these questions, particularly those which relate to trends in women's employment.

The share of women in the total population of the USSR is decreasing, though in 1989 it still exceeded that of men, at 53 per cent of the population. The larger proportion of women in the Soviet population is the outcome of two factors: the loss of men during the Second World War and a higher life expectancy for women. In 1989 women's life expectancy was 74 years as compared with 64.6 years for men (*Narodnoe Khoziaistvo SSSR v 1989*, 1990: 43).

The current situation of women's employment in the USSR exhibits a number of interesting features. The country is characterised by one of the highest rates of female employment in the world. The percentage of women in paid employment as compared to men has been changing as follows; in 1959 89 per cent of men were in employment and 70 per cent of women. By 1979 84 per cent of women were economically active, a figure which dropped back to 80 per cent against 87 per cent of men in 1989.

Percentage changes in women's involvement in paid employment over time is reflected in data set out in Table 1.1.

Industrialisation of the economy in the 1930s was accompanied by huge inflows of women into paid work. This trend became stronger during the

Table 1.1 The percentage of women in the total number of workers and employees

1919	1924	1940	1960	1970	1980	1985	1986	1987	1988
40.9	27.7	38.9	47.2	50.8	51.2	50.9	50.8	50.6	50.6

Source: Zhenshchiny v SSSR, 1960: 31; *Zhenshchiny i Deti v SSSR*, 1961: 120; *Zhenshchiny v SSSR*, 1975: 27; *Zhenshchiny v SSSR*, 1986: 7; *Zhenshchiny v SSSR*, 1989: 17

Table 1.2 The percentage of women in the average annual number of workers and employees by Union Republics, 1989

Republics	%
The USSR	51
Armenia	48
Azerbaijan	43
Belorussia	53
Estonia	54
Georgia	47
Kazakhstan	49
Kirghizia	49
Latvia	55
Lithuania	53
Moldavia	53
Russia	52
Tadzhikistan	39
Turkmenia	42
The Ukraine	52
Uzbekistan	43

Source: Narodnoe Khoziaistvo v SSSR 1989, 1990: 56

Second World War, by the end of which the proportion of women in the labour force was 56 per cent. During the post-war period women's share of employment began to decrease, until the 1970s when we see another upswing. What these trends suggest is that during periods of extensive economic growth women are more actively involved in the economy while during periods of economic reform such as the New Economic Policy, the 1965 reform and the present period there is a discernible outflow of women from the labour force. Depending on the economic strategy women are either called upon to be actively involved in paid work or alternatively are urged to go back to their families and fulfil their womanly mission.

Despite a high rate of female employment in the USSR, there are marked republican variations. Table 1.2 illustrates the level of variation. While the average is 50.6 per cent there is a 15 point fluctuation across the country as a whole, from a high of 55 per cent in Latvia to 39 per cent in Tadzhikistan. The relatively low rate of female employment in Central Asia and the Caucasus corresponds to a higher fertility rate in these regions. At the same time it is difficult to say whether this is cause or effect; are higher fertility rates the reason for the lower levels of employment or the other way round? One thing is clear, the Central Asian part of the USSR has different reproductory rates and female employment levels from the European part of the country.

Table 1.3 Female employment, by percentage, in different branches of the economy

	1980	1989
Commerce	12.9	12.8
Health	8.9	10.3
Education	11.8	14.0
Culture and arts	2.0	2.4
Science	3.8	3.6
Management	3.5	2.7
Collective farms	10.9	8.9
Industry, construction, transport, public services	46.2	45.3

Source: Narodnoe Khoziaistvo SSSR v 1989, 1990: 53–4

Table 1.4 Percentage of women in selected professions

Professions	%
Librarians	91
Book-keepers	89
Economists	87
Teachers	70
Physicians	67
Engineers	58
Agriculturalists	45

Source: unpublished

Women's employment is also characterised by its uneven distribution across sectors and industries.

A number of 'feminised' branches and professions can be identified. These are primarily the administration of credits and state insurance where the share of women in the labour force was 87 per cent in 1989; commerce and public catering – 82 per cent; health care, physical culture and social security – 81 per cent; information and computing – 81 per cent; public education – 75 per cent; culture – 72 per cent; clothing – 89 per cent; textiles – 70 per cent; and bakery – 72 per cent. Table 1.4 shows the percentage of women in professional occupations.

Many women in the Soviet Union have jobs which are low-skill but require hard manual labour, for instance in the construction industry 25 per cent of manual workers are women. Newly created, mechanised and automated jobs are usually filled by men.

Undoubtedly the biggest problem for the female labour force is the difficulty of combining the functions of mother and worker. Popular consciousness still holds firmly to the patriarchal view that there is a natural division between the roles of men and women. According to this view women are mothers and carers, men are bread-winners, protectors and public figures. A traditional sexual division of labour within the home is justified and preserved, which results in a double burden of work for women. Women have two shifts, one at work, another at home. The total weekly amount of work including paid employment and domestic labour is for women 76.8 hours, compared to 59.4 hours for men (*Sotsial'noe Razvitie i Uroven' Zhizni Naseleniia SSSR*, 1989: 261).

Data from various studies show that mothers and wives spend 2.5 times more time on housework than fathers and husbands. During their 'home shift' women walk about 15 to 20 km and carry out over 50 operations in the home, only 15 per cent of which are mechanised.

In the earliest stages of their careers, which as a rule coincide with the initial period of family life and the appearance of children (the first child usually being born during the second year of family life, the second within 6.6 years) women spend a great deal of time on child-care. Women may even change jobs and professions to ones which they regard as more compatible with their family duties. Nevertheless a number of surveys indicate high levels of fatigue amongst women workers. A prevalent view is, 'I'm glad that I do repetitious work, I use up so much energy and concentration on queueing and housework that I'm glad that I don't have to think during work as well'.

Another consequence of women's dual role is that the positions that they hold often do not correspond to their professional training. According to our data about 25 per cent of women do not acquire any further training and keep on working with the same qualifications that they had on entry into the labour market. Nowadays, when re-training and skill enhancement are essential, women's absence from these opportunities must have some impact on economic development as well as individual career development.

Finally we will consider the findings of a survey (1989) carried out by the Institute for Socio-economic Studies of the Population, on the status of women workers at the Kama Machine Building Plant. The survey examined women's views on work and the family and the issue of combining the two. Women assembly workers as well as women engineers and technicians were asked to answer the question, 'If your husband earned more what would you prefer?', using a range of pre-set responses. The results are shown in Table 1.5.

The responses indicate that, despite the hardships, most women would prefer to combine the functions of mother and worker.

Thus we can argue that women's employment profiles have certain characteristics and these result in social and economic problems for

Table 1.5 Working women's preferences

Answers	Workers %	Engineers and Technicians %
Keep present job	26	20
Work part-time	32	64
Have a more attractive job	30	12
Give up working	12	4

Table 1.6 Monthly wages, by percentage, for men and women

Wages	Men	Women
under 150 roubles	16.0	43.0
200–300 roubles	35.0	14.5
over 300 roubles	11.0	2.0

Source: Zhenshchiny v SSSR, 1990: 4

women. Initially women have the same characteristics as men as far as health, educational and professional qualifications are concerned. But women take jobs of a lower level and which have a 'horizontal' character, that is, that they have little opportunity for promotion in those jobs. Amongst the employed population women remain better educated than men and the rate of growth of women's educational achievement exceeds that of men. From 1979 to 1989 the percentage of men with secondary and higher education increased by 13 per cent and the share of women by 19 per cent. Even in rural areas women's educational level exceeded that of men amongst the working population. In 1988–9, 54 per cent of all university students were women.

The number of women in managerial positions is small, therefore the overall structure of female employment is in the shape of a pyramid; the higher the social status the smaller the share of women at that level. Even in the professions there is gender segregation; certain occupations are practically closed to women, for example the highest echelons of power, foreign affairs and high technology industries.

While wages are not sex dependent average wages for women are a third less than those of men. Table 1.6 shows that the proportion of women is much higher among the low-wage group.

In addition feminised industries, that is, industries where women constitute upwards of 70 per cent of the workforce, have the lowest average wages (Table 1.7).

With the transition to the market economy the problems which we

Table 1.7 Average monthly wages of workers and employees by industry, 1988

Industries	Roubles
Economy as a whole	240.4
Industry	263.7
Agriculture	233.5
Construction	316.9
Transportation	287.7
Commerce, catering*	187.1
Public services*	180.6
Health care, social security*	163.3
Public education*	175.5
Culture*	136.2

* = feminised industries
Source: *Sotsial'noe Razvitie i Uroven' Zhizni Naseleniia SSSR*, 1989: 93

have already identified as characterising female employment are becoming more acute as economic reforms marginalise the female labour force. The market economy and new, multiple forms of ownership have brought with them a more intensive use of labour and a requirement for higher professional standards. Unavoidable redundancies due to privatisation, structural adjustment and the conversion of defence industries will result in greater competition for jobs. As the female labour force has lower qualifications and complicated employment rights women will not be able to compete with men in the labour market on equal terms. Over the last two years it has become apparent that women are more likely than men to be made redundant. Overall 60 per cent of those made redundant have been women and 80 per cent of all managerial workers made redundant have been women. Currently women are the first to be fired but not the first to be hired if there are vacancies.

Thus a separate labour market for women is forming; it is segregated, confined to a limited set of occupations and professions, it is marked by lower wages and professional qualifications, it has poor working conditions, it is characterised by 'horizontal' mobility and more part-time work – in short, all the features of a secondary labour market. Women as a socially disadvantaged group run more risk of an intensification of work, prolongation of the working day and exposure to health and safety hazards.

There is already a feminisation of poverty and this is likely to increase. Unemployed women, single mothers, single women past the age of retirement (whose pensions average only 70 per cent of those enjoyed by men), women taking maternity leave and women who are part-time workers are all in an increasingly vulnerable situation as far as redundancies, rising inflation and further income differentials are concerned.

It is clear that the situation demands on the one hand special measures for the social protection of women and on the other a need to change the current stereotypes of appropriate gender roles in the family and society as a whole. Some steps have already been taken in this direction. The president of the USSR sent a message to the Supreme Soviet in which he proposed to make a decree on 'urgent measures to improve the status of women, mothers and children, to consolidate the family' (*Pravda*, 1 April 1990). In its decree of 14 April 1990 Parliament issued a resolution making some significant amendments to legislation affecting women:

- Payment for child-care up to 18 months to be increased to the level of minimum wages;
- Maternity leave to be extended to 70 days before and 56 days after delivery;
- Child-care leave of up to 3 years can be taken by the mother, father, grandmother, grandfather or other relatives either full-time or part-time.

The latter is particularly important because it legally states the principle of equal opportunities and opens up the possibility of more egalitarian types of gender relations. However, what happens in practice may be quite different. Opinion polls indicate that such radical proposals are ahead of public opinion.

WHAT SHOULD BE DONE?

A number of measures aimed at the upgrading of women at work should be introduced and should include: the creation of a system for professional re-training of women after maternity leave; special training courses for women with children; changing the procedures for hiring women and those governing promotion; and improving the working conditions of women as a whole.

These are only guidelines; each requires a set of measures differentiated by region, enterprise and specific problem area. Researchers from the USSR Academy of Sciences have formulated proposals for a state programme to improve the status of women, mothers, children and the family.

Previous experience of intensive economic reforms indicates that they tend to be accompanied by a considerable reduction in employment rates and the further consolidation of a two-sector labour market. What this currently means in the Soviet Union is that there is a primary, 'progressive' sector which is more capital intensive and utilises 'core' workers. The secondary, 'traditional' sector is labour intensive and utilises labour less efficiently.

As long as the responsibility for parenthood remains squarely with the mothers, for whom a growing set of rights has been designed, they are more likely to end up in the secondary sector. Younger men will constitute the core labour force and women will continue to lose jobs because of technological change and job cuts, or to get dead-end, unattractive jobs instead.

In order to avoid the negative consequences of these developments for women a specially designed employment policy should be pursued, using both administrative and economic measures. Enterprises would be instructed to hire a certain number of women and also to ensure that no more than 50 per cent of those in any redundancy programme are women. This is a short-term measure. The second measure would be an economic mechanism which would overcome sex discrimination in profit distribution within an enterprise. A certain share of the profits in an enterprise would be lodged in a 'children's fund' to cover the expenses of bringing up a new generation. The children's fund would be administered by the collective of workers in an enterprise and funds would be disbursed for various kinds of compensation, for instance the care of sick children, the running of the crèches and other pre-school institutions. Children who use the crèche but whose parents do not work in the enterprise should also be included in the children's fund. This is important because already there are cases where enterprises which have turned to self-financing and cost-accounting methods have withdrawn crèche places from non-enterprise children. It is hoped that this measure would stimulate the construction of pre-school institutions from decentralised investment. Free enterprise, co-operatives and private business are integral parts of the transition to the market economy. Co-operatives which have private business will absorb some of the surplus labour from state-owned enterprises. Thus it is necessary to take special organisational measures to ensure that the needs of women workers are recognised, for instance in re-training programmes. At the same time it is necessary to ensure that labour laws are observed at these enterprises especially those which are private.

Many social problems, including gender-related ones become more acute with the transition to a market economy. Amongst the issues which need to be addressed urgently are the need to increase the competitiveness of the female labour force, women's careers and increased political activity on the part of women. To be able to consider such problems special approaches are needed. On the one hand it is necessary to use the whole set of economic tools from taxes to credits as a way of encouraging employers to value women workers. On the other, it is vital to change societal stereotypes of gender roles. Most urgently the issue of equal parenthood must be addressed, through education and the use of the media.

REFERENCES

Sotsial' noe Razvitie i Uroven' Zhizni Naseleniia SSSR (1989) Goskomstat SSSR, Moscow.
Narodnoe Khoziaistvo SSSR v 1989 (1990) Finansy i Statistika, Moscow.
Zhenshchiny v SSSR (1960), Moscow.
Zhenshchiny i Deti v SSSR (1961) Statistika, Moscow.
Zhenshchiny v SSSR (1975) Statistika, Moscow.
Zhenshchiny v SSSR (1986) Finansy i Statistika, Moscow.
Zhenshchiny v SSSR (1990) Finansy i Statistika, Moscow.

2 'Watering another man's garden'

Gender, employment and educational reforms in China

Shirin Rai

PATERNALISM AND PATRIARCHY

The 1980s saw tremendous changes in the economic and political ethos of China. After the political puritanism, social egalitarianism and isolationism of the Maoist years, the new leadership set a new agenda for the Chinese people. China was to modernise its economy to become a strong, powerful international force. For Chinese women this changed agenda has had particular consequences. In this paper I explore some of these and their wider implications in the context of education and employment policies for Chinese women in the 1980s.

Although patriarchy is a disputed concept I use it here as a term to capture 'the specificities of the subjection and oppression of *women* and to distinguish this from other forms of domination' (Pateman, 1990: 35). It therefore includes in its ambit the father-centred family and kinship networks, symbolic systems, and socio-economic structures. Analysing the position of women in China Judith Stacey has argued that China's socialist revolution reached backward to move forward; that the Chinese Communist leaders made a compromise with the patriarchal system to gain the support of the peasantry for the revolution at the expense of women (Stacey, 1983: 254). Kay Ann Johnson makes a similar point in her study of the family in socialist China (Johnson, 1983). This element of collusion, while no doubt present, raises the issue of whether this was a deliberate betrayal of women by the Communist Party of China (CPC) leadership, or was it a more general gender-blindness that resulted in its non-engagement with patriarchy. The Chinese Communist leaders failed to confront the various forms of patriarchy subjecting women to oppression, while believing themselves to be the champions of women's emancipation.

As orthodox Marxism lacks a conceptual framework within which to analyse the nature of an autonomous 'sex–gender system' (Stacey, 1983:

263), the Chinese leaders of all political convictions labelled discrimination against women in socialist China as a remnant of a 'feudal
ideology' (Johnson, 1983: 214). An analysis of the autonomous power of
patriarchy was replaced by a notion of 'public dependency' which
employs a paternalistic, welfare ideology to 'protect' women from
oppression of the civil society (see Hernes, 1984). (The term 'civil
society' is used here not in the specific Habermasian construction as a
product of the separation of the individual citizen from the monarch in
the seventeenth century, but as a concept encompassing all institutions
that exist outside the boundaries of the state.) The civil society was itself
cast in an unfractured mould – as reflecting 'feudal' or 'bourgeois'
prejudices, and was therefore a legitimate target of the state reform
policies. The state became the guarantor of women's rights against a
system of social oppression. The Chinese Communists regarded themselves as engaged not just in class war but also in social liberation:
'Women hold up half the heaven' was a favourite epigram of Mao. The post-
revolutionary Chinese state was both socialist and developmentalist in
nature. It was thus highly interventionist. This allowed it to effect the
course of family life, the position of the woman within the family and
within the public domain through policy-making and implementation.
The legal system, the strategies of political mobilisation and of control,
and economic policy were all used to fashion the role that the woman
played in society. While the needs of the revolution dictated the terms
of a compromise with patriarchy, the urgent need for economic
reconstruction meant that women had to be mobilised for production in
the public sphere. Their 'liberation' became part of the grander plan for
China's modernisation. It also fitted in with the importance of waged
work in the Marxist analysis of women's liberation. The gender-
blindness of these constructed meanings of 'reconstruction', 'economic
modernisation', and 'national interest' was not questioned. Equality of
women thus came to be seen as an ideological, not a gender issue.

Under this paternalistic political system Chinese women did make
significant gains in social status and economic position. The
comparisons with a feudal, Confucian past are many, and favourable.
The very process of participating in the revolution, of bearing arms, of
being subject of progressive legislation directed at their position within
the family and in the work-place, of increased opportunities of
education, and even of official political discourse emphasising the
equality of the sexes, all benefited, and have been taken advantage of by,
women. The Land Reform Law and the Marriage Law of 1950 were the
two most important pieces of legislation aimed at fundamentally

changing the position of Chinese women. While both had limited success in empowering women in their own right – land remained registered in the male-headed family's name – they did strengthen the woman's economic and social position especially at the time of divorce. Emphasis on waged work also developed the notion of economic independence. The social status for the woman as an individual in her own right that was part of the constitutional provisions was a revolutionary break with the Chinese past. Further, under a socialist and developmentalist state women were able to make use of the various officially sanctioned organisations, the rhetoric, rights and 'liberties', to their advantage. The official socialist ideology, especially as interpreted by Mao, created a collectivist political ethic – though based on the traditional family collective effort – that affected women in particular ways. The path of 'individual problem-solving', of 'perfecting individual lives' was precluded in favour of collective endeavour. It also allowed women to situate their own struggle against the family in a broader context of national reconstruction which then legitimised their break with 'feudal traditions'. The nation needed women's skills, enthusiasm, and effort; the family could not restrain them within the confines of the courtyard. The various political mobilisational movements launched under Mao – from the Land Reform, to the Great Leap Forward, and even the Cultural Revolution – brought millions of women into the public domain (see Young, 1989: 233–47, and Prazniak, 1989). Collusion and resistance, petitions and protests were employed as political strategies by women and their organisations to improve their position in the new political system. However, the question of confrontation with and opposition to patriarchy in socialist China remained largely unaddressed.

As Hernes points out in her study of the Scandinavian welfare system, 'welfare is not synonymous with power and with the ability to shape and influence one's own status' (1984: 26). This is a significant distinction to draw in a system that is restrictive of independent political movements. In the name of proletarian dictatorship, the Chinese Communists built a political system that concentrated power in the hands of the Communist Party. Mass organisations were set up, but these functioned primarily as mobilisational units, or transmission belts rather than autonomous interests representing organisations (see Rai, 1991, Chapter 1). The Chinese Women's Federation was one such organisation. At its annual conference in 1978 its tasks were defined: 'resolutely implement the Party's general and specific policies and fully arouse enthusiasm among the broad masses of women, and how to mobilize the women to carry out the general task for the new period is the new problem for the women's movement' (Croll, 1983: 123). The old argument of gender versus class was employed by the state to underline the primacy of the '(non)-gendered' political system rather than confrontration with patriarchy. The lack of autonomous women's organisations, and an unmonitored access to the public sphere meant that the effects of patriarchy could be challenged only in official discourse, and in an officially 'licenced' public space. The agenda of debate was drawn up not by women themselves but by the agencies of the state. For example, the agricultural policy after the Great Leap Forward of 1958 'maintained the traditional family and community structures' (Johnson, 1983: 216). The communes remained as loose administrative structures, while the 'team' based on a few families in a village became the unit of agricultural production. The patriarchal family thus remained integral to agricultural production. Even in the formal representative political bodies women remained greatly underrepresented. Only 21 per cent of the deputies to the national and provincial people's congresses are women, and they form 29 per cent of cadres at all levels. Further, as Vivienne Shue points out in her study of the Chinese state (1988), the various economic and political policies pursued by a centralised state often left enough spaces for local officials, organisations, and individuals to circumvent many of the most radical social policies. Policies on marriage, divorce, and property rights of women were frequently subverted by conservative male cadres. During the Maoist period, the rural and urban production units were asked to become 'self-reliant', leading to a siege mentality among villages and factories, and further increasing the importance of these cadres.

'MAIN CONTRADICTIONS' AND GRAND STRATEGIES

In 1976 Mao Zedong, architect of China's revolution and its economic strategy, died. It was the end of an era. The new leadership soon repudiated the radicalism of Mao, and the policies that resulted from it. The highly centralised system of economic planning came under critical scrutiny; it was blamed for China's economic stagnation. The principal contradiction faced by China was identified as 'between the growing material and cultural needs of the people and backward production'. China's new leaders set up another grand design for resolving China's problems – that of 'four modernisations'. These were modernisation of industry, agriculture, science and technology, and defence. The economics of modernisation was to be based upon ideas of rationalisation, efficiency, and competition. The market was the mechanism that was to realise these ideas. This was made politically acceptable by placing

China at a 'primary stage of socialism' rather than well down the road to Communism as Mao had claimed. The centralised political state intervening in, and controlling every aspect of individual life in China was to give way to a more flexible, less directive state. In other words, the state was to 'get off the people's back'.

During the early 1980s the agricultural communes set up in 1958–9 were decollectivised, and an 'individual and family responsibility system' of contractual production was set up. In industry collective management by 'revolutionary committees' was replaced by 'one-man [sic]- management'; the service industry was opened to private enterprise both in the cities and the countryside. China was 'opened up' to western investment, and price controls were to be lifted to allow the forces of supply and demand to set realistic prices, which would encourage production and enterprise and generate profit for reinvestment and expansion. Under the policy of 'breaking the iron rice bowl' job tenure was replaced by a contract system that was to encourage competition and increase productivity. China's was to be a 'planned commodity economy based on public ownership' (Zhao, 1987: xi). The role of the state in the economy was to formulate policy and to use 'economic levers as price, finance, taxation and credit for intervention and regulation' (1987: ix), significantly reducing the scope of the 'command economy' of the traditional socialist type.

While the events of Tiananmen Square in 1989 have demonstrated the reluctance of the state to withdraw from the public political sphere, the Chinese leadership has kept to the economic strategy based upon the market. This strategy has affected, and continues to affect, the position of Chinese women in both the private and the public sphere. Many questions arise regarding the post-Mao economic reforms and their impact on women. First, has there been a withdrawal of the state from the political and economic spheres that particularly affect women, or is the state continuing to influence the position of women in the Chinese society as much today as it was in Mao's time? In other words, is a 'rationalising' market-oriented political system necessarily less interventionist than a centralised socialist one? An answer to this question would allow us to unravel the relationship between the state and the civil society in a socialist country, which might throw some light upon the relationship between the two in the present context of politico-economic reform. Second, has there been a revival of 'feudal practices' with a partial withdrawal of the 'protection' of the state, or are we witnessing in the functioning of the market a continued impact of patriarchy that was not challenged by a paternalistic state? As Honig and Hershatter point out, 'The situation of women in the 1980s, and the public debate over what their social role should become, was shaped by the past but was not a reenactment of it' (Honig and Hershatter, 1989: 6). Third, the question of marginality is also important in the context of these reforms – in the context of a 'public patriarchy' that twins with the private, are the rights of women to remain marginal to the 'main contra-diction'. In this case economic modernisation – defined by a party/state in whose policy-making women have little or no influence? I propose to find answers to some of these questions by examining the impact of the post-Mao education policy at the two ends of the educational spectrum – the enrolment and drop-out rates of girls in primary schools, and at the point when they leave the educational system as graduates and begin to look for employment.

GENDER, EDUCATION AND ECONOMIC IMPERATIVES

Education, said Deng Xiaoping, was the greatest casualty of the Maoist period, and its reform was an urgent priority for the four modernisations to succeed. Standards of education had fallen sharply during the years of the turmoil of the Cultural Revolution. China was far behind the developed world in scientific and technological fields of knowledge, the two areas needed most to modernise the stagnant economy of the country. Intellectuals had been alienated, quality had been sacrificed for quantity, discipline loosened and initiative stifled in education generally. To set things to right, more conventional educational institutions, enrolment procedures, investment patterns and curricula were to be introduced (Deng, 1984: 80–6). Describing the 'major tasks' for the post-Mao leadership, Zhao Ziyang, the then prime minister, said, 'Give first priority to the expansion of scientific, technological and educational undertakings, so as to push forward economic development through advances in science and technology and improved quality of the work force' (Zhao, 1987: vii). The reforms in education were to be tied to the needs of the economy, and the principles of the market – competition, demand and supply, lessening dependence on state subsidies, diversification of the types of institutions and sources of funding – were introduced. There was an increased emphasis on investment in the higher education sector as compared to the primary and secondary sectors. The 'open door' policy was applied to education; foreign investment and exchange programmes were set up and encouraged. The first World Bank aid programmes were also concentrated in higher education (Hayhoe, 1989: 161). Together with this went the rehabilitation of the intelligentsia in the social and political hierarchy of the country; they were made part of the 'working class', as 'mental workers'.

Many educational institutions such as the *minban* (people's) schools that had experimented in informal, flexible educational practices in the countryside, were gradually abolished. In 1977 a national examination was introduced for enrolment into institutions of higher education, vocational training was emphasised, and educational institutions were encouraged to supplement state funding by tapping other sources, for example, charging parents school fees, getting sponsorship from various state-owned and private industries and individuals. Economic resources were scarce, which meant that they had to be concentrated in a small number of institutions (called 'key point' institutions) at all levels of the educational pyramid (SEC, 1985). A Compulsory Education Law was promulgated in 1985 to eradicate illiteracy. Finally, as part of the opening up of the labour market, college graduates were gradually to be allowed to compete for jobs outside the state allocation system. As the 1980s rolled on, the impact of these reforms on the education, employment, and the social position of women in China began to cause concern. These concerns have been increasingly reflected in a series of surveys carried out by various organisations, including statistical bureaus which have mushroomed in the last decade, and in a press that is increasingly identifying controversial issues for analysis. The increased access of the foreign, especially Hong Kong press, to the Chinese hinterland has also helped to increase the pool of information on issues such as the education and employment of girls and women.

Two issues regarding women and education were hotly debated in 1988 in the Chinese press. The first was the increasing drop-out rates among schoolgirls, especially in the rural areas. The second was the difficulty faced by women college graduates in finding employment under the partially opened job market. These debates reveal both the depths of prejudice against women in Chinese society, and the resistance by women to discrimination born of such prejudice. They also illustrate the gendered biases of the economic policies pursued by a modernising state that refuses to confront the issue of 'public patriarchy'. Further, they show how yet again the politics of gender are defined away by the Chinese state in the name of another global, universalistic dogma – modernisation instead of revolution.

MARKET 'RATIONALITY' AND SCHOOLING FOR GIRLS

The expansion of female education in China occurred mainly in two periods: 1950 to 1958, and 1966 to 1976 (Table 2.1). These mark the beginning of Communist rule in China, and the Cultural Revolution (see Lavely *et al.*, 1990: 61). These are both periods of high state initiative

Table 2.1 Number of female students as percentage of total enrolment

Year	Higher education	Regular secondary schools	Primary schools	Teacher training
1949	19.8	–	–	–
1951	22.5	25.6	28.0	26.0
1955	25.9	26.9	33.4	27.1
1958	23.3	31.3	38.5	31.5
1973	30.8	33.0	40.7	–
1975	32.6	39.3	45.2	–
1976	33.0	40.4	45.5	–
1978	24.1	41.5	44.9	29.8
1983	26.9	39.5	43.7	37.2
1987	33.0	40.8	45.4	–

Sources: SEC, 1984: 40 and *Chinese Education*, Summer 1989: 7

and intervention, and also of high levels of political mobilisation of the masses in China. During the 1980s there has been a fall in the rate of literacy among girls despite the promulgation of the 1985 Compulsory Education Law and the drop-out rates among girl pupils in schools are rising. 'In 1987, there were more than 2. 7 million unschooled children between the ages of 7 and 11, and 83 per cent of them were girls', reported *Liaowang* (*Outlook*) from Hongkong (8 May 1989 JPRS-CAR–89–074). 'Of the 230 million people who are illiterate, 70 per cent are female, and of the 2 million new illiterate people that emerge each year, 80 per cent are female.' The journal *Pai Shing* reported that in 1985 three million girls stopped studying, or about 7 per cent of all children (*Pai Shing*; 1 June 1989; JPRS-CAR–89–090). 'Many of the schools in the Yao Autonomous Region in Guangxi do not have a single female student' (*ibid.*).

There are, however, regional and sectoral disparities that have to be taken into account when examining the education of girls. The more economically developed the region the more are the resources available for education and the larger the number of girls able to take advantage of these. With the relative success of the one-child family in the urban areas, the emphasis on education of girls has been higher, further underscoring the rural/urban divide in this sphere.

'In the post-Mao reform period, primary school attainment has levelled off and secondary school attainment has declined by roughly 25 per cent in rural areas; urban attainment has been affected to a far lesser degree' (Lavely *et al.*, 1990: 61–2).This difference can be attributed to two state policy initiatives: rural reform and a population policy. Decollectivisation of agriculture has increased the need for child labour, and has also undermined the one-child population policy in the countryside.

An important economic reform introduced by the post-Mao leadership was the decollectivisation of agriculture and the encouragement to 'sideline production' in individual households. The state has encouraged family-based rural enterprises in rural China, and an open market for the trade of the products produced by peasant families under the 'individual and family responsibility system'. A 'courtyard economy' has flourished in the countryside, with rural women in particular engaged in three different projects: handicrafts, raising small livestock, and cultivation of fruit and vegetables. Since 1989, 550,000 rural women have engaged in handicraft art and earned 187 million yuan in foreign currency (*Women of China* (*WoC*), May 1990: 17). While engaged in such production the mothers need their daughters to look after the younger children, and to help in house chores. Child labour has particularly affected the education of girls. 'By digging asparagus alone, a ten-year-old girl can make 850 yuan a year, accounting for 15 per cent of the total income of the family', reported *Jiaoyu pinglun* (*CE* Summer 1989: 58).

China spends only 2 per cent of its national income on education (*WoC*, September 1989: 2). This is less than other developing countries, for example India. The communes used to be responsible for education at the village level. With decollectivisation, and a political rejection of Maoist 'egalitarianism', China's peasants are refusing to contribute towards local education. As the local county budgets are sorely stretched by economic infrastructural demands, funds for education are scarce. In the early stages of reform, there were reports of schools being stripped of all wooden furniture and beams by peasants for burning; those who objected were labelled 'ultra-leftists'. The local party cadres, left without support of the higher authorities, and insecure of their own positions dared not oppose the peasants. Between 1982 and 1986, the number of elementary schools in the rural areas of Shaanxi Province, for example, dropped by 288 so that 575,000 students were unable to continue their studies, reported *Pai Hsing* (JPRS-CAR-89-090). By the mid-1980s the local schools began to charge fees. The enterprise culture encouraged by the state meant that the schools which could afford to raise fees disproportionately to expenditure did so, further exacerbating the problem:

> According to data from Taoyuan County, tuition and incidentals were 7.6 yuan, 10 yuan, 19 yuan, and 22.2 yuan in 1985 for lower elementary school, higher elementary school, junior middle school,

and senior middle school respectively, but these charges went up to 18.5 yuan, 28 yuan, 55 yuan, and 87.8 yuan in 1988.

(CE, 1989: 36)

Choices had to be made within the confines of the family income; the girls lost out.

When the communes were disbanded the villages were freed from what had become little state bureaucracies functioning relatively independently. It is necessary, said a report in the *Peasant Daily* in July 1989,

> to place emphasis on strengthening the self-reform mechanisms within society. In recent years, a number of autonomous organisations, such as 'wedding and funeral councils' ... have been set up by villagers in various places. These are good organisational forms ... we can leave the education of the peasants to these organisations. Communist Party members ... should join these organisations as ordinary people.
>
> (JPRS-CAR–89–073)

While such a policy created more space for local organisations in the rural society to emerge, these did not always benefit women (see Rai, 1988) or girls' education. Values of traditional peasant society are re-asserting themselves after being frozen for the last forty years, indicating the limitations and failures of mobilisational and of the directive politics of the Maoist period. They also pointed up the social ambiguities in and prejudices of the civil society, the importance of a legal and legislative support for certain groups, and the space required for oppositional groups to function autonomously. The *Educational Review* reports that child marriage is on the increase and is affecting girls' education:

> Mercenary marriage is now widely practiced in rural areas despite repeated banning, and the price of betrothal gifts has gone up incessantly. To raise funds for their sons' marriage, many parents are forced to have their daughters engaged at an early age so that betrothal gifts can be taken in early.
>
> *(CE*, 1989: 57)

Education among the child brides of Zhoutian Township of Changding County, for example, the article continued, is even lower than among other girls. The county has 'seventy-six school age girls, and twenty-four of them are child brides. Six child brides are denied education, and ten of them go to school off and on.' Parents are also afraid to educate their girls. The drudgery of rural life is such that even with the incentive of greater individual profit both boys and girls want to head for the bright lights of the city. With the relaxation that has come in the residential passport (*hukuo*) system, which tied the people to their place of birth for life, the danger of rural emigration has increased. Girls are valuable for both their income as well as the betrothal gifts that they bring, and education is seen as a threat to their acceptance of their lot. Together with this is a culture which looks upon the daughter as a temporary member of the family, as a guest who will depart to another village upon marriage: 'To educate a daughter is to water another man's garden', warns an old Chinese proverb.

The reforms in education have also done away with the flexibility of the *minban* schools of the Maoist period. In the 1960s and 1970s these schools took the realities of peasant life into account, and fashioned both curricula and timetables for schools so that they could accommodate girls who had household responsibilities. While this system did not challenge gendered division of household labour, and was poor in the level of schooling it provided, it did allow the girls to join schools and get some education. Demands are now being made for flexibility in schooling for girls, and to make education 'relevant to the lives of peasant girls' (*CE*, 1989: 61). Patriarchy is to remain unchallenged; paternalistic welfare tries to step in yet again.

However, women's organisations are taking issue with this situation. Through exhortations, debate, and discussion, the question of education for girls is being made a public issue. There has also been direct opposition to the decline in girls' education – by girls themselves. *Peasant Daily* reported that 'a group of girls in Jia Cui village, Guanxi, have gone on strike, refusing to do housework unless their parents allow them to go to school. They are aged 8 to 15' (FBIS/88/234/45).

OF WORKERS, MOTHERS AND HOODLUMS

Universities are undergoing some radical changes under the post-Mao leadership. The introduction of the market-based economic policies has affected the administration and financing of these institutions. With the introduction of the market into the economy, the state gradually began to relax the job allocation system. This deregulation of job allocation was to be completed by 1993. Although the events during June 1989, and unintended problems resulting from the introduction of the scheme, have slowed down the process, the reform itself is to go ahead in the long run. Its implication for women's employment and social position are significant. Further, the question of employment for women in the context of the market also sheds light on the unproblematic, ungendered way the concept of work has been dealt with in socialist China. As in most liberal societies, in China too, two models have been generally applied to the study of work: the job model and the gender model (Feldberg and Glenn, 1984). The premise of both is the male-headed family. However, unlike liberal theorists of work, the Chinese Communists did not derive social status for men from their professions and for women from their roles as wives or mothers, even though the latter roles remained important to the construction of the woman's social identity. They did not, however, problematise division of labour, either at the work-place or in the family. Women thus continued to be concentrated in light, low-paid jobs, and held responsible for household work. When this question was addressed during the Cultural Revolution, women were asked to be more like men; 'whatever men can do, women can do too' was one of the slogans of the period. To prove that they were good workers women had to be 'desexualised'. A woman lecturer was irritated when I questioned her about problems she faced in the university as a woman: 'I don't think very much about the fact that I am a woman; I am a teacher.' The partiality of any explanation of work/gender discrimination that does not take into account the question of patriarchy becomes obvious here. A dual systems approach to work evolved in part as a response to the Marxist theory of capitalist-segmented labour market (see Walby, 1988: 22). If patriarchy predates capitalism and cannot therefore be explained entirely by it, then the overthrowing of capitalism is not the uprooting of patriarchy. That battle has yet to be waged and won. And if, as in China, market forces are introduced into the job allocation system, this question becomes even more urgent. Whether the segmented labour market theory takes into account the independent factor of patriarchy when explaining gendered discrimination or not, what it does underline is the correlation, nay the necessity, of this discrimination to the efficient working of capitalist economy (see Connell, 1987: 41–6). These are questions that the Chinese Communists have not confronted, as will be evident from the discussion below.

In 1987, 33 per cent of the total number of university students in China were women (*CE*, Summer 1989: 7). This means that the per-centage of women in higher education has not even doubled since the 1950s, when it was about 17 per cent (de Beauvoir, 1958: 151). University graduates in China are in a privileged position where employment is concerned. Their skills are needed by the state, and also, since the reforms were introduced, by private enterprises. Jobs in China have been allocated according to a central plan drawn up by the Ministry of Planning, which accepted the help of the State Education Commission in placing graduates. Areas of need for graduates were identified and matched with the available pool of graduating students, taking into consideration their preferences, and their areas of residence. The large majority of university graduates were sent to teach in either schools or provincial universities, and they did not like this prospect; the jobs are low-paid and low-status. Women graduates, more than the men, are type-cast as school teachers and allocated these jobs. In line with economic reforms, China's graduates have seen a gradual, cautious, but significant opening up of the job allocation system to the market forces. Individual firms and companies now come to the university campuses for direct recruitment. Under such a system women still lose out.

As the question regarding the nature of work, gender, and patriarchy has remained largely unworked out, women's employment – while being much higher than in most western countries – has remained contingent upon the larger economic plans and needs. In the 1950s, 1970s, and again in the 1980s, women were encouraged to leave their jobs and retreat to the private sphere as mothers and wives as a solution for the problem of urban unemployment. In 1987, an article in *Women of China* on the conflict between motherhood and a career for a woman lecturer started a debate that led many young women to question, if not state policy, the gendered system of discrimination in employment. The 'feminist' woman lecturer had written,

> An idea has begun to fix itself in my mind and assert itself. If there were the choice – to stay at home or continue work – I would choose to stay at home without any hesitation. My friends think this would be a step backward and a financial loss for me. But if I could stay at home just temporarily, I explain, my husband, who has a promising future, could devote more time to his work. Our child would be more healthy for growing up in a more family-like atmosphere, enjoying his right to receive love from both his parents, and I could give more attention to his intellectual development and early education. My husband at the same time could enjoy a quiet and comfortable atmosphere after a day's hard awork. Wouldn't my sacrifices reap proportionally greater benefits?
>
> (Wu Daiying, 1987: 1–2)

Two questions arise here. The first is the twinning of child-bearing and child rearing, which a non-confrontation with patriarchy has allowed the party/state in China to leave unaddressed. The second is the labelling of successful women as 'exceptional', thus of no threat to the sex–gender system. Exceptional women achieve as long as they do not live like women but try and become more like men (see Eisenstein, 1989: 334); that is, they don't get married and don't have children. A woman physicist at Hangzhou University who is 42 and unmarried thought this to be the price she had to pay for academic recognition. Had she been married she could not have afforded the time or the energy to do well professionally in a job which requires mental and physical strength, perseverance, courage and determination – all these being exceptional qualities in women. This argument is used, in the case of women students, for not hiring graduate women for more 'demanding', and therefore better-paid jobs.

Zhongguo Funubao reported that in 1986, 'among the unemployed young people in the country, the proportion of women rose to 61. 5 per cent. . . . On top of that, in the current reform to simplify structure and reduce authorized size, many organisations and outfits start out by laying off women' (*CE*, Summer 1989: 28). It is becoming increasingly difficult to find employment for women graduates in post-Mao China. Concern with profitability, cultural and social prejudices, and the withdrawal of a radical political rhetoric of the state is creating a situation that is squeezing women out of the job market. In 1984 'the ratio between male and female science and technological personnel in the country was 2.1 : 1; between males and females holding the title of engineer or the equivalent, 4.4 : 1; and between males and females with a senior engineer title, 7.6 : 1' (*ibid.*: 29). Two factors are particularly important in this fall of graduate female employment. First is the woman's child-bearing role. 'We would rather take in a male hoodlum than a woman. A hoodlum can be reformed, but you cannot get a woman to give up child-bearing', remarked a manager of an enterprise (*ibid.*: 83).

Until the economic reforms were initiated during the 1980s every industrial and commercial enterprise in China or the neighbourhood committees in the housing areas took responsibility for running crèches so that the mothers could go back to work as early as possible. With the emphasis shifting to profitability, and the introduction of private enterprise, the new managers regard the expenditure on crèches, and maternity leave as a cut in profits. 'Childbearing is the first economic problem one encounters in the hiring of women. To relieve the employer's worry, we must start with economic [initiative] . . . Childbirth is the concern of the whole society. Why should the factories alone be required to bear all the losses', the managers argue (*Zhongguo Funubao* 257, *CE*, Summer 1989: 84). Many 'people of insight' have this advice to offer the state: 'The losses *caused* [my italics] by women bearing children for the regeneration of the human race should not be borne by factories . . . If the government can subsidise or the enterprises can retain part of the profit [for birth subsidies] . . . the employers' misgivings about hiring women would be dispelled' (*CE*, Summer 1989: 86).

The managers find various ways to exclude women from employment. In any tests that the graduates have to take to get a job, women have to score significantly higher: 'We also take women, but they must pass a test', said the manager of the Beijing Garment Import and Export Corporation. '60 points for men and 90 points for women. . . . This . . . is giving them opportunity. If you are good, you can compete!' (*Zhongguo Funubao* 315, *ibid.*: 12). However, higher scores in the 1987 examinations failed to get women graduates of the German language course in the Foreign Languages department at Hangzhou University the better jobs in the hotel or travel industries. The management did not think that the women could devote their full energies to their jobs and also care for a family. Maternity leave and benefits were costs that managers were not willing to meet. These are, of course, the better-paid jobs and have much higher status than the teaching jobs in small towns. The women students who spoke to me about this had approached the university authorities regarding this continuing discrimination, but got no support from them. They felt bitter, frustrated and angry but also helpless to change things.

As contractual work begins to replace tenured employment, the managers can refuse to renew their contracts: 'Among contract women workers there is a sense of insecurity of losing their jobs. One contract woman worker in Nanning Glutamate Factory had performed the normal procedures for marriage registration. The factory, however, terminated the contract on the pretext that she violated the factory policy of late marriage.' Factory officials also 'encourage' women to take early retirement in return for 60–70 per cent of their salary as pensions. (The normal retirement age for women is 5 years earlier than for men.) Another way is to ask women to take a 'prolonged maternity leave' of up to 3 years at 75 per cent of their pay. This allows the management to cut back on crèche facilities in their factories. The Chinese Women's Federation 'perceived it as no more than a thinly disguised plan to move women out of the workforce' (Honig and Hershatter, 1988: 253). The rationalisation and efficiency of the market means that women in positions of authority also fall in with the profitable option. A party secretary, and a deputy manager of Keli High Technology Corporation felt that, 'though I am a woman manager, I still want fewer women in my corporation . . . [women] would marry, get pregnant and take maternity leave. When their children were young they would sometimes have to ask for leave to care for them . . . when there were more women in the work unit, there were greater costs' (*WoC*, December 1989: 35). In 1987, 20 per cent of the Beijing University graduates sent by the placement office to various enterprises were rejected because of their sex (*Zhongguo Funubao* 257, *CE*, Summer 1989: 74). In 1988, among the graduates of the Chinese People's University rejected by employers, 80 per cent were women (*Zhongguo Laodong Kexue* 5, *CE*, Summer 1989: 41).

The ethic of the market is also used by managers to 'prove' the undesirability of employing women. Women are not suited to the competitive thinking and work ethic required in the market place: 'In the future', writes an enthusiast, 'the principle of the survival of the fittest will become one of the major factors in the new, dynamic employment system. If you fit, you will be well received; if you fail to fit, you will be eliminated. This will hold true for all members of the society – no tolerance and no excuse'. And the women graduates are not fit enough to appreciate the new system! They have, we are told, a psychological barrier to the values of the market. In Henan of the 66 women surveyed, 90 per cent wanted to work in state-owned enterprises. They 'believed these enterprises are an "iron rice bowl" that guarantee a stable income. They have yet to realise that they are facing the challenge of the survival of the fittest', commented the spokesperson for the Investigative Group, Women's Work Commission, All-China Federation of Trade Unions (*ibid.*: 44).

It would be wrong to suggest, however, that these attacks on women's rights to work are not being resisted. There has been a growing pressure on the state from women's organisation to intervene, and from public opinion, as reflected in the various discussions and debates published in women's magazines. The response from the state – fractured and localised as it is – has been to encourage industrial enterprises to recruit more women, but also to experiment with institutional devices to protect the interests of women. Subsidised funds to pay for women's maternity leave benefits have been one such experiment. One such initiative came in 1988 in Nantong, which is a textile industry town. Public debate on the decreasing number of women employed by the industry led the city to create a Delivery and Child-Bearing Fund for Women Employees. Every year textile companies contribute 20 yuan per employee into this fund, and will be able to draw 1,000 yuan from it for each woman employee who gives birth. In 1989, the No. 1 Textile Mill for example, turned over 140,000 yuan to the city's Delivery and Child-Bearing Fund and received over 400,000 yuan, which the company used to pay salaries and welfare benefits for women workers on maternity leave. This has drawn approval not only from the factories, but also from the Women's Federation (*WoC*, September 1990: 22–4). What such schemes do not confront is the gendered division of labour that is the root of the problem of women's employment. The mayor of Nantong, endorsing the need to 'protect' the interests of women's employment said, 'The responsibility of giving birth and bringing up children that women shoulder is by no means a private or a domestic matter, but it is their great contribution to the development of the society' (*ibid.*: 22). However, there has been no direct intervention by the state to confront the problem.

The problems faced by women graduates have provoked a public display of anger by the women themselves and by their families. One commented, 'in today's attempt to build the Chinese economy and to implement the Four Modernisations, do we or don't we need knowledge? Do we or don't we need talent? If the answer is yes, then female university graduates should be respected and utilised' (Honig and Hershatter, 1988: 250). An article on public and private responsibilities of women in *Zhongguo Funu* concluded, 'Men taking part in politics requires opportunity and ability; women taking part in politics requires opportunity, ability, and family support. The unfairness of this situation demands our consideration' (*WoC*, April 1990: 3). Chinese women studying the growing employment problem of graduate women have emphasised that women do not want to leave work; that it is the values of the society that are pushing them in that direction: 'Most women are worried that having no job may jeopardise their position' (*Zhongguo Funubao*, 20 June 1988: 2, *CE*, Summer 1989: 51). While a survey of 500 married couples in Shanghai by the Shanghai Academy of Social Sciences found that '23.7 per cent of married women are willing to return home to concentrate on household matters', most of them saw this as a contingency measure rather than choice (*ibid.*: 50). Such articles, studies, and surveys by women emphasise the need to counter 'the feudalistic idea of "holding man superior to woman" '. The language of rights is also being used, as is the argument against profit being the only criterion of recruitment. Women are calling upon other women to stand up for their own rights, and are berating those who encourage women to devalue themselves: 'news media in recent years ... fail to call upon women to make unremitting efforts to improve themselves' (*ibid.*: 93).

CONCLUSION

Readdressing the questions raised at the beginning of this chapter in the light of the discussion about education and employment, we are still without a clear picture. The logic of the market, that is, being employed as an answer to the stagnation of the economy under centralised planning, does not confront many issues of development. First, while the state has been loosening its control of certain areas of the economy, its political primacy remains intact. This situation is anomalous because, on the one hand, any withdrawal of the state from the economic sphere leads to the needs of the market taking precedence over even welfare policies that might benefit women. On the other hand, the political monopoly of the Communist Party of China denies women the autonomous space to organise in the defence of their own rights. Second, the market has a centralising aspect which is detrimental to the needs of women. Marketisation of the Chinese economy has denied space to alternative economic structures, methods of production, administration, and exchange; this has affected women adversely. At the level of individual units of production – both in rural and urban economy – there is evidence of growing centralisation of management powers. In the countryside, the family responsibility system has meant increased power to the male head of the family; in the factories the 'one-man management system' has increased the power of the manager. The consequences for the position of women in China can be seen in the above discussion regarding education and employment. However, the operation of the market also has the potential of creating a 'public sphere' that is essential to the formation of interest groups. Competition for resources, jobs, and profit, encouraged by the market, also creates 'possibility spaces' within which individual needs can be aired. The contradiction between individual interests, and centralised political power, on the one hand, and the logic of the market on the other, can produce strains that can be exploited by interest groups to their own advantage.

As regards the question about the revival of feudal practices in Chinese civil society, it would be unwise to deny the fundamental break that Communism in China has made with that past. The changes in the legal and social position of women have been real, and significant. However, the gender-blindness that characterised CPC policies from its inception has not been rectified. With the withdrawal of the radical rhetoric of an interventionist state, the unresolved question of 'feudal practices' is emerging yet again. However, as already pointed out, this revival of patriarchal values is also accompanied by a refusal by the state to release its stranglehold on political power. Some of the problems faced by Chinese women today are those of a traditional patriarchal society, others of a statist one.

The marginality of women's problems, needs and rights is not in doubt in China today. The project of modernisation has taken overarching precedence over any other interests. In August 1937 Mao had written, 'whatever happens, there is no doubt at all that at every stage in the development of a process, there is only one principal contradiction that plays the leading role ... while the rest occupy a secondary and subordinate position' (Mao, 1977: 332). Despite the repudiation of Maoist politics in other areas, the post-Mao leadership continues to regard social contradictions in the same light as did Mao.

The post-Mao reforms in China have resulted in a re-examination of the relationship between the state and civil society. While the introduction of new economic forms by a politically centralised state has been welcomed by many on the grounds that it can allow the re-emergence of a critical public sphere and a civil society, the fact of continued political centralisation undermines the promise of critical debate. And the re-emergent civil society creates new problems for women. Civil society, while providing an alternative focus to the political institutions of the state also supports and reinforces unchallenged orthodoxies by which women suffer. While civil society can be subversive of a centralising state, its opposition to the state can and often does have roots in traditional values, and systems that are not necessarily beneficial to all groups comprising it. In China this is becoming evident in the nature of spontaneous organisations and values emerging from an unreconstructed patriarchal civil society. The celebration of 'Virtuous Wives Day' is on the increase in the countryside. On this day 'the whole village turns out at the threshing ground, beating drums and gongs, to watch the village leaders pin red flowers on the jackets of virtuous wives and present them with certificates of merit'. Those selected for this decoration may have 'cared for a mentally ill husband for years, concentrated all their affection on their children when they were widowed, or helped their husband make a fortune' (*WoC*, April 1987). In this context the role of a socialist or welfare state becomes less straightforward to analyse. Whereas civil society provides a space for subversion of the state, the legal and institutional instruments at the disposal of the state can be used to subvert the traditional values of this civil society. The willingness of the state to do this is of crucial importance in this situation. By loosening its control over the economic sphere, and significantly diluting the radical socio-political rhetoric of equality, and by giving legitimacy to market relations in civil society, the state continues to participate in the patriarchal oppression of the women. The 'liberation' of civil society from the centralised state takes on a different complexion in this context. The question of the relationship between the state and civil society thus remains a complex one, and one that is as yet unresolved.

REFERENCES

de Beauvoir, Simone (1958) *The Long March*, André Deutsch and Weidenfeld & Nicolson, London.

Chinese Education. A Journal of Translation (CE), Summer 1989, White Plains, New York.

Connell, R.W. (1987) *Gender and Power*, Polity Press, Cambridge.

Croll, Elizabeth (1983) *Chinese Women Since Mao*, Zed Books, London.

Deng Xiaoping (1984) *Selected Works*, Foreign Languages Press, Beijing.

Eisenstein, Zillah (1989) 'Reflections on a politics of difference', in Sonia Kruks, Rayna Rapp and M.B. Young (eds) *Promisory Notes: Women in the Transition to Socialism*, Monthly Review Press, New York.

Feldberg, R. and Glenn, E.N. (1984) 'Male and female: job versus gender models in the sociology of work', in J. Siltanen and M. Stanworth (eds) *Women and the Public Sphere*, St Martin's Press, New York.

Foreign Broadcasts Information Service (FBIS).

Hayhoe, Ruth (1989) *China's Universities and the Open Door*, M.E. Sharpe, Armonk, New York.

Hernes, Helga Maria (1984) 'Women and Welfare State: the transition from private to public dependence', in Harriet Holter (ed.) *Patriarchy in a Welfare Society*, Universitetsforlaget, Oslo.

Honig, Emily and Hershatter, Gail (1988) *Personal Voices: Chinese Women in the 1980s*, Stanford University Press, Stanford, Calif.

Huang Wei (1989) 'The plight of Chinese intellectual women', in *Women of China*, December.

Johnson, Kay Ann (1983) *Women, the Family, and Peasant Revolution in China*, University of Chicago Press, London.

Joint Publication Research Supplement (JPRS).

Lavely, William, Xiao Zhenyu, Li Bohua and Freedman, Ronald (1990) 'The rise in female education in China: national and regional patterns', *China Quarterly* no. 121: 61–93.

Mao Zedong (1977) *Selected Works*, Vol. V, Foreign Languages Press, Beijing.

Pateman, Carol (1990), 'Contract and ideology: a reply to Coole', in *Politics*, vol. 10, no. 1.

Prazniak, Roxanne (1989), 'Feminist humanism: Socialism and Neofeminism in the writings of Zhang Jie', in Arif Dirlik and Maurice Meisner (eds) *Marxism and the Chinese Experience*, M.E. Sharpe, New York.

Rai, Shirin M. (1988) 'Market merry-go-round', in *China Now*, no. 125, Summer.

Rai, Shirin M. (1991) *Resistance and Reaction: University Politics in Post-Mao China*, Harvester-Wheatsheaf, London.

Shue, Vivienne (1988) *The Reach of the State*, Stanford University Press, Stanford, Calif.

Stacey, Judith (1983) *Patriarchy and Socialist Revolution in China*, University of California Press, Berkeley, Calif.

State Education Commission of China (SEC) (1984) *Achievement of Education in China: Statistics 1949–1983*, People's Education Press, Beijing.

State Education Commission of China (SEC) (1985) *Reform of China's Educational Structure: Decision of the CPC Central Committee*, Foreign Languages Press, Beijing.

Walby, Sylvia (1988) *Gender Segregation at Work*, Open University Press, Milton Keynes.

Women of China (WoC) (Journal of the Women's Federation of China, Beijing).

Wu Daiying (1987) 'Each to her own choice', in *Women of China*, March.

Xiao Ming (1990) 'Nantong's delivery and child-bearing fund for women employees', in *Women of China*, March.

Xiao Ming and Liu Hong (1990) 'Conflicts between public and private responsibility', in *Women of China*, April.

Young, Marilyn B. (1989) 'Chicken Little in China: women after the Cultural Revolution', in Sonia Kruks, Rayna Rapp and Marilyn B. Young (eds) *Promisory Notes: Women in Transition to Socialism*, Monthly Review Press, New York.

Zhao Ziyang (1987) 'Advance along the road of socialism with Chinese characteristics', in *13th National Congress of the Communist Party of China*, Beijing Review Publications, Beijing.

3 Gender and political participation in rural China

Zhang Junzuo

THE QUESTION OF GENDER AND RURAL INSTITUTIONS

Agricultural development in China has unfolded within two major institutional structures of production in the past four decades. These are the people's commune system between the 1950s and the late 1970s and the household responsibility system from the 1980s up to now. The role and status of rural women in this developmental process are fairly complex with regard to their economic, political and social participation. Particular institutional forms of agricultural production, the political and socio-economic policies characterised by the development strategies adopted by the Central Committee of the Chinese Communist Party, and the process of implementing them during the different periods of economic development have affected the participation of women in different areas of rural life. Thus one could assume that the perception of the role and status of rural women in society would alter, following the fundamental changes in organisational structures of agricultural production.

One way of measuring change in the status of women is by studying the numbers of women who hold responsible positions in the Communist Party, government organs and production units (Croll, 1985: 44). An editorial in *Beijing Review* (7–13 March 1988: 23) claimed, 'the falling number of women leading members was already becoming evident before the 13th National Party Congress in 1987. An official of the All-China Women's Federation revealed that in the 1987 re-election of leading bodies at the county and township levels, the number of women representatives was found to be down in 12 provinces and munici-palities. In some areas there was not a single woman in county and township government.' A fierce debate over the question of women's participation in politics arose from this (Zhou, 1988). While many urged that attention must be paid to the existing decline of women cadres at local level of leadership bodies (*Zhongguo Funu*, 1982, no. 6: 4 and no. 4: 45; 1984, no. 12: 40), others found it hard to conclude that women's political status had changed negatively (*Renmin Ribao*, 8 March 1988: 3). Johnson suggests that:

> Although the bias towards economic emancipation was somewhat amended during recent years and women have been mobilised to participate in political processes, there were few references to the need to take specific political action to further sex equality. This omission reflects a strong emphasis in socialist policies which conceptualises the ending of women's subordination as derivative and reliant in the first instance on broader, political and socio-economic changes.
>
> (1981: 702)

According to Nelson, the effects of development policies designed for rural areas show that they have, at least until very recently, systematically 'neglected rural women' (1979).

This chapter will focus on a comparative examination of rural women's political participation during the two major institutional phases of agricultural production. Within this context we will speculate about the future political prospects of Chinese rural women.

RURAL WOMEN'S POLITICAL PARTICIPATION AND MOBILISATION

The establishment of the All-China Women's Democratic Federation (1949) was an official recognition of the importance of women's position in political decision-making. The Marriage Law (1950) and the Labour Insurance Regulations (1951) had allowed women to exercise their choice in marriage and divorce and to join in the labour force. In the early years of the People's Republic the Chinese Communist Party concentrated on the reorganisation of the relations of production and the transformation of institutional structures. This strategy was adopted in order to achieve rapid growth in agricultural production, to support state industry and to guarantee a basic living standard for all the population. In June 1950 the central government promulgated the Land Reform Law, after which the land reform movement of 1950–2 gradually spread to most parts of China (Liu and Wu 1986: 47). The major policy towards women was to encourage them to take part in production activities and to achieve equality with men in economic affairs. The Communist Party eliminated the landlord class, changed land ownership, redistributed land among the peasants, and later formed agricultural producer co-operatives, expanded the arable land and maximised the use of resources. The Peasant Associations were organised, which were expected to have a minimum of 30 to 40 per cent women members (Davin, 1976: 140). With the protection of the Marriage Law and the Labour Regulations,[1] rural women as a social group were not only self-supporting but also began having equal status in the family and equal rights in social production (Yao, 1983: 159).

In early 1953 the Central Committee of the Chinese Communist Party decided to develop co-operatives in agricultural production. Women involved in production were considered as a great contributing force to agriculture. Mao Zedong in his book of 1955 entitled *Socialist Upsurge in China's Countryside* wrote,

> Before the co-operative transformation of agriculture, surplus labour power was a problem in many parts of the country. Since then many co-operatives have felt the pinch of a labour shortage and the need to mobilise the masses of women who did not work in the fields before, to take their place on the labour front ... the principle of equal pay for equal work for men and women must be enforced to encourage women to engage in productive activity.
>
> (Mao, 1977: 269)

The Communist Party made a decision to allow rural women to participate in agricultural production. Women were to be recruited into production not only to give them an independent economic role in society but also to ensure that they could benefit society through work. Mao claimed in 1955 that 'Women form a great resource of labour-power in China. This resource should be tapped in the struggle to build a great socialist country' (*Zhongguo Funu*, 1956, no. 3: 1; Mao, 1977: 269). By 1952, 60 per cent of rural women participated in agricultural production and received pay for it. During the rural co-operativisation and collectivisation movements (1953–7) more than 120 million rural women were occupied in collective agricultural production in China (*Funu Bao*, 9 October 1989).

In 1958 the people's commune system was initiated, based on the Chinese Communist Party's long-term strategy for economic growth. Mao Zedong suggested that the communes' advantage was that they combined 'industry, agriculture, commerce, education and military affairs, thus making the task of leadership easier' (Liu and Wu, 1986: 233). The three tiers of the commune system – the commune, the production brigade and the production team in which the ownership of the means of production was vested – became the dominant institutional structure in the rural sector. The production team was the basic unit of production. It was responsible for labour use and assignment of production tasks. Income distribution was based on the work point system.[2] Up to the end of 1956 the work points for women's income were one quarter of the total in many co-operatives in rural China (*Funu Bao*, 9 October 1989). Communes were linked to the central government through the counties and provinces. This was one way that administrative management could achieve a balance between the centralisation sought by the Chinese government and the decentralised structures which ensured that local authorities and community leaders in general had a large influence on local production and other social activities. The commune system was readjusted and consolidated in 1962. Altogether 74,000 people's communes were set up, embracing 700,000 collective production brigades and 7 million production teams in the whole countryside (Burns, 1988: 36). During the Great Leap Forward (1958–9), a demand for women's labour had resulted in 90 per cent of the working age women in rural areas being mobilised in social production (Croll, 1985: 27). Up to the late 1970s around 80 per cent of peasant women worked in collective agriculture, constituting at least 40 per cent of the collective labour force in the countryside (Croll, 1983: 23).

The All-China Women's Federation was organised at rural grass-roots level in a structure which closely followed the three tiers of the people's communes. At the commune level there was a 'basic-level congress of women' and at brigade and team level every brigade and every production team had its own women cadres to take care of the special problems pertaining to women. Women cadres were elected from among the women in these tiers, and functioned as full-time, specialised women cadres. The members of the women's congresses were elected in the production teams. The women cadres served an integrated political function, since they were in charge of organising women's work and at the same time had a permanent seat in the administrative committee of the team or the brigade. In general they also had a seat in the women's congresses at commune level (Hemmel and Sindbjerg, 1984: 8, 69). The framework within which these basic-level congresses were set up was analogous to the organisation of the people's congresses, with delegates of members at each level, for example village, county, province, and national level (*ibid.*: 8). Women's basic-level conferences met periodically, and involved women from production teams, brigades and communes of the province. The national congress of women met every few years.

The government introduced 'labour protection' and 'equal work for equal pay' legislation, and organised women into separate groups to promote their entry into production. Some collective facilities, such as nurseries, public dining halls, canteens, old people's homes (*jing lao yuan*), mills and sewing groups, were set up in order to release women from the 'double burden' (that is, participation in social production and reproduction) to enable them to contribute more effectively in production, education and political activity. The Women's Federation at different levels aimed to organise labour participation in communes, unite all women in social activities, raise their levels of socialist understanding and vocational skills and protect their rights in all respects (Yao, 1983: 164). Education and training activities were given more attention and were directed towards the leaders of women's groups and production teams. During this period 'women leaders were encouraged to regard their work among women as an independent contribution of great political significance for the fortunes of women and the country' (Croll, 1985: 20). In the late 1950s over 5,500 peasant women had taken the leader or deputy leader positions at the commune level. By 1958 over 16 million women were lifted out of illiteracy (*Zhongguo Funu*, 1959, no. 20: 1). Women cadres were present in 70 to 80 per cent of the 750,000 agricultural co-operatives in 1956. The total number of female cadres was 500,000 in rural China during the mid-1950s (*Funu Bao*, 9 October 1989). The rise of female education and training occurred mainly in two periods – from 1950 to 1958, and the late 1960s to mid-1970s (Lavely *et al.*, 1990: 61).

However, the fact that women's associations were organs of the state makes it reasonable to assert that the Women's Federation from its very beginning aimed at organising 'downwards'. It was organised as a vehicle for policy implementation and mobilisation of women into the labour force, rather than as a local self-governing organisation responding to the reality of rural women in their specific environment. By duplicating the political command structures in the Women's Federation at every level, women's participation was reinforced at each level of the organisational structures, and women's interests were promoted from the 'outside' or from 'above'. This means that the access of women to political advancement was through *imposed* structures of participation. Women's political position relied on a conventional socialist assumption that women's liberation was but part of the programme of the Chinese Communist Party. Such an approach clearly emphasised the primacy of political equality above gender equality.

Between the 1950s and the late 1970s the liberation of women as a political goal was merged with the 'tapping' of women as an unused labour resource. Rural women's political participation was strongly influenced during the periods of intense political movements, for example, the Socialist Education Movement, the Great Leap Forward, as well as Anti-Confucian Movement and Lin Biao Campaign during the period of the ten-year Cultural Revolution. The gender issue was, however, placed in second position after the political goals defined by the party: 'Genuine equality between the sexes can only be realised in the process of the socialist transformation of society as a whole' (*Zhongguo Funu*, 1956, no. 3: 1; Mao, 1977: 263). The advent of the Socialist Education Movement and the Cultural Revolution meant a shift in attention towards women's issues. The tone of debate became more radicalised, but this was in the direction of promoting women's work through politics. The political education of women was considered paramount.

However, in the Xinghe Brigade in Hua County of Guangdong province where Tao Zhu[3] had made a two-month investigation of the rural situation in 1964, women constituted 54.3 per cent of the total population and 55.4 per cent of the labour force. In the brigade's peasant association women constituted 56.6 per cent of the membership as against 36.7 per cent of the leading body. Women constituted 13.5 per cent of the cadres and 14.9 per cent of the party members and 52.5 per cent of the Young Communist League. They made up 38.2 per cent of the military members. Tao Zhu, in a influential speech delivered at the Women's Federation meeting in Guangdong on the 29 May 1965, said,

> Women's work has its own characteristics, for instance the problems concerned with marriage and birth planning which have to be given specific attention, but apart from these issues, some problems still remain to be solved. For instance, there are too few women in the Party, leading positions and the local military. The political influence of women therefore has been limited. Special attention should be paid to receiving female party members and female military members and to promoting more women to be in the positions of leadership. To this end, particular attention should be paid to education of women. As the improvement of their political status is achieved, women's political consciousness will be heightened, education levels can be improved and then the marriage issue can be solved as well.
>
> (*Zhongguo Funu*, 1965, no. 8: 1)

According to Tao Zhu, there were too few women in party and leading positions in the Xinhe Brigade. He suggested that each production team should have its own women cadres to take care of the women's work. Women cadres working in a county's Women's Federation should 'go down' to the level of communes and brigades. They could take the job of vice-director of a commune's political department, or become a brigade's political director. Thus the county's Women's Federation would be able to have the contacts with the grass-roots level to get further working experiences so as to promote women's work in the whole county. Tao Zhu said, 'Women's work is just a part of political work' (*ibid.*).

Women's political participation in rural China during the first thirty years of the People's Republic of China was embedded in overlapping political structures which linked women's work with political mobilisation from above. Participation in social production was high, owing to the requirements of agriculture-based economy. There was a certain degree of economic equality between men and women[4] and the universal participation of women in non-domestic work gave them status. The Chinese socialist ideology brought some social justice to women's position in society. A popular Cultural Revolution slogan was 'Women hold up half the sky'. Chinese women enjoyed greater equality with men than their counterparts in most other developing countries (Aziz, 1978: 68). Rural women, in practice at least, had achieved significant results in political participation, employment, education and some change in family status. But until the reforms started in 1978 the fundamental problem for women's political participation was its compartmentalisation and subordination to national policies. The ambiguity was that the policies were declared to be emancipatory. Women's self-awareness was not a precondition for being liberated in the development process: their liberation was 'given' to them. But artificial, *planned*, *man-made* opportunities for female participation in rural politics are vulnerable to policy shifts in that the very organisations for women's participation can be turned against their interests, and the achievements of these institutions are likely to disappear once the initiative ceases to come from the 'outside' or 'above'. As pointed out by Burns, 'in general, political participation has meant, for most Chinese, mobilization into various forms of elite-determined political activity in support of party and state policies. Political participation in this view is a method of policy implementation' (1988: 33). Burns holds that

> Political participation in rural China was largely restricted to influ-
> encing the implementation of a relatively narrow range of economic
> policies. Absent from economic concern was a wide range of what
> might be called 'potential' issues such as the provision and distribution
> of housing, education, social welfare, transportation, and the regulation
> of labour. There is little evidence to show that peasants have
> attempted to influence policies beyond those that had an immediate
> impact on their livelihood, narrowly conceived in economic terms.
>
> (1988: 59)

In the case of rural women's political status, economic influence is insufficient to ensure political participation. This implies that when political influence diminishes and is replaced by economic influences, the economic forces at best are gender-blind or – as we shall see – rather hostile to the improvement of women's political status.

RURAL WOMEN, ENTREPRENEURSHIP AND LOSS OF POLITICAL INFLUENCE

Beginning in 1978, a dramatic change in the structure of agricultural production resulted from the implementation of the household responsibility system. (In this a contract specified a target output in farm production and the full responsibility for carrying out production was taken by the individual farm household as the basic unit of operational production.) The commune system was quickly abandoned in accordance with the 1982 constitution, and replaced by 58,016 townships and 830,302 villagers' committees[5] which are 'self-governing organisations' (China Rural Statistical Yearbook 1988: 14–15; Du, 1989: 190). In the beginning of the 1980s this dramatic change was fully developed by a series of rural economic reforms related to income distribution, the market environment and a price system for agrarian products. Peasants have subsequently gained much more freedom in managing land and making production plans, and production output is directly linked to the income of the producers by a contract which specifies a target output. Under the responsibility system, the ownership of the means of production was reorganised and the farming household became the dominant unit.[6] The reason for these changes was the need to enhance the peasants' productive motivation and enthusiasm, to contribute to the diversification of rural economy and increase rural incomes, and to introduce the incentives and the discipline of the market-place into the rural economy.

Under this system women in the countryside can also contract land or engage in sideline production and other diversified economic activities. They do not any more need to be organised or mobilised by the leaders of women's organisations to participate in production. Particularly during the first years of the economic reforms, women in many places in rural China took advantage of new employment opportunities and became involved in agro-economic occupations. Statistics from Shandong and Hebei provinces show that in 1980 women were 40 to 60 per cent of the total workforce in diversified agriculture; women were 80 per cent of the total employees in handicrafts and agriculture (*Funu Bao*, 9 October 1989). *Renmin Ribao* reported on 8 March 1986 that in Guangdong province there were 1.4 million specialised households which were mainly run by women, and in

Guizhou province over 47,000 specialised households (*zhuangye hu*) were managed by women of minority nationality. The female labour force at township level reached 163 million in 1984, 45.33 per cent of the total labour force in the townships of the whole countryside. By 1988 the number of female workers in rural enterprises in China was 35 million, 41 per cent of the total of 85 million workers (*Funu Bao*, 9 October 1989).

Issues of rural women's political participation however have been overshadowed by policies directed at getting rich first and facilitating economic growth. The degree of women's political participation is now much more dependent on their own *participatory capability*, and is based on their ability to represent *nouveau riche* peasants or specialised households. However, in many places in rural China, the decline in the number of women cadres has been sharp over the last ten years. Data from several articles in *Chinese Sociology and Anthropology* (Autumn 1987) show that the number of leading women cadres at various levels is now smaller than before. In Heilongjiang province leading women cadres at county level decreased from 9.04 per cent in 1951 to 3.9 per cent in 1980. Now women constitute only 1.5 per cent of the total cadres in this province. In Hebei province up to the end of June 1985 women constituted 4.9 per cent of the members of the leading bodies at county level. Among county heads, they made up only 3 per cent. In Anhui province at the end of 1984, the percentage of women cadres in the province was 23.2 per cent, but at the county level they accounted for only 7.1 per cent and at the district level 6.2 per cent (Cong, 1987: 40; Chen, 1987: 26–7). Data from the Henan provincial investigation into women's participation in leading bodies show that in 1990, among 80,000 cadres at the township level of the province, only 6,000 were women cadres, constituting 8 per cent of the total (*Nongmin Ribao*, 10 April 1991). Attention was drawn in the press to the problems and difficulties of rural women being accepted by the Communist Party (Liu and Ren, 1987: 55; *Zhongguo Funu*, 1984, no. 10: 48). Data from Burns (1988: 180) showed that in 1956, 69.1 per cent of party members were of peasant origin. Since 1979, although the party admitted 800,000 new members, it recruited only 10 per cent of them from among the peasantry. Recent data indicate that only 40 per cent of the party members are peasants. There does not exist published data on women's party membership, but after the general decline in the proportion of rural members, rural women's status must have been affected.

The popular Maoist slogan, 'Women hold up half the sky' has been overridden by a new one: 'The reforms have brought new challenges to women.' The status of women will now be seriously affected by various interacting factors, such as income, employment, education, work style of cadres and rural social welfare, which are all related to the socio-economic policies already introduced by the Chinese government. These factors can in turn affect women's position in the political system.

Women's political rights in rural China not only derive from their officially declared equal rights, but are also based on their position in the social life of their own communities. Their political participation has its foundation in the framework of the communities. Traditionally, women would go to the husband's village after marriage; men would not move to their in-laws' house at marriage because the team saw this as an intrusion upon their property. The marriage pattern is almost universally exogamous. The household registration system (*hukuo*) which was introduced in 1958 (Christiansen, 1990; Potter and Potter, 1990: 296–312) cemented this tradition by fixing people to their place of origin – their native village. Therefore, a woman's political participation was limited because she had to move away from her own family and friendship networks to a village where her husband could monopolise the networks. In pre-1978 China a formal structure which was based on official policies for political influence *did* provide political participation for rural women, and therefore in this period women could move into the realm of political power. In the post-reform period this 'man-made' support fell away. Women were exposed to a situation where informal networks grew in importance, since more economic decision-making was left with the households.

As mentioned earlier, one of the most striking features of the responsibility system in rural China is that production output is directly linked with household income and that contracted households organise their own production. This gives individual households comprehensive access to and control over given amounts of land and other resources. Labour use becomes the most important factor in production. Recent studies on women's participation in social production show that women are not welcome in employment, especially in places with a labour surplus, and that they have been forced to take up unskilled work with low pay (*Women of China*, March 1989, no. 3: 1). Where there is labour shortage, peasants want to have more children in order to get more working hands in the household, which has pushed women towards staying at home and reproducing, regardless of family planning. There is now evidence of one million children without birth registration (*Renmin Ribao*, 30 June 1988). There is also a growing pressure on women to produce sons as land becomes a transferable property, and male labour more valuable for fulfilling contracts. A serious imbalance in survival rate between infant boys and girls in some areas (in some cases the ratio is 5 : 1) was reported by the Women's Federation of Anhui province (*Renmin Ribao*, 7 April 1983: 4).

From the early 1980s, the policy of the Party's Central Committee on reorganising the ranks of cadres was to recruit cadres who were younger, more educated and more specialised. The policy is that 'cadres in the countryside do not withdraw from production ... Those who succeed in elections among peasants will be cadres and those who fail will be peasants' (Du, 1989: 190). Women cadres no longer function as full-time, specialised cadres. Women's groups originally organised for particular political studies and production activities have been abandoned since the disappearance of the commune system. This has made it difficult for women to act as a conscious group both defending and promoting their interests. Davin (1976: 64) observed that in the 1950s 'the Party continued to stress the importance of work amongst women. Discussion and statements on problems connected with women appeared in the press constantly and the work of women's associations in both town and villages was frequently mentioned.' During the economic reform period this general concern has declined. Many Women's Federation branches at the local level in rural China are 'in name only', owing to the loss of their working duties. In many cases, even the work of birth control may not be the responsibility of women. The leader of the village or a specific person from the higher authority might be directly in charge of its implementation, since family planning is regarded as a national concern.

We have few figures which indicate the real situation of rural women's political power in social production. In April 1991 I interviewed an official of the All-China Women's Federation, who told me that since the implementation of economic reforms, no women are involved in political work at local level on a full-time basis. Women's political participation is not regarded as an independent activity; it must be based on economic participation. She therefore considered the increase in women's *participatory capability* as central to improving the status and role of women in social production.

Policies dating from the early 1950s were in theory meant to promote women's position and were generally concerned with 'equal pay for equal work', the sexual division of labour, the strength of women's organisations and education and the transformation of private house-work into public industry, but now they were all promoted in a highly political and ideological sense. Now the official position on women has shifted from political campaigns to economic activity as a central task, following the overall changes in the strategies for economic development (*Zhongguo Funu*, 1979, no. 1: 5 and 6: 20; 1985, no. 1: 2–3). The current policies towards women are to promote women's self-development, which means that women are to be responsible for their own efforts in achieving economic, political and social status. Social attitudes towards women are reflected in the principles of women's 'four selfs' – namely, self-respect, self-confidence, self-reliance and self-improvement (*zizun, zixing, zili, ziqian*) (*Women of China*, 1989, no. 1: 1) – which were first officially raised at the Sixth National Women's Congress in September 1988.

CONCLUSION

The two institutional structures of rural society in China offered women opportunities for equal treatment each in its own way and re-socialised society to bring about a new identification of women's role and status. Women in rural China have achieved some impressive goals in terms of their economic independence, political power and social status. The common opinion is that women's participation in politics is an important basis for women's liberation and that women's political power determines the degree of women's liberation in society (*Zhongguo Funu*, 1990, no. 7: 5).

At the 80th International Woman's Day in 1990, the Communist Party General Secretary Jiang Zemin gave a speech which reflected the official interpretation of women's liberation. He said,

> Women's liberation is a historical process; the degree of women's liberation not only depends on the level of socio-economic development, but is also intimately linked to the non-economic, ideological sphere ... Without the leadership of the Chinese Communist Party and without the guarantees of the socialist system, there is no way that women's liberation could exist. To continue to adhere to the leadership of the Communist Party and to follow the socialist road is the only choice for the Chinese people and is the only way for the liberation of the Chinese woman.
>
> (*Renmin Ribao*, 8 March 1990: 1)

Jiang takes Mao's famous statement, 'the day when Chinese women stand up is the day on which the Chinese revolution has been victorious', to emphasise his view on the relations between Chinese women's liberation and the Chinese socialist revolution. Thus the position of the party on women ostensibly has not changed. The link between social development and the liberation of women is still the dominant idea. But the question remains as to whether the Chinese Communist Party and the state will commit themselves to propagating and supporting women's liberation. If so, is it by creating 'man-made' frameworks for women's political participation, like the mobilisation strategies of the 1950s and 1970s or by actually recruiting able women into senior decision-making posts at all levels? Alternatively, can Jiang's speech be understood to mean that women's issues must wait until socio-economic and non-economic inequalities have been solved?

I shall not attempt to draw specific conclusions from Jiang's words, but it is, however, obvious that there exist two scenarios as far as women's liberation is concerned, particularly in relation to political participation: the struggle for self-liberation in political life, and public and social support for the liberation of women. If we accept that the social policies give women equal rights with men, and it is up to women themselves to achieve equal participation in politics through competition, then the subsequent struggle for equality would also lead to self-liberation. This would also ensure that women's interests were promoted and realised in such a way as to avoid any accusation of unequal or 'softer' treatment. However, the idea of self-liberation presumes equal social conditions for men and women, and even when law and official policy (albeit at its declarative level) are egalitarian, the reality may be very different. Inequalities exist which are unfavourable to women's political participation, for example the rural traditions of exogamous marriage and the negative impact of social ideologies about the personality of women and women's position in social life, etc. Equal political rights, therefore, would be a necessary but not sufficient factor in encouraging women, as a social group, to make major strides towards equal political power. Under such 'equality' women would not gain a significant proportion of political power and would not have sufficient influence on policy-making on women's equal economic and social rights.

In order to become politically active, women must not only fight for themselves, but society as a whole should also be rid of politically unequal institutions. Such a process can only be initiated if the bias against women is identified and actively removed by state and society. Mobilisation of women as instruments for central policy implementation does not lead to greater political participation in real terms, but neither do *laissez-faire* policies. The active public and social support for women's political participation in rural China is certainly strongly needed.

NOTES

1 For women's traditional relationship to production, see Delia Davin, 'Women in the countryside of China', in *Women in Chinese Society*, Stanford University Press, Stanford, Calif., 1975, pp. 116–24.

2 After deduction of agricultural tax and state procurement quotas, the income distribution was carried out by the team leader at the end of the year according to the work points earned by each member of the team.

3 A member of the Central Committee, the first secretary of the Central Committee for Central and South China and Vice-Premier.

4 It is general knowledge that the work point system was slightly disadvantageous for women, but the relative equality in economic terms was significant.

5 Townships are the lowest level of state authority, while villagers' committees are organised by the peasants themselves.

6 The public ownership of the means of production within the commune system was retained in principle, but the actual possession of the means of production was distributed among the families of members of the collectives, who obtained 'use right' and signed production contracts.

REFERENCES

Aziz, Sartaj (1978) *Rural Development: Learning from China*, Holmes & Meier Publishers, New York.

Burns, John P. (1988) *Political Participation in Rural China*, University of California Press, Berkeley.

Cai Chang (1959) 'Dang de Zongluxian . . .', *Zhongguo Funu*, vol.136, no. 20: 1–3.

Chen Zhiping (1987) 'Attention should be paid to training and promotion of women cadres', *Chinese Sociology and Anthropology*, vol. XX, no. 1: 26–31.

China Rural Statistical Yearbook 1988 (1989) China Statistics Press, Beijing.

Christiansen, Flemming (1990) 'Social division and peasant mobility in mainland China: The implication of the hu-k'ou system', *Issues and Studies*, April.

Cong Fenghui (1987) 'On training and promoting female cadres', *Chinese Sociology and Anthropology*, vol. XX, no. 1: 29–43.

Croll, Elisabeth (1981) Review of *Asian Women in Transition*, *China Quarterly*, no. 88: 701–3.

Croll, Elisabeth (1983) *Chinese Women Since Mao*, M.E. Sharpe, Armonk, NY.

Croll, Elisabeth (1985) *Women and Rural Development in China*, International Labour Office, Geneva.

Davin, Delia (1976) *Woman-Work: Women and the Party in Revolutionary China*, Clarendon Press, Oxford.

Du Runsheng (1989) *Many People, Little Land: China's Rural Economic Reform*, Foreign Languages Press, Beijing.

Hao Jiangxiu (1985) 'Fulien gongzuo ...', *Zhongguo Funu*, vol. 317, no. 1: 2–3.

Hemmel, Vibeke and Sindbjerg, Pia (1984) *Women in Rural China: Policy Towards Women Before and After the Cultural Revolution*, Scandinavian Institute of Asian Studies, Curzon Press Ltd, London, chs 1, 2, 3.

Hsu Kwang (1974) 'Women's liberation is a component part of the proletarian revolution', *Beijing Review*, 8 March, no. 10: 12.

Jiang Zemin (1990) 'Quandang Quanshehui ...', *Renmin Ribao*, 8 March: 1–2.

Johnson (1981) *China Quarterly*, no. 88.

Kang Keqin (1979) 'Ba funu gangzuo ...', *Zhongguo Funu*, vol. 245, no. 1: 5.

Lavely, William, Xiao Zhenyu, Li Bohua and Freedman, Ronald (1990) 'The rise in female education in China: national and regional patterns', *China Quarterly*, no. 121: 61–93.

Li Jingwen (1959) 'Yao fahui funu ...', *Zhongguo Funu*, vol. 284, no. 4: 45.

Li Xiaojiang (1986) 'Zhongguo dangdai funu ...', *Zhongguo Funu*, vol. 329, no. 1: 6–7.

Liu Hexian (1984) 'Nongcun funu ...', *Zhongguo Funu*, vol. 314, no. 10: 48.

Liu Ruilong (1956) 'Zhengqu jinnian ...', *Zhongguo Funu*, no. 3: 2.

Liu Suinian and Wu Qungan (eds) (1986) *China's Socialist Economy: An Outline History (1949–84)*, published by *Beijing Review*, Beijing.

Liu Yuzun and Ren Fei (1987) 'Attention should be paid to the problem of rural women being accepted by the Communist Party', *Chinese Sociology and Anthropology*, vol. XX, no. 1: 55.

Mao Zedong (1956) 'Guanyu Fadong ...', *Zhongguo Funu*, no. 3: 1.

Mao Zedong (1972) 'The great union of the popular masses', *China Quarterly*, no. 49: 76–87.

Mao Zedong (1977) *Selected Works*, vol. v, Foreign Languages Press, Beijing.

Nelson, Nici (1979) *Why Has Development Neglected Rural Women?*, Pergamon, Oxford.

Office of Investigation and Study, Anhui Provincial Women's Federation (1987) 'How women can become achievers', *Chinese Sociology and Anthropology*, vol. XX, no.1: 32–8.

Potter, Sulamith Heins and Potter, Jack M. (1990) *China's Peasants: The Anthropology of a Revolution*, Cambridge University Press, Cambridge.

Tao Zhu (1965) 'Zai quanguo fulian ...', *Zhongguo Funu*, vol. 219, no. 8: 1–4.

Wang Huanyun (1979) 'Zhongdian zhuanyi ...', *Zhongguo Funu*, vol. 250, no. 6: 20.

Yao Lee, Esther S. (1983) *Chinese Women: Past and Present*, Ide House, Mesquite, Texas.

Zhang Liying (1989) 'Women become "surplus" ', *Women of China (Zhongguo Funu*, English version), no. 3: 1.

Zin Zainong (1984) 'Xiwang Zhongshi . . .', *Zhongguo Funu*, vol. 316, no. 12: 40.

Zhou Zheng (1988) 'Why fewer women at leading posts?', *Beijing Review*, March vol. 31, no. 10: 7–13.

4 Uneven burdens

Women in rural Poland

Frances Pine

She carries on her shoulders
the house, the garden, the farm,
the cows, the pigs, the calves and the children.

Her back wonders
why it doesn't break.
Her hands wonder
why they don't fall off.
She doesn't wonder.
  (from 'Peasant Woman', Anna Swirszczynska)[1]

Women have often been described as bearing the double burden of domestic responsibility and waged employment in contemporary Polish society. For many rural women, the burden appears to be not double but triple or greater, extending to agricultural labour as well as domestic and waged work. Caring for the children and the home, feeding the animals and tending the crops, going out to work in a factory production line or behind a shop counter, standing in queues for basic foods for hours on end, spinning wool in the evening, travelling to the market before work to sell eggs: the sheer enormity of the everyday tasks of one ordinary rural woman seems overwhelming.

During the socialist period,[2] some aspects of rural women's lives, particularly those concerned with health care and education, improved considerably; many remained unchanged. However, this article is not concerned specifically with the failure of Polish socialism to live up to its promises in terms of women, although this is one implicit aspect of what I shall discuss in the following pages. Nor is it a defense of the parts of socialist policy on 'women's' issues which actually worked, although it is important to remember that there were these. Neither, finally, is it an attempt to predict in any other than the most rudimentary ways the sorts of changes which the move from a centrally planned economy to a demand-based free market are likely to bring for Polish women. That is another piece of work altogether, and one for which at the moment, although we have some insights based both on past attitudes and current trends, we need more information before embarking upon. What this article does represent is an attempt to examine the ways in which women's lives in one area of rural Poland were shaped during the socialist period, not in terms of state policy but under the conditions of 'actual existing socialism'. In some ways, as will become clear as the discussion progresses, socialism as a theoretical construct has little place in the overall picture. This in itself must speak volumes about the relationship between the state, formal legislation, and the daily lives of real people.

The double failure of the Polish socialist state to address the inequalities experienced both by women and by peasants merely reinforces an established legacy of prejudice and discrimination. Even with positive legislation, attitudes and cultural ideologies are slow to change; neither the integration of peasants nor of women into the dominant society was successfully accomplished in the socialist period, and there is little reason to anticipate a sudden improvement in the situation of rural Poles, or of women generally, with the new order. Indeed, there may be very good reasons for expecting the position of women, and rural women in particular, to deteriorate as the austerity programme runs its course. These, I would argue, arise from a series of inter-related factors, and include (1) the association of women with the household and with caring activities; (2) the valorisation of men's work and the undervaluing of that of women; (3) established ideologies, including those of the Catholic Church, of 'natural' female and male roles and character, and of the 'natural' inter-relation between men and women; and finally, (4) the cultural tolerance of alcoholism and violence as acceptable, or at least understandable, male responses to frustration and deprivation. In so far as the rural woman is 'the angel in the house', she is the one who works herself to the bone for very little recognition or compensation, and sometimes gets battered in the process. In the region of southern Poland where I have done research,[3] women are expected to be strong, hard-working and independent, and have a significant power base in their ownership of land and property. None the less, their work is both economically and culturally undervalued in relation to that of men, and they are subject to a series of gender-linked constraints which the socialist state did little to alleviate and which seem likely to carry over into the market economy.

THE PODHALE

The Podhale is the name given to the area of south-western Poland which stretches from the low foothills of the Tatra Mountains to the high peaks on the border with Czechoslovakia. The people of the Podhale are the Gorale, or highlanders. Formerly pastoralists, they are now primarily dairy farmers and subsistence cultivators, and are also engaged in a variety of economic activities outside farming. The Gorale are known throughout Poland as a fiercely independent and lawless people. The stereotypical Gorale woman, often depicted in the paintings and writings of the Mloda Polska group, is strong and beautiful, with a kind of earthy sensuality. The Gorale man has a reputation for heavy drinking, fighting and blood feuding, and generally colourful behaviour. While these gendered stereotypes have no more accuracy than any other collective ascriptions of ethnic characteristics, they do reflect in part the Gorale's own self-image and representations of femininity and masculinity. In terms of the present discussion, this is an important point because the social and economic lives of the peasant women are to some extent both predicated on and constrained by these ideologies of gender.

Until as late as the 1960s the Podhale, like many peripheral mountain regions throughout Europe, was an extremely poor and isolated area. Its poverty and backwardness had long-established historical roots. The southern region of Poland fell under Austrian rule during the Partition Period (1772–1918). Under Austrian law land was divided according to principles of partible inheritance, which gave equal rights to all offspring, both male and female. Partible inheritance is a paradoxical system. Ideally it is highly egalitarian, and it gives women a source of economic power, at least in formal terms, in their equal right to own the most valuable resource in a peasant community – land. However, it also creates intense fragmentation of land holdings. By the beginning of the twentieth century fragmentation in the Podhale had become acute, with many families holding as little as one or two hectares, and many others being landless. This pattern of fragmentation, combined with poor soil and a short growing season – winters are long and severe in the mountains, with the first frosts beginning in October or November and the last snow still on the ground as late as April – limited the possibility of even subsistence farming. Many peasants, both male and female, were forced by economic necessity to work as day labourers in agriculture and to send their daughters into domestic service from a very early age. In the late nineteenth and early twentieth centuries, during the years of epidemic, crop failure and potato famine, there was a massive migration from the Podhale, most significantly to Chicago. Both the pattern of diversifying labour and that of emigration to Chicago were to have a significant effect on the way in which Gorale communities responded to the confused economic climate of the later socialist period.

In the years between the two World Wars the Podhale remained backward and poverty-stricken, although the mountain town of Zakopane, nestled in the heart of the breathtakingly beautiful high Tatras, gained increasing popularity within Poland as a tourist resort. The more remote villages, however, benefited little from the growing tourist trade during this period. Some girls and young women went to work in Zakopane as domestic servants, a practice which continued until the Second World War. Women and children occasionally took small quantities of local produce, baskets of eggs and jugs of tiny wild strawberries and bilberries, to Zakopane to sell to the women of the 'big houses', but on the whole they were more likely to sell their wares in regional markets. And the amount of surplus produce they had to sell was minimal. In the village in which I did my research people today recall that as children they would walk bare-footed to the local Thursday market 9 kilometres away, in order to sell half a dozen eggs for their mothers. Until the beginning of the socialist period, Podhale villages were isolated and inward looking. The peasant economy revolved around family labour for subsistence cultivation and there were long periods of food shortage, during which poorer villagers were forced to mortgage or sell their lands, or to work on the farms of wealthier neighbours, or on the large estates, in order to survive.

Economic growth in the Podhale began in the 1950s, when the socialist regime embarked on a programme to rebuild the country's war-shattered economy and to establish industry in rural areas. Simultaneously, there was a great input into infrastructure development, with roads and railways built and extended, and communication networks developed. New social policies were introduced in these years, including legislation for compulsory education until the age of 16, provision for schools and training colleges, and for pre-school care for the children of those who worked in the state sector. Pensions were established for those who worked in the state sector, and health and dental coverage was provided, for self-employed farmers as well as for state workers.

In agriculture itself, the relationship between the state and the peasant farmers was complex and often hostile. Throughout Poland the peasants fiercely resisted government efforts to collectivise land by organising against the state and refusing to deliver produce. Faced with such extreme opposition, the government abandoned its collectivisation programmes by the mid-1950s, introducing instead co-operatives for the marketing and distribution of produce, and 'agricultural circles' for distribution of farm equipment. As a result, more than 80 per cent of Polish farming remained in private hands during the entire socialist period.

In many parts of Poland, including the Podhale, individual holdings are extremely small; the average size nationally is under five hectares, and many smallholdings are in fact little more than market gardens. In the Podhale specifically, decades of fragmentation and partible inheritance had created farms uniformly small even by Polish standards; in the village where I worked, no holding was large enough to be redistributed under the post-war anti-kulak legislation.[4] Fragmentation was exacerbated by the custom of including land in marriage settlements and dowry payments, resulting in one family working several tiny strip fields scattered over several villages. Today, many Podhale family holdings are too small to be viable for subsistence, let alone for production for the market, and villagers resort to a variety of other economic activities either to supplement farming, or as their main source of income. Agricultural labour is still highly valued, however, and is seen as the most important and essentially the 'real' work. With the exception of a small number of specialist farmers, who run dairy, meat or poultry farms as quite successful businesses, the main structure of agriculture, based on labour-intensive, minimally mechanised household production, has changed little even in the post-war years.

DIVISIONS OF LABOUR

The domestic sphere: women as carers and nurturers

The labour of village women is central to both the domestic economy and the running of the farm; these two spheres of activity are rarely distinguished but rather are subsumed under a general concept of women's economic responsibilities within the peasant family. Extended families are still common in the Podhale, with a single household often consisting of an aged grandparent, a married couple and their unmarried children, and one married daughter or son, her or his spouse, and their young children. Domestic labour is the responsibility of the women and girls, under the direction of the *gospodyni*, the senior woman. Men may perform many of the domestic tasks without losing face if women are ill or engaged elsewhere, but the work is still seen as properly that of women. A Gorale woman is expected to be hard-working and strong, and is judged on the basis of these characteristics, and on her role as a mother. There is extensive informal co-operation among women in domestic labour, not only within individual households but between them as well; this extends from shared child-care, help with sewing and knitting, and cooking for weddings and other feasts, to more extensive help in unusual situations such as during illness and after childbirth. Many villagers are connected to others by ties of kinship or marriage, and the informal mutual aid system provides a local 'safety net' for closely knit groups of women. However, the hierarchical organisation of the household, under the direction of the senior couple, can also create tension between generations of women, particularly between mother-in-law and daughter-in-law.

In addition to their domestic responsibilities, women are also involved in most stages of agricultural production. Feeding the livestock, collecting eggs, and milking cows are seen as women's work, except in the case of specialist farms, where the entire enterprise is much larger and more lucrative and men take over the direction of these activities, if not their actual performance. Farmyard work is not distinguished from labour within the house itself; it also involves food preparation, feeding and cleaning, and is characterised as part of a woman's *robota*, her daily domestic routine. As such, it tends to be undervalued in relation to work in the fields, which is seen as under men's jurisdiction.

Valorisation of male labour

Work in the fields is organised on the basis of age and gender, although, as with domestic labour, these categories are flexible and can be adapted to meet a household's specific needs. Ideally, men do the work which involves horses or tractors and machinery; this includes breaking the soil and ploughing, spreading fertiliser, sowing grain, and cutting the crop for harvest. Women perform the manual, more labour-intensive tasks: weeding, following the horse and planting potatoes by hand, raking hay, and bundling cut grain in the fields. While the *gospodyni* is responsible for organising the labour of women and children, the entire process is under the direction of the *gazda*, the senior man, and it is he who gives the *gospodyni* her instructions. Again, this is an ideal division of authority; in fact, many women participate freely in discussions and decision-making about farming matters, but the actual authority is perceived as male. Here we can speak of the invisibility of women's labour; embedded in the total process of production, it is rarely identified as skilled work in its own right. However, as in the domestic sphere, a woman is expected to be hard-working and capable. Most farm work is performed by the members of the family alone. It is only when the larger tasks which require more than one horse or a labour force greater than that of one family, such as potato planting and picking or threshing, are undertaken, that circles of families exchange labour on a reciprocal basis. At these times the senior man of the farm whose fields are being worked directs the entire operation, and the women provide food for all of the workers as well as working in the fields themselves. This is a formal sphere of co-operation, and is viewed as being primarily male work, although both women and children are active participants. Unlike the informal co-operation which takes place among groups of female kin, the need to account and to reciprocate accurately underlines the public and economic nature of such activities, and the value which is accorded them, both economically and as links of interdependence between households.

Ideologically, the man is associated with the farm and with productivity, and the woman with the household and reproduction. Farm work is valued above all other kinds of labour, and a man is judged as hard-working (*practowity*) or lazy or beggarly (*dziad*) on the basis of his success as a farmer. A woman who is viewed as lazy, or slovenly in the care of her house, is also considered *dziad*, but she has no independent reputation as a farmer unless she has neither husband nor son or other resident male. Such a woman is viewed with pity, and her farm is considered to be inefficiently run, because she must rely either on help from kin, who come to her after they have done their own work and often send women and children rather than men, or on hired hands. While many women do efficiently and effectively run farms if their husbands are ill, incapacitated by alcohol or age, or are absent migrant workers, they tend to be considered more as temporary caretakers, holding things together until their husbands return or their sons are of an age to take over, than as legitimate farmers in their own right. Thus, male identity and prestige can be seen as linked to social and economical roles extending from farming and reaching beyond the family, while female identity and value revolve around the roles of wife and mother. By far the most important aspect in assessing a woman's reputation is her maternal role. Women who neglect their children are very harshly judged, while adult women without children are seen as the most pitiful of creatures. A man's reputation, on the other hand, is linked to his farming skills, as I have said, and to his strength and control in relation both to other men and to women, which I shall discuss below.

While agriculture remains highly valued in cultural terms, farming now takes second place to other activities in the economies of many households. Both men and women work outside farming as waged workers, as self-employed or privately contracted labourers, or as traders, dealers and intermediaries on an informal basis.

Peasant-workers: the continuation of gendered divisions

As the Podhale was opened up to light industry and as the socialist bureaucracy extended throughout the countryside, many villagers were able to obtain work in the state sector during the socialist period. By far the most common jobs for both men and women were in factories. Near the village where I did research, a shoe factory, a ski factory and several other small enterprises were opened in the late 1950s. Most of the work provided by these operations was unskilled and lowly paid; the few villagers I knew who rose to take up administrative jobs in factories were men. The handful of village women who have entered the sphere of white collar work have been those who have achieved a higher level of education, and who work in banks or for the state bureaucracy in town. Although official policy accorded women equal opportunity, it seems that the likelihood of women achieving administrative posts, and hence more responsibility and higher pay, has been limited by the female pattern of a broken or intermittent work career.

Typically, a young woman attends school until the age of 16, and then goes straight to work, either in the waged sector or as an apprentice to a female kinswoman in a craft or trade. Most women marry between the ages of 18 and 22, and continue working, both in agriculture and for pay, until the birth of their first child. Waged work carries 16 weeks maternity leave on full pay, with an option to stay off work for up to three years, either unpaid or with social benefits. The most common pattern which I observed was for a woman to return to work six months after the birth of her first child, leaving it in the care of her mother or mother-in-law. However, after the birth of a second or third child, women tend not to return to work, but rather to take over increasing responsibility for farm labour, and to supplement their household income by informal work such as sewing, knitting or spinning, and sometimes marketing these products or farm surplus such as eggs or cheese. They are likely to return to work when their children are of school age, unless they have established themselves as successful market-women, seamstresses, or the like. When women do return to waged work after a long gap, they are likely to begin again at the bottom; frequently village women of this age work as cleaners, or as cooks or waitresses. One obvious factor determining this type of work pattern is lack of adequate child-care facilities; although many villages do have state-run pre-schools, they have become progressively more expensive over recent years, and peasant families are frequently unable to meet the costs, or prefer to leave their children in the care of their female kin while they are involved in part-time work such as marketing. An obvious advantage of work such as sewing and knitting is that it can be done at home, and therefore combined with both child-care and agricultural labour. A further influence on women's work patterns is the extent to which their responsibility for farm labour may intensify if their husbands or other male household members engage increasingly in non-farming activities.

All of these factors are connected to the developmental cycle of the farming household. When women are childless, or have one child, they are able to work in regular employment as well as on the farm. At this time too their mother or mother-in-law is likely to be young and fit enough to help with child-care and to carry out a lot of the domestic and agricultural tasks. However, as a woman has more children, the demands on her time multiply, and simultaneously, her older female kin are often physically less able to help and tend, in fact, to delegate more and more of the female household and farm work to her. This period also coincides with the time in her husband's life when he is most likely to be occupied extensively outside farming, either in an enterprise of his own, or in a middle-income factory job. Thus, as men become steadily more established in non-farming work, women move in and out of external economic activities which tend to revolve around the core work of farm and household. At this stage of their lives, women are more prone to be engaged in some sort of home-based production or trading than they are to be classic 'peasant-workers'.

Again, the exception to this pattern is the woman who receives some kind of higher education other than manual training. Although the pay received by women working in low and middle level jobs in the state sector has been consistently low, such work has the advantage of being physically undemanding. It also gives the women a network of 'contacts' in similar positions, who can be approached for help in obtaining food and consumer goods, and arranging favours as diverse as finding jobs for relatives, helping obtain passports, providing contacts with doctors and other specialists or jumping the queue for a car or a tractor. Such informal networks became increasingly important in Poland during the late 1970s and 1980s, as systems of distribution broke down and more and more of a family's daily and extraordinary needs were met not through official channels but through personal contacts and favours arranged *na lewo* ('on the left', informally).[5]

INFORMAL WORK

The economy of the Podhale changed considerably during the first two decades of the socialist regime, with the development of industry and infrastructure growth. It was during the profligate Gierek years in the

1970s, however, that the area really took off economically. This can be linked primarily to the growth of two different but interrelated spheres: tourism and the informal economy. I have discussed the development of these two areas in detail elsewhere (Pine, 1987; 1991; Pine and Bogdanowicz, 1982) and shall only touch on it briefly here. What is important in the context of this article is the way in which women elaborated upon activities traditionally associated with the established domestic sphere in order to create new sources of income for themselves and their families.

The tourist industry began to flourish in the 1970s in the Podhale, as improved roads and railways created greater ease of access to the smaller villages. Previously focused on Zakopane, tourism expanded outwards from this centre into quieter, more remote but equally picturesque villages. People came from Poland and from the rest of Eastern Europe to ski in the winter, and to walk and generally benefit from the clean mountain air in the summer. Villagers realised that they could earn money by letting rooms and providing other services for the visitors. A tremendous building boom began in the early 1970s. This was a time when unrestrained borrowing of hard currency at the national level had created a huge foreign debt and a desperate need for dollars. Many goods were available only for western currency, in official government shops, with no questions asked regarding the source of the money. Returning migrants, both women and men, used their American earnings to purchase building materials, and often to purchase the necessary permission for building as well. Three- and four-storey brick houses shot up over the countryside, replacing the traditional two-roomed wooden cottages. Most families continued to live in the basement, eating and sleeping in one or two rooms, while all of the other rooms were let out, either formally through the tourist board or informally, through connections and word of mouth.

Male and female patterns in the informal economy

This growth in the tourist and building trades had different implications for male and for female labour. Basically, each extended the sphere with which they were already predominantly associated into the external market. Men, traditionally the builders of their own houses and outbuildings, began to find employment as builders, carpenters, roofers and plasterers. This work was conducted almost exclusively in the informal sector, often with unofficially obtained materials, and was both highly paid and untaxed. It usually involved groups of men recruited through kinship and neighbourhood ties in very much the same way as agricultural labour; however, although some such work was reciprocal, exchanged and accounted just as agricultural labour, most was contracted on the basis of remuneration received from a particular client.

The impact of tourism on female labour was different in so far as the types of money-making schemes developed by women tended to involve family members only, rather than recruiting from more extended networks, and to derive from the domestic economy. Women let rooms to tourists, provided them with milk and eggs, knitted sweaters for them and sold them wool, and cooked meals for them. Basically, the women, like the men, were elaborating their 'traditional' gender tasks, and extending them out from the household economy into the the market. However, while male agricultural work is valued highly, and its extension into external economic ventures equally so, female participation in the tourist industry is considered far less significant. Women's earnings from such activities tend to be viewed as 'pin money'. Again, it could be argued that for women the tourist trade provides a realm of activity which is barely distinguishable from labour in the domestic sphere generally. Just as male work is public, based on formally recruited groups and highly paid, female work is seen as private, embedded in the household economy, and neither particularly economically lucrative nor culturally valued.[6]

IDEOLOGIES OF GENDER – COMMUNITY, STATE AND CHURCH

Gorale ideals of female and male

I suggested at the beginning of this article that four factors particularly influence the situation of women in rural Poland. The association of women with the household, and with caring activities, and the undervaluing of female work in relation to that of the male have been the focus of the previous pages. Let us now consider the way in which these patterns are upheld by cultural ideas about maleness and femaleness, and, albeit in different ways, by the (overt) ideology of the Catholic Church and the (implicit) ideology of the state.

Among the Gorale, various characteristics, not always consistent, are linked with ideal femaleness and maleness. As should be clear from the foregoing discussion, local ideologies of gender are inextricably linked to work. A good woman is hard-working, self-sacrificing, strong and stoical. A good man is a reliable provider, a strong and steady worker, and a good farmer. These are representations of femininity and masculinity at their most positive, or in an ideal light.

Female power

Women are also associated with fertility and, in sometimes contradictory ways, with sexual purity. Fertility is obviously connected with child-bearing, the most valued female attribute. The connection between females and fertility is also ritually elaborated in various contexts relating to the physical structure of the house, the fecundity, health and affluence of household members, and the successful sowing and abundant harvesting of crops (Pine, 1990). Here there is clearly a strong association between female power and what could be considered 'natural' womanhood or femininity.[7] Women at their most dangerous represent fertility and power out of male control. Hence a woman who bears one illegitimate child is not excluded or stigmatised, while a woman who does not marry and is viewed as promiscuous, who bears several illegitimate children to different fathers, or who openly commits adultery, was likely in the past to have been associated with witchcraft, and is still viewed with deep suspicion bordering on fear. The symmetry between positive femininity, both 'natural' and social, and the perpetuation of the household and family, and negative femininity, both 'natural' and social, and the threat to their wellbeing seems clear.

Male power: from strength to violence

Rituals involving men, on the other hand, underline patriarchal authority rather than fertility, and both role as household head and role in the community. Positive notions of masculinity are tied up with physical strength and courage, and a certain kind of machismo. Thus, men are expected to be somewhat wild in youth, to drink with their peers, and to fight to defend their male kin and co-villagers. However, when the 'natural' strength and wildness of men is not controlled in adulthood, it becomes dangerous. Just as men are expected to be tough, and even violent, in certain public situations, they are also expected to protect the home and the family. The negative side of this ideal of powerful masculinity develops when men continue to drink excessively after marriage and turn their violence inwards, towards their wives. While such behaviour is by no means condoned, it clearly derives at least partly from positive images of male power, and as such may be tolerated as 'part of man's nature' against which women have little defense. Most men are not excessively violent, but the association between some contexts of violence and positive masculinity makes the *potential* for domestic violence something with which most women live. In the construction of both masculinity and femininity, therefore, certain attributes are celebrated in some contexts, tolerated in others, and in yet others regarded as threatening when out of control. In relation to behaviour out of control, however, the women appear to be the victims regardless of whether it is their own behaviour, or that of men which is excessive. They risk loosing their public reputation and being subjected to gossip and exclusion if the excess is seen as lying with themselves, and are in danger of physical abuse when it lies with the man.

Worker–heroines to angel–mothers: images of the state and the Church

The gender ideals which the villagers themselves hold are reinforced in various ways by both the state and the Church. Immediately after the Second World War, when the losses of war had devastated the Polish male population, the state went to great lengths to foster the image of the socialist woman who could do everything. Official posters showed smiling young women on tractors, and mothers carrying farm tools in one hand and resting a fat and healthy baby on the other hip. However, by the 1970s these representations had undergone considerable change. On the one hand, the birth-rate was not increasing sufficiently. On the other, the official policy of full employment created a situation in which certain sectors of the economy, notably the service sector and the administrative bureaucracy, were over-subscribed. It was during the late 1970s that articles depicting the plight of children left at home while their mothers went out to work first became noticeable. Maternal deprivation was blamed for everything from moral apathy to delinquency and crime.

At this time as well an unlikely, although not wholly unprecedented, alliance arose between the state and the Catholic Church on the subject of abortion and birth control. Birth control was extremely difficult to obtain in Poland during these years, and in rural areas many young people had heard only of condoms and the rhythm method.[8] Rates of abortion, on the other hand, were high, particularly in urban areas.[9] The state embarked on a highly emotive pro-natal campaign, with the obvious backing of the Church. Motherhood was celebrated, and pictures of 'unborn babies' were posted in churches and public buildings. In rural areas such as the Podhale, where the population is almost uniformly practising Catholic, where birth-rates are already high and a strong cultural emphasis is placed on motherhood, these images reinforced existing views of women's 'natural' function.[10] The teachings of the Polish Catholic Church place enormous emphasis on Mary as the all-embracing, all-nurturing mother, who provides the sacred prototype for those of her sex. The problems facing women having to deal with large families in conditions of poverty, particularly during periods of acute shortages of food and consumer goods, are rarely alluded to in such contexts.

CONCLUSIONS

The association of women with 'natural' motherhood in rural ideology, reinforced continually by the central position held by Mary in both Polish Catholicism and nationalism[11] and juxtaposed to the real hardship of many mothers' real lives, is symptomatic of the problems, practical and ideological, faced by women under 'actual existing socialism'. In Eastern Europe, as in the west, there has been no necessary or automatic correlation between formal policies concerning women's rights and actual practice. Legislation guaranteeing women's rights in the family, in the work-place, and over their own bodies was passed in Poland as early as the 1950s, and is on paper most impressive.[12] In actuality the situation, particularly for rural women, has been far more complex. In the Podhale, socialist policy, in terms of any wide-spread improvement in women's roles in the family and the economy, was most conspicuous by its absence. Rather, the peasant communities continued to revolve around long-established patterns of gender divisions in most areas of life. In situations in which state intervention was apparent, as in the growth of wage labour and infrastructure development, the peasants were only partly integrated, and little attempt was made to break down the structures of inequality between men and women implicit in the rural division of labour. Both men and women continued to develop their own strategies for survival, outside the state, as they had done for decades. For women particularly, the socialist period provided mixed experience. Health care improved, although in rural areas it lagged behind the cities; increasing availability of domestic appliances reduced some of the drudgery of women's labour, although problems with distribution of goods and parts of appliances again were particularly acute in non-urban regions; education allowed some women access to the white collar sector of employment. However, as men become increasingly involved in wage labour and entrepreneurial activities outside farming, women have taken over more of the farm labour, with little increase in either prestige or economic reward. Women's own work and employment patterns tend to be constrained by responsibilities for caring for children, the family and increasingly, the farm. For many rural women, therefore, the development of industry and associated work has merely increased the already formidable load that they carry. It remains to be seen whether the new structure of Poland will do more to lessen the burdens of these women.

In rural areas, where female labour actually accounts for a large proportion of total agricultural production, the situation is further complicated by the fact that women's contribution is often not formally recognised, either by the state or by the people themselves. The work of women is often hidden within the family production unit of the peasant household economy, and hence often undervalued and not specifically compensated; in this it is similar to domestic labour, except that it is part of a process of production rather than reproduction. It could in fact be argued that the agricultural work of women is viewed primarily as an extension of their domestic, marital and family responsibilities, and that this fact adds to its undervalued status and even its invisibility. A second feature which characterises the economic roles of rural women is that work outside the household and the farm is often sporadic and informal, rather than regular and waged. Marketing of small surpluses such as eggs and cheese, crafts such as weaving, spinning and sewing on commission or for middle women to sell to larger traders, hawking single items of imported clothing or of jewelry in the market square or on the street corner, cooking, baking and letting rooms to tourists are all activities which peasant women engage in to earn money, but which are neither really included in formal concepts of work and employment, nor protected by any kind of state legislation or benefit scheme. Equally significantly, all of these typical female activities can in some sense be interpreted as extensions of non-waged domestic labour. However, it is important to remember that not all rural women are excluded, either by choice or by prejudice, from regular waged labour. Many in fact are, for at least some periods of their lives, classic 'peasant-workers', engaged partly in agricultural production and partly in formal waged labour. While few of these women could afford to give up their waged work, the work itself is often part-time, temporary or sporadic, and usually badly paid.

The picture which emerges from even so cursory an overview as this is one in which rural women, with all of the skill of long experience, continually engage in a precarious balancing act, juggling domestic labour and child-care, agricultural labour, and either formal or informal paid employment. However, a large part of this work is rendered invisible by its inclusion into a pervasive 'domestic' sphere, or is undervalued, irregular, and underpaid.

It is too early yet to tell what future the new civil society will hold for Polish women. The shops are full now, at least in the cities, and the queues have disappeared, but their absence owes more to astronomically high prices[13] than to any new style of quick and easy purchasing. Articles now appear in newspapers and magazines claiming to reveal women's desire to shed some of their burdens and remain at home with their children. It is difficult not to view the revelation of such aspirations as a convenient response to increasing levels of unemployment;[14] when regular paid work is scarce, as we know from experience in the west, the female worker is often construed as a threat to the males' opportunities for jobs and income. Then the image of the family home in which the angel-mother provides safety and security for her children becomes a useful and powerful ideological tool to justify the exclusion of women from the workforce. In Poland the opposition between the 'good' mother–housewife and the 'bad' working woman itself contains a paradox. On the one hand, it is clearly understandable why women would express a preference against engaging in paid work. Many have worked for decades in hazardous, stressful jobs, for long hours with low pay and little even approximate job satisfaction; the combined demands of a job and running a household under extremely difficult and time-consuming conditions such as those which have been prevalent in Poland are exhausting, stressful and may leave little time for any other activities, such as leisure time with children and family.[15] On the other hand, however, the home itself is often less than a haven, or even a safe place. Domestic appliances are scarce and expensive, and domestic labour hard and time-consuming. Male alcohol abuse is endemic, and is often accompanied by domestic violence. Housing is in short supply and living conditions, particularly in cities, tend to be crowded, while many of the buildings themselves are crumbling and in a state of neglect and general disrepair. In other words, the domestic sphere and the workplace are often equally unsatisfactory for women.

A related problem in the construction of this paradox is the issue of choice. What the discussion of the advantages and disadvantages of women's employment often overlooks or ignores is that, of course, many women have no choice but to take on paid work. Wages are low for most workers, in both rural and urban areas, and costs of living high and rising. Women on their own with children to support, or with dependent elderly kin, are not in a position to rely on a man's earnings. Although paid work may become increasingly hard for women to obtain, many cannot afford to stay at home without an income. In rural society, as I have tried to show here, even the division between female domestic and economic spheres is in many ways as unclear today as it was a hundred years ago.

To some extent, this article represents a plea for consideration and understanding of a long-term historical process: many of the problems which face Polish women today, particularly in rural areas, have roots which extend beyond the socialist period into pre-socialist history. For instance, during the Partition Period, when Polish national culture was forced underground in many regions, men took the more active political and social roles, while women came to represent the transmission of culture, in the form of language and Catholicism, within the home (Siemienska, 1987). This division between public and private roles provided the basis for a set of deeply entrenched attitudes which justified, at least in cultural terms, and perpetuated, the separation of female and male spheres. The powerful Polish Catholic Church has long advocated a view of women as mothers and nurturers, providing the moral background and psychic strength in an often troubled and disconnected society. These attitudes are deeply ingrained and go a long way in explaining the almost complete lack, until extremely recently, of any women's movement in Poland. As far as the peasantry specifically is concerned, the relationship between women's status and ideologies of gender is even more complex. The division of labour in 'traditional' peasant farming is based almost solely on gender and age. There is a long-established mutual distrust between peasants and urban Poles. This stems on the one hand from the consistent failure of consecutive governments to create any effective pro-peasant policy in terms of price and distribution of produce, access to education and training, and general equal opportunity, and on the other from the urban populations' view of the peasantry as a self-interested and grasping social group who hoard food and fail to deliver in order to force up prices. All of these conditions predate the imposition of the socialist state on Poland; in so far as socialism can be blamed for the present situation of rural women, it is for sins of omission rather than of commission. While it is easy to document the persistent failure of consecutive socialist governments to implement policy which would radically change women's overall situation, it should also be remembered that the record of capitalist governments, with regard to rural underdevelopment, is certainly no better and may in fact be worse. In this sense, it could be argued that there is little in the experience of women under capitalism which would indicate that a demand economy heralds the birth of a new era for rural women. These are problems with which the new Polish civil society has yet to come to terms.

NOTES

I am grateful to Annie Phizacklea and Marjory Lang for their careful reading of an earlier draft of this essay, and for the clarity of their comments and criticisms, all of which were most helpful.

1 In Anna Swir, *Fat Like the Sun*, translated by Grazyna Baran and Margaret Marshment, The Women's Press, London, 1986.
2 The socialist government was established in Poland in 1947, and one-party rule was overturned by the Solidarity victories in the elections of 1989.
3 Material in this article was gathered during field-work in 1977–9, 1981, 1984 and 1989. I gratefully acknowledge support from the then Social Science Research Council in 1977–9, and from the Economic and Social Research Council (Project R00231489) in 1989. I also thank the British Council and the Central Research Fund for help in the earlier research periods.
4 This applied usually to farms of 50 hectares or more.
5 See Wedel, 1986 for a detailed description of the informal economy during these years.
6 I have argued elsewhere (Pine, 1991) that this type of gendered division of labour, and particularly the elaboration of female domestic tasks into poorly paid services in the informal sector, may best be considered far less as a failure of socialist policy than as a typical pattern of underdevelopment, all too familiar from rural areas in the 'Third World'. Thus I would argue that the situation of many Polish peasant women is more usefully viewed in terms of rural underdevelopment than of factors associated with a centrally planned socialist economy.
7 I am not introducing a female: nature/male: culture dichotomy (Ortner, 1974) here; rather, my argument is that the 'natural' aspect of both males and females can be either positive or negative, as can the 'cultural' or what I would prefer to call 'social' side of each.
8 In 1977, when I began my research, IUDs were sold over the counter in Pewexs, the official hard currency shops, but few people knew what they were, or where to get them inserted. Diaphragms were relatively unknown even in urban areas, and Prewentin, the spermicide cream for use with a diaphragm, was continually out of stock in chemists.
9 Polish abortion laws were liberalised in 1956, permitting terminations for social as well as medical reasons. By 1973 official statistics recorded 25.8 abortions per 100 pregnancies (Jancar, 1978: 70).
10 Abortion remains a contested area in Poland, as the hot debates during the 1989 election campaigns and more recent attempts, so far unsuccessful, to outlaw abortion completely, demonstrate.
11 Marian cults are widespread in Poland: Mary is referred to as the Queen of Poland and the Black Madonna of Czestachowa is particularly viewed as the guardian of the Polish nation.
12 See for example Lasok, 1968 for discussion of the Marriage Act of 1945 and the Family Law Code of 1950.
13 In June 1991 inflation was estimated at about 70 per cent. This actually reflects a drop, dating from the beginning of the austerity programme, from about 150 per cent per month in 1990.
14 Unemployment is now officially recognised to be about 1.5–2 million, or about 5 per cent of the adult working population. This is a rise from zero unemployment in the socialist period, and it does not take into account hidden unemployment, caused by temporary factory closures, etc., to which the female workforce is particularly susceptible.
15 See Sokolowska, 1963 for a discussion of conditions for working women in the early socialist period, and Bujwid *et al.*, 1988 for a devastating critique of the later period. A short but excellent English summary of women's position in the late socialist period is in Kolankiewicz and Lewis, 1988: 60–2.

REFERENCES

Bujwid *et al.* (1988) *Kobieta Polska Lat Osiemdziesiatych*, NOWA, Warsaw.

Jancar, Barbara W. (1978) *Women Under Communism*, Johns Hopkins University Press, Baltimore, Md.

Kolankiewicz, George and Lewis, Paul (1988) *Poland: Politics, Economics and Society*, Frances Pinter, London.

Lasok, Dominik (1968) *Polish Family Law*, A.W. Sijthoff, Leiden.

Ortner, Shelley (1974) 'Is female to male as nature is to culture?', in M.Z. Rosaldo and L. Lamphere (eds) *Women, Culture and Society*, Stanford University Press, Stanford, Calif.

Pine, Frances (1987) 'Kinship, marriage and social change in a Polish highland village', PhD thesis, University of London.

Pine, Frances (1990) 'Naming the house and naming the land: kinship and social groups in the Polish highlands', forthcoming in Janet Carsten and Stephen Hugh-Jones (eds) *Houses: Buildings, Groups and Categories*.

Pine, Frances (1991) 'Women, domestic economy and entrepreneurial activity in rural Poland', in C.M. Hann (ed.) (1992) *Anthropological Approaches to Socialism*, Routledge, London.

Pine, Frances and Bogdanowicz Przemek (1982) 'Policy, response and alternative strategy: the process of change in a Polish highland village', *Dialectal Anthropology*, vol. 7, no. 2.

Siemienska, Renata (1987) 'Women and social movements in Poland', *Women and Politics*, Winter, vol. 64.

Sokolowska, Magdelana (1963) *Kobieta Pracujaca*, Wiedza Powszechnia, Warsaw.

Wedel, Janine (1986) *The Private Poland*, Facts on File Inc., New York.

Part II

The construction and reconstruction of gendered identities

5 Population policy and reform

The Soviet Union, Eastern Europe and China

Delia Davin

INTRODUCTION

For a woman, effective control over her own fertility is a prerequisite for
achieving choice in other areas of her life and for playing a full role in
society. In the twentieth century scientific advances gradually improved
the range of contraceptives available. Although some problems with
side-effects and reliability remain, potentially a woman may now decide
the number of her children and the timing of their births. For this potential to become a reality women need access to information, medical
services and supplies. Access may be obstructed by a lack of resources,
state policy, ignorance, religious taboos and a number of other factors.
The degree of access to modern birth control therefore differs greatly
from one country to another.

Socialist states, despite a commitment to women's emancipation,
have at times failed to give women control over their fertility, or have even
denied it to them. The perceived interests of the state have been given
priority over those of the individual. Where birth control is concerned,
this has often meant sacrificing the interests of individual women.

In this article I will examine the effects of the economic, political and
social reforms introduced in the 1980s in China, the Soviet Union, East
Germany, Poland, Hungary, Czechoslovakia and Romania on the
availability of birth control, which I use to include both contraception
and abortion. Before the reforms, in all these countries, there was
official concern about demographic trends which were seen as running
counter to national interests. In each country, the availability of
contraception and abortion was affected, to a greater or lesser degree,
by an explicit population policy, whether anti-natalist as in China, or
pro-natalist as in the Soviet Union and Eastern Europe. The reforms
have created a different but equally varied pattern. In China and
Vietnam, where population growth rates are high, state intervention to

reduce fertility has intensified. In countries where pro-natalist policies prevailed previously because low birth-rates were causing concern, demographic trends are now less of a preoccupation, but other factors specific to individual countries influence the availability of abortion and levels of contraceptive use.

In many ways, the impression of a common pattern given by the nearly-universal upheavals in what used to be known as the socialist or the Communist bloc, is quite misleading. In the past, the fact that the countries in which the Communist Party was in power had a shared ideology, and similar institutional structures in the political and economic spheres, tended to mask the profoundly important differences between them. These national differences, arising from pre-socialist histories and cultures and from varied levels of economic development were always important. Now that the mask of ideological uniformity has been ripped away, they are impossible to ignore.

The unparalleled power of the state in countries ruled by a single party, its great organisational ability, and the general acceptance that individuals' interests should be subordinated to national ones, meant interventionist population policies had a tremendous impact on the lives of ordinary citizens, and especially of women. Policy makers did sometimes pay lip service to women's welfare in justifying policy. But arguments couched in these terms, that abortion or contraception were bad for women's health, or that repeated child-bearing exhausted women and was a barrier to sex equality, tended to change conveniently to match the prevailing wind. A review of state policies on reproduction in some individual countries will show that they developed mainly in response to specific national circumstances, with ideology increasingly a minor factor.

THE SOVIET UNION, 1920s–1930s

In the early days of the Soviet Union, the debate on contraception and abortion related them clearly to women's emancipation. Following Marx, Engels and Bebel, Lenin believed that the oppression of women arose from their exclusion from the labour force, and he saw the power to control births as a necessary precondition to women's participation in work and politics. However, when the Soviet government became the first in the world to legalise abortion in 1920, the motive was to reduce the rate of harmful illegal abortions as much as to give women choice. Although terminations were to be performed on demand and free of charge in Soviet hospitals the hope was expressed that the 'serious evil' of abortion could be eliminated in the future (Lapidus, 1978: 60–1).

Like much other radical early Soviet social legislation, this liberal decree did not survive the 1930s. As war began to threaten, Stalin's government took various measures to reinforce the traditional hierarchical family and to promote population growth. Abortion was outlawed for first pregnancies in 1935, and in 1936 for all cases except where the health of the woman was seriously endangered by pregnancy, or there was a threat of inherited disease (Buckley, 1989: 129–31). Those who performed illegal abortions were henceforth to be punished by imprisonment, while women who underwent them were to receive a 'social reprimand' for a first offence, and fines for subsequent ones. Some ideological justification was attempted. It was said that the 1920s legislation had been appropriate, given the difficult conditions of the time, but now that Soviet society had made maternity so much easier, there was no need for it.

As contraception was hardly available at the time in the Soviet Union, abortion was a major means of birth control and its prohibition in effect deprived women of control over their fertility or forced them to seek illegal terminations. Not only was this hardly discussed as a problem, the very wish for control was condemned, while on the other hand motherhood was vaunted as showing social responsibility. Women were said to have a duty to bear children.

Since the 1930s state policy in the USSR has always been informed by pro-natalism, although the tactics employed to raise fertility have varied over time. The bizarre promotion of decorations for prolific mothers, whereby five births brought a second class Motherhood award, and a woman might progress through various other distinctions to the final acccolade of Heroine Mother for producing ten, dates from 1944. There was legislation designed to penalise the childless, and, to a lesser degree, small families. Citizens with no children paid 6 per cent of their incomes in tax, those with a single child 1 per cent and those with two children, only 0.5 per cent. Maternity and child benefits were expanded, and while single women lost the right to sue the fathers for maintenance, they gained the right to significant financial aid from the state (Buckley, 1989: 134). The population loss suffered by the Soviet Union during the Second World War was so great that its true extent was not fully revealed until the 1980s. Inevitably, these pro-natalist policies were continued in the post-war years.

THE SOVIET UNION, EASTERN EUROPE AND CHINA IN THE 1950s

Soviet policies were more or less copied in the Eastern European countries after the war, both because of the political tendency to treat the Soviet Union as a model, and because these countries, too, were concerned to build up their populations. This was especially the case in Poland and East Germany where population losses had also been heavy. In Eastern, as in Western Europe, the war was followed by a baby boom. Both the Soviet Union and the countries of Eastern Europe, with the exception of East Germany, initially experienced high birth-rates (Berent, 1970: 35). At the time of the establishment of the People's Republic in 1949, China had suffered decades of war, invasion and civil war. Birth-rates, death-rates and infant mortality rates were all high. With peace, civil order and the growth of public health and medical services, population growth began to accelerate. Hardly surprisingly, China never followed the Soviet model of pro-natalist policies. Indeed, as we shall see, the results of the first modern census in 1953 gave rise to worries that China's population was growing too fast. However, powerful figures in the Party still argued that there was no cause for concern and Marxists were still inhibited from arguing the case for population control by their rejection on theoretical grounds of what had been dubbed Malthusianism. Although contraceptives were available, at least in the cities, efforts to promote family planning were sporadic and limited until the 1960s.

Abortion was once more made legal in the Soviet Union in 1955. This measure, apparently a contradiction of the well-established pro-natalist policy, requires some explanation. It should perhaps be seen as part of a general easing of repression characteristic of the period of de-Stalinisation, but also as a response to the very high rate of illegal abortion prevailing at the time. Back-street operations, often performed in bad conditions, were doing harm to women's health, and no doubt to their fertility (Buckley, 1989: 158). After 1955, although hospital abortions were usually performed in a harsh, unsympathetic environ-ment, often without anaesthetics, Soviet law did, in effect, allow abortion on demand with a minimum of bureaucracy (Peers, 1985: 134).

The Soviet lead in legalising abortion was copied within a few years by China and the countries of Eastern Europe, except for Albania and East Germany. By 1960 Poland, Czechoslovakia, Bulgaria, Hungary, Romania, Yugoslavia and China allowed abortion on request, or on broad social grounds (Francome, 1984: 128–32). As in the Soviet case, legalisation was in part an attempt to deal with the problem of illegal abortions. It was also said that legalisation was a response to popular demand and would give women more control. In fact, still concerned to try to maintain or increase birth-rates, Eastern bloc governments were slow to promote, or to make widely available, the modern means of contraception which came into use in the west in the 1960s. Abortion developed as, and tended to remain, the major means of birth control both in the Soviet Union and in Eastern Europe (Ketting, 1990).

The high post-war birth-rates which had prevailed in all of Eastern Europe except the German Democratic Republic (GDR), and had given governments the confidence for abortion law reform, began to fall in the 1950s. The fall came earlier in Czechoslovakia, Hungary and Bulgaria, and somewhat later to the Soviet Union, Poland and Romania, but by the early 1960s it was causing very general concern. In Bulgaria, Hungary and Romania net reproduction rates fell below replacement level (Berent, 1970: 47). China, by contrast, except in three famine years, maintained high birth-rates and rates of natural increase until the 1970s.

EXPLANATIONS FOR LOW BIRTH-RATES

The legalisation of abortion was often blamed for the steep fall in the birth-rate with which it had coincided. In fact, of course, abortion could provide the means but not the motive for people in this period to have fewer children. To understand Eastern Europe's falling birth-rates more clearly, we have to look further.

In the 1950s there was a decline in the proportion of women of reproductive age in the population as a whole, but in the 1960s the proportion actually rose. Neither this factor, nor others such as nuptuality rates and the age composition of married women provide a complete explanation (Berent, 1970: 49). Marital fertility itself was falling; in other words, right across Eastern Europe and the Soviet Union, couples were deciding to limit the number of children they would have. These decisions produced the fall in the birth-rates.

The post-war flight from motherhood was by no means unique to Eastern Europe. Although the birth-rate tended to fall a bit further and faster in the east, Western Europe experienced similar trends in this period. Historically, industrialisation and urbanisation have been associated with falls in fertility. There is also a positive correlation between women's education, high levels of female participation in the labour force, and smaller completed families.

In the decades after the Second World War, both the USSR and the countries of Eastern Europe carried out industrialisation programmes. Industrialisation, together with an ideological commitment to women's economic participation, meant that particularly large numbers of women were drawn into the labour force (Frenkel, 1976: 45). Social measures such as the provision of child-care were taken to facilitate this. Education, including female education, was given a high priority by the state. Housing, by contrast, was rather neglected; many of the cities of

Eastern Europe suffered and still suffer chronic housing shortages. No doubt all these factors played a part in bringing about smaller family sizes. The association with urbanisation can certainly be easily demonstrated by fertility differentials between urban and rural populations, although even rural populations wre increasingly influenced by the new trends.

Family planning surveys began in the late 1950s in Czechoslovakia and Hungary, and some ten years later provided some helpful confirmation of influences on family size (Frenkel, 1976: 35). They reveal an interesting divergence between the number of children women said they would wish for, and the number they actually expected to have. The ideal was already a small modern family of two or three children, but the surveys indicate that most expected to limit their families to only one or two children. When asked why they expected to have fewer children than they would like, women spoke of employment, income, housing and child-care. The wife's wage was seen as necessary to the family budget, and she could only manage one or two children while still holding down a job. In 1971, in a Czech survey of women applying for abortions, 11.2 per cent gave dissatisfaction with housing conditions as their motive (Mazur, 1975: 423). In the same period, a Polish survey indicated that 12.7 per cent of married women aged 20 to 24 would have an extra child if their housing conditions were improved (Mazur, 1975: 424).

OFFICIAL ATTITUDES TO FERTILITY TRENDS

As falling birth-rates in Eastern Europe increasingly became a matter of official concern, various policies were developed to try to arrest or reverse the trend. This reaction itself calls for some explanation. Birth-rate falls of nearly the same magnitude in Western Europe in the same period caused little anxiety except in France. Perhaps the sort of defensive nationalism of which the desire for population growth is a part was the result of the instability of national entities and national frontiers in Eastern Europe in recent history. In some countries the wish to make good the terrrible population losses of the Second World War was also important. Ethnic factors contributed to official concern. Birth-rates in some Asian republics of the USSR were double those of European Russia, giving rise to concern in European-dominated Moscow that Asians would one day become the majority in the Union (Lapidus, 1978: 295–8). Elsewhere in Eastern Europe there was comparable unease at the higher birth-rates of gypsies, and of the minority Muslim groups in Yugoslavia and of the Turks in Bulgaria (Tanner, 1989: 24).

On the economic front, the demand for labour created by

industrialisation was intensified by low labour productivity in both industry and agriculture (Heitlinger, 1976: 123). Political factors precluded the solution of bringing in the migrant labour common in Western Europe in this period. Labour shortage therefore also contributed to official pro-natalism.

The Chinese experience in this period was very different. The first modern census in 1953 showed that the population was 583 million, a total which some found worryingly high. Limited public education campaigns about family planning reached the urban population in the 1950s (Kane, 1987: 64–7). Abortion, barrier contraceptives and sterilisation for contraceptive purposes were made available at least in the cities (Banister, 1987: 149). However, demographers and economists who argued on economic grounds for a fertility limitation policy came under fierce ideological attack in 1958. They were accused of being followers of Malthus and were told that a large population could be turned to China's advantage. Family planning was promoted again in a cautious campaign in the early 1960s, with the emphasis on limiting births to safeguard the health of mothers and children. Some government leaders were worried about China's rapidly increasing population, especially after a census in 1964 not disclosed to the outside world, but political differences on this issue deferred the introduction of a stronger state policy until the 1970s.

It was in the 1960s that the differences in state policy on population and reproduction between China and the European socialist bloc became pronounced. Moreover, within Eastern Europe each state also developed its own distinctive policies in this period. All were basically concerned to maintain or increase birth-rates, but while the Soviet Union continued a permissive policy on the termination of pregnancy and the GDR liberalised its law for the first time, Hungary made its abortion law somewhat more restrictive, and, most dramatically, Romania attempted to prevent access to both abortion and contraception almost completely. Given these differences, the recent history of birth control in this area is best dealt with country by country.

THE SOVIET UNION FROM THE 1960s

The continuation of easy access to abortion in the Soviet Union did not mean that there was no debate on the subject. Some blamed it for the declining birth-rates. Opponents of prohibition pointed out that abortion was the instrument, not the basic cause of low fertility and attempted to redirect the debate towards finding ways to make people want larger families (Lapidus, 1978: 298).

Discussion of pro-natalist measures began to show a more sophisticated appreciation of their effects and to hint at class and ethnic dimensions. For example, one demographer argued that the aim should be to increase the number of first, second and third parity births, while the encouragement of fourth and higher parity births should cease. In this way fertility could be increased in areas where it was low (European Russia), and be reduced in areas where it was high (the Asian republics) (Lapidus, 1978: 298). Articles in women's magazines intended for a readership in the Asian republics still stressed the advantages of women's participation in the labour force, while those for European Russian emphasised motherhood (Bridger, 1987: 133).

The sociologist Boris Urlanis argued that the Hungarian model of a high flat-rate child benefit produced an unfortunate distortion because it was most significant to low-income families (Lapidus, 1978: 307). Echoing the fears of the neo-Malthusians of the nineteenth century that better educated people would leave reproduction to those with the lowest attainments, he urged a progressive scale of benefits which would give more to high-earning families and thus offer meaningful incentives across the social scale.

Contraception has been very poorly developed in the Soviet Union (Holland and McKevitt 1985: 152). Although it has been acknowledged for years that it is harmful to rely on abortion for birth control, the pro-natalist climate appears to have inhibited the discussion or promotion of contraception. Barrier methods were often the only ones available and there were many complaints about the quality of Soviet condoms (Hansson, 1984: 21, 48 and 62). The USSR was extremely late in approving the use of the pill (Scott, 1976: 151). Even today it is officially recognised that supplies of both intrauterine devices and oral contraceptives are inadequate. In the rural areas they are often simply unobtainable (Bridger, 1987: 130; Manuilova, 1990: 9–10).

The abortion rate remains very high, and it is not unusual for a woman to have four or five terminations in her fertile life, with negative consequences for both physical and mental health. Although anaesthetics are now more generally used for terminations than they were in the past, they are not universal. Some women prefer to pay for an illegal abortion, not because they could not obtain a legal one, but because the payment will guarantee them better care and perhaps even a vacuum suction abortion – until recently difficult to obtain in the Soviet Union (Holland and McKevitt, 1984: 152; Hansson and Liden, 1984: 63–4).

In the era of Gorbachev's reforms there was much official rhetoric about protecting motherhood, improving women's lives and so on (Buckley, 1989: 224–33). The reforms have produced a system more sensitive to popular pressure and at last some effort is being made to make modern contraception and contraceptive information available to Soviet women. With only an estimated 13.3 per cent of all women of child-bearing age employing modern contraception, there is a long way to go (Manuilova, 1990: 10). There is evidence of a small decrease in the number of surgical abortions being carried out, though this appears to be due to an increase in the number of early vacuum suction abortions rather than more effective contraception. A new state medical and social programme is being developed with a strong emphasis on training medical personnel in the use of modern contraceptives. Help and advice has been accepted from the International Planned Parenthood Federation (IPPF) of which the USSR was an associate member. It is a tragedy for women that when at long last the will to develop a good, nation-wide delivery system for birth control advice and supplies seems to exist, the political and economic chaos facing the former Soviet Union may obstruct it.

EAST GERMANY

Even before the 1960s, the German Democratic Republic had followed the pattern of the Soviet Union in birth control policies less closely than the other countries of the Eastern bloc. Although immediate post-war legislation changed the Third Reich's absolute prohibition of abortion, to allow terminations to women under 16 or over 40 or to those who had already had five children (Francome, 1984: 130), full liberalisation was brought in only in 1972. Abortion up to twelve weeks was then offered on demand. After twelve weeks, as was usual in Eastern Europe, medical grounds were required. The ratio of legal terminations to live births has fallen steeply since from 57 : 100 in 1972 to 37 : 100 in 1988 (Mehlan, 1990: 17). This level is lower than those of the rest of the Eastern bloc (Hamand, 1989: 7).

The GDR was the first of the Eastern European countries to introduce modern contraception. Family planning centres were set up in the mid-1960s to offer free advice and supplies. The pill was imported from the Netherlands from 1965 and home manufacture began soon afterwards.

Rather surprisingly, given the anti-reform Communist leadership of the GDR up to 1989, attitudes on family and sex education at this time were less puritanical than elsewhere in Eastern Europe. The one-third of all children born outside wedlock suffered no legal discrimination and lone mothers were eligible for extra benefits. Birth-rates stayed constantly low after the war, and emigration to the west, often through illegal channels, resulted in further demographic loss. The population of the GDR fell from 18.4 million in 1950 to 16.4 million in 1989. Yet pro-natalist policy in the GDR was characterised not by depriving women of the means of controlling their fertility, but rather by trying to make motherhood or parenthood easier and more attractive. The proportion of young women who were in the labour force was 97 per cent, probably the highest in the world. To keep young mothers at work, the government provided good maternity leave and benefits, child allowances and subsidies for child-care and children's clothes.

The late 1980s brought the end of a tyrannical and unpopular regime in the GDR. The reunification which followed will no doubt ultimately confer economic benefits and individual freedoms on many of its former citizens. Yet it has to be recognised that in various areas which concern women and reproduction, there were losses as well. It is significant that abortion was one of the real sticking-points when the agreement on reunification was drawn up. Federal German law on the termination of pregnancy (although liberally interpreted in some states) is far more restrictive than that of the east. The agreement finally reached in 1990 allowed the East German status quo to continue for two years, after which new legal arrangements will have to be made for the united country (Koch, 1990: 4; Neumann, 1990: 2). It is not yet clear what these are likely to be.

Many of the welfare measures of the former GDR which were beneficial to women are disappearing. They were expensive and do not fit the now dominant West German pattern. Moreover their rationale is gone. Unemployment is a growing problem in the east now that it is open to competition from the more efficient west. Women's jobs will no doubt often be the first to go. The labour market in West Germany is saturated, having already had to absorb refugees and migrants not only from East Germany, but also from the other countries of Eastern Europe. Without a labour shortage, the expense of a pro-natalist welfare programme and subsidised child-care is no longer seen as worthwhile.

POLAND

The history of birth control provision in Poland has been deeply influenced by the strength and social conservatism of Polish Catholicism. Of Poland's population of 38 million, 95 per cent are professed Catholics. The Church was already involved in opposition to the activities of voluntary organisations promoting the use of contraceptives before the war. After the war, the entry of the state into this arena produced a complicated situation. One-sixth of Poland's pre-war population of 35 million had died as a result of extermination or the hostilities, and numbers were further reduced by frontier changes and emigration, so that its population stood at 21 million in 1945. Predictably the new Communist government adopted pro-natalist policies. Birth-rates were high and by the 1980s the country's population had attained its pre-war levels (Kozakiewicz, 1986: 197–209).

Following the general East European pattern, abortion was legalised in Poland in 1956. In 1957, a non-governmental organisation, the Society for Conscious Motherhood, was established, taking its name from a pre-war family planning organisation. Its purpose has been to inform people of their legal right to abortion, to organise sex education, to manufacture contraceptives, and to set up and run family planning clinics. This reliance on a non-governmental organisation, unusual in a Communist country, was tactically convenient for the government, which could appear neutral, while the society absorbed the attacks of the Church. Until 1982, the society did not even receive subsidies from the state but relied heavily on advice and help from the IPPF, of which it became a member in 1959.

The attitude of the government to the society fluctuated in accordance with changes in its own relations with the Church. A fall in the birth-rate from 30 per thousand in 1956 to 18.7 in 1968 produced expressions of concern from both the government and the Church. Edward Gierek's government, which came to power in 1970 with some discreet help from the Church, was strongly pro-natalist. The incentives it offered, together with an increase in the proportion of young adults in the population, and an upswing in the economy soon produced an increase in the population growth rate.

Gierek also created considerable difficulties for the Society for Conscious Motherhood, which in 1970 had become the Polish Family Planning Association. In 1975 he personally insisted that it change its name to the Family Development Association (Towarzystwo Rozwoju Rodziny (TRR)). In 1976 the allocation to the TRR of the paper on which it depended for its publications was cut. It was made more difficult for the TRR to collect donations, the import of contraceptives was cut, and home production reduced.

In 1980–1, the growth of Solidarity gave Catholic opposition to contraception, abortion, sex education and to the TRR itself, a stronger voice. Fierce attacks were launched on the TRR, which lost one-third of its members and much of its income. Although Solidarity at the national level did not take a position on these matters, some of its branches did. Moreover it acted as an umbrella for Catholic organisations such as

'Gaudium Vitae' and 'Care for Life' to campaign, using anti-abortion material supplied by 'Life' organisations in the United States. The imposition of martial law in December 1981 brought a proscription of these organisations, and of Solidarity itself, which lasted until July 1983. Solidarity's widespread support, and identification with popular nationalism, unfortunately lent a sort of respectability to the conservative positions on sexual matters held by many of its leaders, which persecution could only enhance.

Ironically, the government, which in reality shared this conservatism if it shared little else with Solidarity, soon found it politic to change its treatment of TRR. It needed allies and was in any case becoming concerned that record birth-rates were threatening the country's economic stability. TRR was given grants from the Ministry of Health which allowed it to open new centres as well as recommencing its former activities.

None the less, TRR was a small organisation without the capacity to reach the majority of the population. Although modern contraception was available in Poland in the 1980s, it was used by only a minority of Poles. Of those using any kind of birth control, 76 per cent in the towns and 87 per cent in the villages relied only on the natural methods approved by the Church. Only 2 per cent of women of reproductive age were on the pill and fewer still used the IUD. Teenage pregnancy was a growing problem. The abortion ratio was estimated at 70–100 abortions per 100 live births. Voluntary sterilisation was and remains illegal.

The rise to power of a non-Communist government has brought difficult times for the TRR again. It lost 50–60 per cent of its income when all subsidies to non-governmental organisations were suspended and in 1989 it began to close clinics and cut staff (Kozakiewicz, 1990: 15). This now threatens its very survival. The Polish pro-life organisation, partly financed from the United States, has become very active again with a campaign to prohibit abortion. Newly-drafted laws threatened both the continuation of sex education and the end of legal abortion. In a bill submitted to the Diet in 1989, 'in defence of the conceived child', a punishment of three to five years in prison was laid down for women having an abortion. Harsh penalties were also proposed for those carrying out abortions or helping women to procure them. Members of the Diet who oppose such legislation openly are condemned by the Church and pro-life organisations and may suffer electorally (Kozakiewicz, 1989: 15).

Paradoxically, the Church's opposition to modern birth control has led many women in Poland to rely on 'natural methods' with rather frequent resort to abortion when these fail. As the tragic experience of

Romania shows, a population which has learnt to rely on abortion as a method of controlling births will not cease to use it just because it is made illegal. If the new laws go through, the result will be a great increase in the number of illegal abortions carried out in bad conditions and much consequent suffering for women.

HUNGARY

Hungary modified its stern Stalinist pro-natalist policy by legalising abortion in 1956. Abortion became available on demand to women in the first twelve weeks of pregnancy, extended to eighteen in the case of minors (Francome, 1984: 130). Hungary then developed high abortion rates, peaking in 1969 at 134 terminations per 100 live births (Várkonyi, 1989: 22), and the lowest birth-rates in Eastern Europe (Heitlinger, 1976: 124). From 1967 the government began to introduce a new range of social benefits in an attempt to raise the birth-rate. In 1967 Hungary became the first of the Eastern European countries to introduce a child-care allowance paid for the first three years of the child's life. The amount paid increased with the birth order of the child. In 1985, a more substantial child-care benefit payable for two years was introduced to make it easier for mothers to stay at home with young children. Free obstetric care was made available in 1972 and the 1974 labour law protected the jobs of pregnant women and improved maternity rights (Várkonyi, 1989: 22).

However the new concern with the birth-rate also found expression in some restrictive measures. New regulations in 1973 introduced limitations on abortion. Any woman applying for a termination had to appear before a committee which operated within a hospital out-patient clinic. Her request could be accepted on any of the following grounds: that she was unmarried, already had at least three children, or was over 35 (40 from 1980), that pregnancy presented serious health hazards for her, or that the family had severe housing problems or lived in poverty (Szalai, 1988: 98–100). Although only 7–9 per cent of all applications were refused, women disliked appearing before the committees and feminists claim that the inability of less educated women to present their cases convincingly could cause and exacerbate social inequalities.

The first oral contraceptives were introduced in Hungary in 1967. By the early 1970s, one-quarter of all married women used them. The abortion rate had fallen by about 20 per cent even prior to the restrictive legislation, as women began to switch from abortion to contraception as the primary means of restricting their fertility (Kamarás, 1990: 13–14). It continued to fall in the 1970s and 1980s. Restrictions on abortion were consequently eased in January 1989. The pill was made available to all women over 18 in 1974. The use of IUDs also began to accelerate from the mid-1970s. By the mid-1980s, 54 per cent of married women under 40 took the pill while 26 per cent used IUDs (Mészáros, 1990: 14). In 1987 new regulations permitted sterilisation for contraceptive purposes under specified conditions. Vasectomy is available, but permission to have the operation depends on the age of the applicant and the number of children he has had. A man between 30 and 34 must have three children to qualify, whereas once over 35 he qualifies with two (Várkonyi, 1989: 23).

Pro-natalist policy in Hungary was notably ineffective. The population has actually fallen since 1981. The housing shortage, an extremely high divorce rate, and other problems kept birth-rates low, even when pro-natalist welfare benefits were at their most significant. In the 1980s the value of these benefits was seriously eroded by inflation, and the economic crisis made it impossible to make good the loss. In 1989 the government recognised that it was 'not indispensably necessary to increase the population'.

In Hungary, effective contraception appears to be replacing abortion as the major means by which individuals control their fertility. The process is not yet complete, and family planning experts are unhappy that 25 per cent of married couples still rely on abortion as birth control, that the abortion rate is high, especially among the unmarried, and that one-third of all pregnancies still end in abortion. It is not yet clear what policy the new government, elected in 1990, will adopt on family planning, but it seems certain that current trends towards greater contraceptive use will continue.

CZECHOSLOVAKIA

One of the most urbanised and developed of the socialist countries, Czechoslovakia early experienced falling birth-rates, rivalling Hungary for the lowest rate in Eastern Europe in the early 1960s (Heitlinger, 1976). In the next two decades the rate showed no sharp variation, fluctuating between 14.9 and 17.1 per thousand. As in other Eastern European countries, women seem to have responded to difficult material conditions, the conflicting demands of home and family, and a serious shortage of housing, by limiting their families.

Pre-war Czech family planning clinics were tainted by an involvement in eugenics promoted by Nazi ideology. They were abolished in 1950 and for some years nothing was put in their place. Although the IUD and the pill have both been available since 1966, both ordinary citizens and medical personnel are often resistant to them. Oral contraceptives are available only from gynaecologists (Heddy, 1989: 20). Male and female sterilisations are still permitted only on medical grounds.

Abortion was first legalised in Czechoslovakia in 1920. A new interpretation of the law in 1936 restricted abortion to cases where the mother's life was endangered by the pregnancy. Restrictions were partially relaxed in 1954, and in 1957 a new abortion law was introduced. To obtain a legal abortion a woman had to apply to a local abortion committee. The application could be approved on health grounds, or on specified social grounds, for example the advanced age of the woman, a pre-existing family of three children, the loss or disablement of the husband, breakdown of the marriage, unmarried status, financial stringency, bad housing or rape (Scott, 1976: 144–5). Stiffer charges for abortion were imposed in 1962, and in the early 1970s abortion committees were urged to cut down the number of abortions allowed on social grounds. Each of these measures reflected concern at the falling birth-rate.

By the late 1980s, abortion was still the most commonly used method of fertility control. There were an estimated 75 abortions per 100 live births in 1988. Only about 16 per cent of fertile women used an IUD, and 5 per cent oral contraception (Buresova *et al.*, 1990: 17). Some effort towards change has been made. New regulations in 1987 introduced stiff charges for abortion where gestation had exceeded eight weeks. At the same time, contraceptives were made available free of charge.

The official Czech statement at the Mexico conference on population in 1984 claimed that Czechoslovakia's aim was to maintain a stable population and to concentrate on improving standards of living for families rather than attempting by financial and other incentives to persuade couples to have two or more children.

Family allowances and tax deductions were introduced in Czechoslovakia in the 1940s. Rates were gradually increased, and in 1959 they were made progressive to reward the mothers of large families. In 1962, after a decade of declining birth-rates, maternity leave was extended and minimum retiring ages for women were introduced that were graded on the basis of the number of children they had borne. There were various improvements to maternity benefits during the 1960s, culminating in a one-year maternity allowance for mothers staying at home with their children, introduced in 1970, and extended to two years in 1971. In 1973, family allowances were increased again, and differences in the amounts paid according to the parity of the child were increased. A loan scheme to help young couples to set up house allowed the cancellation of one-fifteenth of the debt on the birth of the first child and of two-fifteenths with each subsequent birth (Heitlinger, 1976: 130).

Priority housing rights for married couples have produced a high marriage rate and a low average age at marriage (Heddy, 1989: 19). The birth-rate did in fact increase in the 1970s, although the increase must be attributed not only to the incentives, but also to the new restrictions on abortion and to a more favourable age composition. It fell again in the late 1970s and continued to do so through the 1980s. Inflation was allowed to halve the value of maternity allowances. The pro-natal programme seems to have become too expensive to maintain.

Since 1989, the main political power has been Civic Forum, in effect a coalition lacking a single ideology. Opinions within Civic Forum on abortion, sex education and family policy vary, and it is not yet clear how they will coalesce. Meanwhile, voices have been raised against abortion and family planning promotion. The advocacy of family planning and existence of legal abortion are all too easily discredited by their association with the old regime and opponents have been quick to take advantage of this. Catholic members of the new parliament are urging the abolition of the abortion law (Buresova *et al.*, 1990: 17).

ROMANIA

Romania, like other Eastern European countries, legalised abortion in 1957, experienced a considerable fall in birth-rates and a high abortion rate, and in the 1960s took measures to try to reverse these trends. The pro-natal programme developed by Romania was unique, however, for its harshness and coerciveness. It was the first of the Eastern European countries to change the permissive abortion regulations of the 1950s. Moreover, while Hungary, Bulgaria and Czechoslovakia in effect amended their laws, in Romania there was a real reversal. A decree of October 1966 limited abortion to women over 45, women who had already had four children, women whose lives were endangered by the pregnancy or cases where there was a risk of congenital malformation (Teitelbaum, 1972: 405).

Whereas other Eastern European countries which restricted abortion simultaneously made contraceptives more easily available, in Romania, both the import and the manufacture of contraceptives were discontinued. They were prescribed only on strictly defined medical grounds, although they were also available to the top Party elite or at exorbitant black market prices.

The immediate effect of these measures was a sharp rise in the birth-rate and a fall in the number of legal abortions. However, the birth-rate soon began to fall again indicating that women were regaining some limited control over their fertility. Even the number of legal abortions began to rise. Indeed, in 1983 it was officially claimed that over half of all pregnancies had been legally terminated on the narrow grounds still permitted. This figure was probably deliberately exaggerated in order to justify the further restrictions on abortion which followed (Tanner, 1989: 10). From 1984, to qualify for an abortion on the grounds of a large family, a woman had to have five living children, all under 18. Not only were doctors who performed illegal abortions liable to be struck off the medical list and sentenced to up to fifteen years in prison, even doctors who had performed only legal abortions were sometimes prosecuted for having performed an excessive number. Intimidated medical personnel often refused to perform terminations even where legal grounds existed.

Women of child-bearing age were 'supervised' by the District Demographic Commission and by the District Health Directorate. After the crackdown of 1984, a third body was added, the District Demographic Command. Employed women were obliged to submit themselves to a monthly medical examination. Any woman who did not attend would lose rights to social security, a pension, and free medical and dental treatment. There were mandatory quarterly pregnancy tests for all women between 20 and 30. Once she had been found to be pregnant, a woman's failure to produce a child at the end of nine months could be taken as evidence of an illegal abortion and charges could be brought against her.

In a further development of the pro-natalist programme, a tax of approximately 10 per cent of salary was introduced for any Romanian not married by the age of 25. Married couples who did not produce a child within two years of marriage had to pay 20 per cent of their joint incomes unless they could prove medical reasons (David, 1990: 9). Justifying his policy, Ceausescu said in September 1986, 'The foetus is the socialist property of the entire society. Giving birth is a patriotic duty which is decisive for the fate of the country. Those who deliberately refuse to have children are deserters trying to escape the laws of national continuity' (Tanner, 1989: 12).

Ceausescu's objective as proclaimed in 1984 was to raise the birth-rate to 20 per thousand in order to increase the population of 23 million to 30 million by the year 2000. By this criterion, the programme was ineffective. The birth-rate had stood at 14.3 per thousand in 1966; the 1967 figure soared to 27.4, but declined again quite rapidly and had reverted to around 14 per thousand by the 1980s.

Romanian women achieved this control over their fertility at very high individual cost. The side-effects of pro-natal policies were horrific. Many women who attempted to abort themselves or who underwent 'back-street' abortions suffered terrible complications such as haemorrhages, perforations of the uterus or other organs, infections, gangrene and so on. Because abortion was a criminal offence, women feared to seek medical help, even when it was clear that things had gone badly wrong. The result could be permanent disability, infertility, psychological trauma, and even death. Maternal mortality rose to alarming heights. Most of these deaths were due to abortion.

The child victims of Romania's population programme have received wide publicity in the early 1990s. The perinatal and infant mortality rates increased in the wake of the prohibition of all forms of family planning, as did the proportion of children born with many forms of mental and physical disability (Grigoroiu-Serbanescu, 1990: 6). Some children were even rejected by their parents and sent to orphanages, either because of disability, or simply because their parents could not manage the difficulties and expense of bringing them up. In the 1980s the state even sold children for hard currency to childless couples in the west, deals which no doubt provided the children with better prospects, but were scarcely consistent with sanctimonious statements about bringing up more Romanians. Exhausted and malnourished mothers often gave birth to weak or premature babies. These children routinely received transfusions of blood not tested for the presence of HIV. The lack of equipment such as disposable syringes in maternity hospitals caused the spread of the infection. Of the 650 cases of HIV infection reported to the Ministry of Health by February 1990, 83 per cent were of children under 4 (Gromyko, 1990: 10–13).

The baby boom of the summer of 1967 caused by the sudden introduction of restrictions in 1966 has put the system under strain at each stage of its existence. Because so many were being born and because large numbers of medical personnel were themselves on maternity leave, women had to be urged to give birth at home that summer (Teitelbaum, 1972: 415). Later it was difficult to provide this huge cohort with adequate schooling and employment. It is pleasing to think members of the bulge generation which Ceausescu so arbitrarily created, as young women and men in their twenties, took an active part in the overthrow of his regime in 1989.

The Provisional Government of the National Salvation Front gave high priority to ridding Romania of its hated population policy. Its second decree, passed on the 25 December 1989, made abortion legal on request up to 12 weeks, and after that for medical reasons (Marinescu, 1990: 4). The hospitals were immediately flooded with women seeking terminations. Western journalists reported that wards were so full that women had to lie two to a bed (Simmons, 1990). Contraception was made available and family planning clinics were set up (Neagu, 1990: 7). Bodies such as the IPPF, Marie Stopes International and the French Family Planning Movement have all been active with help and advice.

The lives of some individuals, disabled or neglected children, women disabled by botched abortions, and families impoverished by the birth of too many babies have been irredeemably damaged. Widespread ignorance about sex, reproduction and health will need time to overcome. In some cases even midwives and other medical personnel are hostile to modern contraception, having been trained during a period when it was unreservedly condemned as dangerous (Gallard, 1990: 7). Women are not only accustomed to use abortion as a means of controlling their fertility, they still tend to try to induce abortions themselves. When they seek legal terminations they often come too late (Puia and Hirtopeanu, 1990: 5). Although the number of post-abortion deaths is down, they do still occur. The legacy of the most interventionist pro-natal programme the world has ever known will take a long time to fade.

CHINA

China's attempt to persuade a majority of couples to restrict themselves to a single child, is the most extreme anti-natal policy the world has seen. Vietnam has followed China in implementing a stern programme of incentives and penalties to persuade its people to limit their families, but has adopted a two-child ideal. This section will focus on China, the most populous of the socialist states. As we have seen there was already concern about population growth in China in the 1950s. An education campaign of 1956–7 about family planning was confined mainly to the cities. Contraceptives were available at least in the big cities. As in Eastern Europe, abortion was legalised in 1957. But unlike the Eastern European countries China also legalised sterilisation for contraceptive purposes in 1957. By 1958, Chinese doctors were reporting their research on vacuum aspiration abortion. This method, pioneered in China and now used all over the world, was to be of immense benefit to women. Less traumatic and less dangerous than older methods, it made abortion statistically safer than carrying the pregnancy to term (Banister, 1987: 149).

However, although the Chinese never promoted a large-scale pro-natal programme – it must have been all too evident that it was unnecessary – anti-natalism was not yet official policy. Indeed, economists and demographers who had argued on economic grounds for population control were attacked and disgraced in the late 1950s (Banister, 1987: 18).

In the early 1960s a new population campaign invited party members to restrict the number of their own children to two, and Premier Zhou Enlai expressed the hope that China's population growth rate could be reduced to under 2 per cent per annum. The main argument used in favour of family planning at this stage was that it would benefit the health of both mothers and children, but it was clear that other concerns underlay the campaign. Oral contraceptives and IUDs were used on a large scale in China from the late 1960s (Tien, 1973).

By the 1970s ideological inhibitions were fading. The official line was now that a planned economy needed a planned population. All couples were urged to follow the slogan, 'few, spaced and late' in planning their families. Before the end of the decade, a family of two children was not only being held up as an ideal, couples were being persuaded to conform to it by political pressure and in some localities with economic incentives.

After Mao's death in 1976, his successors, troubled by the state of the Chinese economy, embarked on a far-reaching programme of economic reform. At the same time, the insistence on social and intellectual conformity which had marked China for two decades was somewhat relaxed.

By contrast, population policy was made stricter than ever. The population had doubled since 1949, and it was calculated that it would do so again in 45 years if each couple had three children (Chen and Tyler, 1982: 67). This relentless growth was now regarded as a drag on economic advance. There was particular worry about the surges in the birth-rate which were expected as the bulge generations of the late 1960s and 1970s began to bear children. From 1979, couples were asked to have only a single child. A complex programme of incentives and penalties was gradually formulated to encourage acceptance (Croll, Davin and Kane, 1985). The very heavy financial and social pressure exerted on couples to conform could be defined as coercive, although public education to gain co-operation by persuasion was attempted. Physical coercion was forbidden, but in some years there were many reports of forced abortions and IUD insertions. The central authorities must bear some responsibility for such abuses for they were due partly to the 'campaign' style adopted, whereby local officials were given 'targets' for births in their areas. If these were met, officials were rewarded, if not, they were fined.

The policy has been largely successful in the cities where the pressures of urban life had earlier persuaded many couples to limit their families to two children or even a single child. It has been much more difficult in the countryside, where children are still needed to swell the family labour force and to support their parents in old age. This problem was exacerbated by the effects of the decollectivisation of the 1980s (Davin, 1988, 1991). The peasant household is now the basic economic unit in the countryside and its income is closely correlated with the amount of labour it can deploy. There is minimal provision for social welfare and peasants normally depend on their sons in old age. The parents of daughters are especially reluctant to limit their families before they have at least one male child. Sons will carry on the family line, and while some girls marry into their husbands' families, boys stay with or near their own parents and support and care for them (Davin, 1988). The authorities have acknowledged the difficulties of implementing the policy in the countryside, and the regulations allow more exemptions to the single child rule in rural areas. The most important of these, announced in 1988, was that peasants whose first child was a girl might be permitted a second child if they left a four year gap (Davin, 1990). This modification was intended to make the policy more acceptable in the countryside and to protect baby girls from the neglect or ill-treatment to which they were vulnerable when their existence prevented their parents from being allowed to try again for a boy. The new regulation is easy to justify on pragmatic grounds, but in effect it lends official support to traditional rural attitudes to women. Government propaganda may continue to insist that a girl is as good as a boy; the new message is clearly acceptance that, for peasant parents at least, she is not.

Women have suffered in many ways from China's strict population policy. They are blamed and sometimes ill-treated if the first child is a daughter (Davin, 1987). The main burden of contraception falls on them as the IUD and the pill are the major methods used. Where contraception fails, they have to abort, although in some cases they may very much want to carry the pregnancy to term. Easy access to abortion means that most terminations take place early, but there have been second and even third trimester abortions where the pregnancy has been successfully concealed for a time. Sterilisation is a common means of contraception for couples who have already had two children and female sterilisations far outnumber male ones. The policing of the policy varies considerably from one area of China to another but often involves extraordinary intrusions on privacy. At its most extreme, in factories for example, supervision involves keeping wall-charts of the menstrual cycles of all the women workers. Women are required to report each time they start a period and this satisfactory evidence of their non-pregnant state is duly entered on the chart.

Girl children have also sometimes been victims of the policy. In some provinces sex ratios among young children favour boys to a worrying degree. The under-reporting of females affects the figures but this is not the full explanation. There have been instances of female infanticide, although these are impossible to quantify. The strength of son-preference in Chinese society tends anyway to make a girl's survival chances poorer than those of her brothers, on whom more of the family resources are concentrated. As pointed out, where a girl's very existence is the obstacle which prevents her parents trying again for a son there may be even more significant neglect.

In China the reforms have produced not a relaxation of population policy, but a new and more severe version of it. Although in many spheres the reforms have been accompanied by far greater individual freedom, state intrusion into private family life in the name of population policy has been on a scale unparalleled even in the years of the Cultural Revolution.

The depth and the early success of China's economic reforms meant that before the Tiananmen massacre of 1989, China was often held up as a reform model. However, China's reforms differed from those in Eastern Europe in the degree to which they were imposed from above. They were on the whole popular, and at times the leadership courted popularity through implementing economic reform, but pressure from below was not the main impetus which produced them.

CONCLUSION

Specific experience of population planning or state intervention to affect birth-rates in the USSR, Eastern Europe and China has been quite diverse. While the USSR and the Eastern European countries have generally pursued pro-natalist policies, China's leaders have moved from moderately encouraging birth control to enforcing it. Despite their pro-natalist position, the USSR and the Eastern European countries legalised abortion in the 1950s, two decades before western European countries began to take this measure. Legalisation in Eastern Europe came at a time when, for various reasons, many people were anxious to have smaller families. Uptake was rapid and birth-rates dropped fast. In Romania, Bulgaria and Hungary, net reproduction rates fell below replacement level.

The USSR and the Eastern European countries were slow to introduce reliable modern contraceptives when these became available in the 1960s, in part because a further negative impact on the birth-rate was feared and also because the well-established availability of abortion reduced the pressure for reliable contraception.

Since the 1960s pro-natalism has inspired an enhanced range of welfare incentives to parenthood in most East European countries, restrictions on abortion and dilatoriness in making modern contraceptives available in some, and the notorious prohibition of abortion and contraception in Romania.

The governments produced by the upheavals of the 1980s in Eastern Europe and the USSR have tended to follow policies influenced by a greater responsiveness to the needs and wishes of their citizens, especially of women, rather than by a desire to maintain numbers. In the region as a whole it seems that access to birth control will be improved as a result of the changes. More countries will go through the process already well underway in Hungary, in many ways a leader in the reforms, whereby dependence on abortion for fertility control is replaced by the use of contraception with abortion as a back-up. However, the access of East German women to abortion seems likely to be restricted when regulations for a reunified country are finally agreed. In Poland and perhaps even in Czechoslovakia, the renewed influence of the Church may result in limitations to abortion. In Poland even the extension of contraceptive knowledge and services is endangered.

Even in the reform era, China presents a sharp contrast to Eastern Europe and the USSR. State policy remains anti- rather than pro-natalist and strenuous efforts are still made to enforce it. The gravity of China's demographic problems probably makes it impossible for any Chinese government to vary this stance significantly, but the lack of any thoroughgoing political reform in China has certainly made it easier for the government to maintain what is a very severe policy. In fact, the one-child family policy and the complex financial, administrative, and social pressures employed to enforce it were introduced at the same time as the economic reforms that in may ways liberalised Chinese society in the 1980s.

It is perhaps hardly surprising that no clear pattern of development in the field of birth control has arisen from the reforms. China has long followed a path quite distinct from that of the European socialist countries. Its demographic problems are in sharp contrast to theirs and necessitate different solutions. Moreover, as reform in China has been very much led from the top, the government has not needed to be so particularly responsive to grass-roots pressure. In June 1989 it explicitly rejected the populist model of reform.

Socialist countries are not of course unique in having attempted to influence the fertility decision of their citizens and to control access to abortion and contraception. However the USSR, the Eastern European countries and China have had in common that the strong, centralised and often exclusive power of the state has allowed state policy on abortion and contraception to have a considerable impact on people's lives. Resistance at a fragmented, individual level, is reflected in, for example, Romania's return to low birth-rates in the 1970s, or the still quite high number of third and higher parity births regularly reported from China. None the less it has been true of all these countries that the state has been able to exert considerable influence over the family size, and control over access to abortion and contraception. Moreover, no other agency has been in a position to challenge this control systematically.

It seems likely that in many countries the state will in the future wish to influence the fertility decisions of its citizens. There is certainly no reason to suppose that the sum of these individual decisions will always produce demographic trends which suit the interests of the country as a whole, and indeed it is clearly theoretically possible that they could produce a rate of population growth or decline that was not compatible with the maintenance of reasonable standards of living. This gives a special relevance to the study of the population policies already undertaken, for a study of this past and current experience helps us as individuals decide which interventions might be acceptable and which could never be.

REFERENCES

Banister, Judith (1987) *China's Changing Population*, Stanford University Press, Stanford, Calif.

Berent, Jerzy (1970) 'Causes of fertility decline in Eastern Europe and the Soviet Union', *Population Studies* vol. 24, no. 1.

Bridger, Susan (1987) *Women in the Soviet Countryside: Women's Roles in Rural Development in the Soviet Union*, Cambridge University Press, Cambridge.

Buckley, Mary (1989) *Women and Ideology in the Soviet Union*, Harvester, London.

Buresova, Alexandra, Sracek, Jiri and Zverina, Jaroslav (1990) 'Family planning in Czechoslovakia: after the "Gentle Revolution" ', *Planned Parenthood in Europe*, vol. 19, no. 2.

Chen, Charles H.C. and Tyler, Carl W. (1982) 'Demographic implications of family size alternatives in the People's Republic of China', *China Quarterly*, no. 89.

Croll, Elisabeth, Davin, Delia and Kane, Penny (1985) *China's One-Child Family Policy*, Macmillan, London.

David, Henry (1990) 'Romania ends compulsory childbearing', *Entre Nous: The European Family Planning Magazine*, no. 14–15.

Davin, Delia (1987) 'Gender and population in the People's Republic of China', in Haleh Afshar (ed.) *Women, State and Ideology: Studies from Africa and Asia*, Macmillan, London.

Davin, Delia (1988) 'The implications of contract agriculture for the employment and status of Chinese peasant women', in Stephan Feuchtwang and Athar Hussain (eds) *Transforming China's Economy in the Eighties*, Zed Books, London.

Davin, Delia (1990) 'Never mind if it's a girl, you can have another try', in Delman, Jorgen, Stubbe Ostergaard, Clemens and Christiansen, Flemming (eds) *Remaking Peasant China: Problems of Rural Development and Institutions at the Start of the 1990s*, Aarhus University Press, Aarhus.

Davin, Delia (1991) 'Chinese models of development and their implications for women', in Haleh Afshar (ed.) *Women, Development and Survival in the Third World*, Longman, London.

Francome, Colin (1984) *Abortion Freedom*, George Allen & Unwin, London.

Frenkel, Izaslaw (1976) 'Attitudes towards family size in some East European countries', *Population Studies*, vol. 30, no. 1.

Gallard, Colette (1990) 'The Mouvement français pour le planning familial: involvement in Romania', *Planned Parenthood in Europe*, vol. 19, no. 2.

Grigoroiu-Serbanescu, Maria (1990) 'How a restrictive abortion policy affected child mental health', *Entre Nous: The European Family Planning Magazine*, no. 14–15.

Gromyko, Alexandre (1990) 'Nosocomial transmission of the HIV virus in the Soviet Union and Romania', *Entre Nous: The European Family Planning Magazine*, no. 14–15.

Hamand, Jeremy (1989) 'German Democratic Republic: a model for the East?' *People*, vol. 16. no. 3.

Hansson, Carola and Liden, Karin (1984) *Moscow Women*, Allison & Busby, London.

Heddy, Julian (1989) 'Czechoslovakia: still not out of the closet', *People*, vol. 16. no. 3.

Heitlinger, Alena (1976) 'Pro-natalist population policies in Czechoslovakia', *Population Studies*, vol. 30. no. 1: 123–35.

Holland, Barbara and McKevitt, Teresa (1985) 'Maternity care in the Soviet Union', in Barbara Holland (ed.) *Soviet Sisterhood*, Fourth Estate, London.

Kane, Penny (1987) *The Second Billion: Population and Family Planning in China*, Ringwood, Vic., Australia, Penguin.

Kamarás, Ferenc (1990) 'Survey of Central and Eastern Europe', *Entre Nous: The European Family Planning Magazine*, no. 14–15.

Ketting, Evert (1990) 'East and West: a common cause', *Planned Parenthood in Europe*, vol. 19, no. 2.

Koch, Hans-Georg (1990) 'German reunification and the Abortion Law', *Planned Parenthood in Europe*, vol. 19, no. 2.

Kozakiewicz, M. (1986) 'Poland: a case study', in Philip Meredith and Lyn Thomas (eds) *Planned Parenthood in Eastern Europe*, Croom Helm, London.

Kozakiewicz, M. (1989) 'Poland: locked in battle with the Catholic Church', *People*, vol. 16, no. 3.

Kozakiewicz, M. (1990) 'Poland's other thirty years' war', *Entre Nous: The European Family Planning Magazine*, no. 14–15.

Lapidus, Gail Warshofsky (1978) *Women in Soviet Society: Equality, Development and Social Change*, University of California Press, Berkeley, Calif.

Manuilova, Irina (1990) 'Family planning in the USSR: the role of the

Soviet family and health association', *Planned Parenthood in Europe*, vol. 19, no. 2.

Marinescu, Bogdan (1990) 'Official statement by the Romanian Vice-Minister of Health', *Entre Nous: The European Family Planning Magazine*, no. 14–15.

Mazur, Peter D. (1975) 'The influence of human fertility on the economic conditions of the rural population in Poland', *Population Studies*, vol. 29, no. 3.

Mehlan, K.-H. (1990) 'How the government tackles family planning in the German Democratic Republic', *Entre Nous: The European Family Planning Magazine*, no. 14–15.

Mészáros, Arpád (1990) 'Birth control in Hungary: changing legal conditions', *Planned Parenthood in Europe*, vol. 19, no. 2.

Neagu, Cristina (1990) 'Bucharest's first family planning clinic since the revolution', *Entre Nous: The European Family Planning Magazine*, no. 14–15.

Neumann, Hans-Georg (1990) 'Thoughts on the present-day family planning situation in the GDR', *Planned Parenthood in Europe*, vol. 19, no. 2.

Puia, Sorin and Hirtopeanu, Christian (1990) 'Coming out of the dark: family planning in Romania', *Planned Parenthood in Europe*, vol. 19. no. 2.

Peers, Jo (1985) 'Workers by hand and womb – Soviet women and the demographic crisis', in Barbara Holland (ed.) *Soviet Sisterhood*, Fourth Estate, London.

Scott, Hilda (1976) *Women and Socialism: Experiences from Eastern Europe*, Allison & Busby, London.

Simmons, Michael (1990) 'Two generations suffer Ceausescu's fertility fetish', *Guardian*, 19 January.

Szalai, Julia (1988) 'Abortion in Hungary', *Feminist Review*, no. 29.

Tanner, Marcus (1989) 'Romania: life on a babyfarm', *People*, vol. 16. no. 3.

Teitelbaum, M.S. (1972) 'Fertility effects of the abolition of legal abortion in Romania', *Population Studies*, vol. 32, no. 2.

Tien, H. Yuan (1973) *China's Population Struggle*, Ohio State University Press, Columbus.

Várkonyi, Anna (1989) 'Hungary: families struggle to make ends meet', *People*, vol 16, no. 3.

6 Whose space is it anyway?

Youth, gender and civil society in the Soviet Union

Hilary Pilkington

One of the most striking components of the reforms aimed at democratising Soviet society, which were first declared at the 1987 January Plenum of the Central Committee of the CPSU and subsequently formalised at its 19th Party Conference, has been the emphasis laid on the role of the individual (*lichnost'*) in bringing about social change. In the early stages of the reform process, this emphasis was understandably interpreted as little more than an ideological justification for short-term reliance on the improvement of individual work performance to realise the policy of 'acceleration' (*uskorenie*). The latter word had been adopted as the ideological code-name for the historically necessary programme for rescuing Soviet society from the economic stagnation (*zastoi*) of the Brezhnev period. Indeed such an interpretation seemed to be borne out by the 19th Party Conference in June 1988, when Gorbachev explicitly linked the need for extensive democratisation to the realisation that the economic crisis was much deeper than originally anticipated (Gorbachev, 1988a: 22). Nevertheless, the democratisation campaign was to develop its own internal dynamic and become, according to Gorbachev, 'not only the means of *perestroika* but the very essence of our socialist system' (Gorbachev, 1988b: 1). Throughout 1988 and the early part of 1989 emphasis was placed on the institutionalisation of the democratisation programme via a gradual transference of power away from the Secretariat, and subsequently the Central Committee and the Politburo, of the CPSU and towards the parliamentary system of the Supreme Soviet and its standing committees. This would, it was claimed, make democratisation 'irreversible'.

The ongoing process of the democratisation of Soviet society has also forced into the open the key question of our epoch, that of the relationship between state and individual. The different components of the integrated programme of *perestroika* have been linked by a crucial recognition that a future Soviet society must be based not on an abstract mass of 'workers', in whose name the party rules, but on the active support of a 'working citizenry'. The need to construct new norms of legitimation is an obvious motivation here. Having publicly torn up the Brezhnevite social contract – according to which public silence was rewarded by 'personal freedom' in the familial sphere (Millar, 1985) – Gorbachev has been forced to redefine the relationship between state and individual and reclaim the public sphere for meaningful activity. The importance of the socio-demographic category of youth is important since youth has been targeted as a key agent of change in this process. Young people have been heralded as the force capable of breaking the chains of the paternalistic state and reconstructing a truly modern Soviet society (Gorbachev, 1988c). According to the reformers' vision, the restructured Soviet citizens of this new society should be active and critical members of a growing civil society whose development would gradually push back the state and, eventually, provide a counterbalance to it.

Gorbachev's, like Thatcher's, concept of a more delimited state and a more 'socially responsible citizen', however, did not necessarily entail a weaker state. On the contrary, the state itself was actively to construct civil society (Scanlan, 1988). The practical embodiment of this impossible theoretical juggling act manifested itself in the Komsomol's prolonged and pathetic attempt to transform itself into an authentic youth movement. The impossibility of the reauthentication of statised movements such as the Komsomol is not rooted in the fact that Soviet society must build a 'civil society' (*grazhdanskoe obshchestvo*) from a state of nothingness, as those who now wish to revive totalitarian theories of Soviet society claim. In fact, of course, the slow-down of growth rates under Brezhnev may have constituted an economic 'stagnation' but society did not, and could not, stand still. The continuing processes of education, urbanisation and increasing stratification of Soviet society meant that long before the advent of reform from above, young people had created their own forms of active public life. Indeed, by the early 1980s, Soviet society was witnessing a new social phenomenon – a plethora of non-formal youth groups – and the advent of *perestroika*, if anything, has encouraged a process of the formalisation not deformalisation of their activity.[1] Although the existence of authentic, non-state organisations and associations is only one manifestation of civil society, their emergence is highly significant since their presence is tangible proof of the existence of some kind of space between the private and the state-governed spheres of society. So far, however, it has been the concern of political scientists to assess the level of development of these non-formal groups and to measure the degree to which they have been institutionalised. This has meant that the groups themselves remain unproblematised and characterised as a naturally 'progressive' element of a nascent civil society.

The aim of this chapter is to challenge this approach by offering a gendered reading of the new space which has been revealed by the redefinition of the relationship between state and individual in Soviet society. This will be attempted via: a consideration of the implications for women of the end of 'paternalism' and the development of a 'modern' society in which a balance is struck between institutions of the state and of 'civil society';[2] and an analysis of the actual relations between the sexes pertaining in civil society, taking the example of the experience of young Russian women in non-formal youth groups. Since the process of change is ongoing, no conclusions will be attempted – the aim is simply to intervene in the interminable debate about the existence or non-existence in a restructuring Soviet society of this space we call 'civil society', by interposing the question, 'Whose space is it anyway?'

THE SOVIET CITIZEN RESTRUCTURED?

In contrast to Eastern Europe, where the notion of 'civil society' has been crucial for opposition movements in identifying a site for the construction of alternative structures to those of the state, in the Soviet Union the discourse of civil society arrived late and has been mono-polised by liberal-Communist reformers. Civil society, they claim, has remained 'underdeveloped', owing to the legacy of pre-revolutionary Russia (where the economic, social and cultural spheres of society had undergone an inadequate evolution), and the constraints placed upon the post-revolutionary state by the need to develop the nation's economy and defend the new system against internal and external enemies. As a result, state power became centralised and dominant and the functions performed by the state and civil society became inverted. This process must now be reversed by state-led efforts to create a new civil society by, 'paring down public interference in economic and socio-cultural life, and encouraging in every way voluntary associations, unions and organisations in order to give free rein to the creative energies and initiative of the people' (Migranian, 1989: 109).

The prevailing notion amongst reformers of the constitution of this new space would appear to conform to a classic liberal concept of civil society as a universal public realm whose development marks the end of the dominance of the paternal relationship between state and individual. In Migranian's words, 'The paternalistic function acquired by the state due to objective conditions should be brought to a minimum as civil society gains in strength' (1989: 109). Perhaps ironically, Migranian later argued that the best political strategy for such a transition was a temporary dictatorship (Migranian, 1990). Others continued to argue for a direct transition and suggested that the Soviet Union look to the Anglo-American experience in order to develop a system of mechanisms for including civic initiative in political practice and allowing the development of a socialist civic society, that is, a society of well-informed, politically competent citizens who manage their affairs independently (Beliaeva, 1988).

The 'universal public realm', however, is not new, uncharted territory but a gendered space which is being reworked within a male-determined political discourse. This is evident from the disruption of the 'civil society as universal public realm' discourse by a second, gender specific discourse. This discourse concerns the importance of the private, moral and family sphere and is built into a gendered notion of citizenship. For Gorbachev, the rights of citizens are tied inherently to their duties (Gorbachev, 1989: 1), and although restructured citizenship will continue to grant women and men equal, and virtually identical, rights before the law, their duties to the state are seen as essentially (and naturally) different. It is this gendered notion of the citizen which has lent the integrated policy of *perestroika* its gendered face.

In the first phase of *perestroika – uskorenie* – the 'rights' of women were defined as the opportunity to return to their 'truly womanly mission' (Gorbachev, 1987: 117), and these rights were to be strengthened through legislation on shorter working days or weeks for women, the encouragement of work from home and the increase in the amount of paid absence from work for mothers with sick children. At the same time the 'duties' of women were defined as 'housework, the upbringing of children and the creation of a good family atmosphere' (*ibid.*) which, it was claimed, women had been obliged to neglect because of their activity in social production. This neglect on the part of women had led to the intensification of a number of social problems in Soviet society, especially the increase in crime, juvenile delinquency, alcohol and drug addiction, poor labour discipline and lack of moral guidance. This had occurred, according to Gorbachev, as 'a paradoxical result of our sincere and politically justified desire to make women equal with men in everything' (*ibid.*). What is important here is the recognition that the restructured notion of citizenship contained a redefinition of equality. Equality was no longer to be seen as 'identity' but constituted in 'difference', the difference being the relocation of women's duties to the moral, spiritual and private sphere.

The second phase of *perestroika* – democratisation of the public sphere – has also proved to be an ambiguous experience for women. For women the receding of the state proved far from immediately liberating: in the first contested elections to the newly formed Congress of People's Deputies in March 1989, just 15.7 per cent of the 2,250 deputies elected were women. This compared extremely unfavourably to their representation under the old system. The percentage of women elected to the Supreme Soviet of the Soviet Union in the 1979 elections was 32 per cent, and in the local soviet elections in 1980, 50 per cent of those elected were women (*Zhenshchiny v SSSR*, 1981: 5). Moreover, 75 of the seats won by women in the Congress of People's Deputies had been reserved for the organisation of women's councils – a privilege designed to enhance the position of the party and thus destined to be short-lived. It should not surprise us, therefore, that there have already been calls from representatives of the official women's organisations for the state to reintervene in order to regulate the voting public's discrimination against women by reserving not less than 30 per cent of the managerial posts in state bodies at all levels for women (Startseva, 1990). In effect this would mark a return to something akin to the pre-democratisation 'quota' system implemented by the party.

In the socio-political sphere of non-formal activity women have not been wholly absent, but they generally remain outside the organisational committees of socio-political groups (see Chapter 11). Consequently, little time is devoted to discussing potentially distinct social and political demands of women and sexual politics remains off the agenda. Just as the 'formals' they criticise, therefore, the *neformaly* (those who work outside the formal structures) have subordinated women's demands to what they consider to be 'all-human' issues. This has not prevented women from putting forward their demands, however. The revival of the system of women's councils (called for by Gorbachev at the 27th Party Congress in 1986) seems at least to have facilitated women's ability to agitate for improved consumer facilities at work although only in a few cases have the women's soviets escaped party domination and definition of their interests (Bessolova, 1989). In general the women's soviets, under the women's committee, have met the same fate as the Komsomol, being unable to transform themselves into an authentic women's movement.

Nevertheless, the last two to three years has seen the emergence of numerous authentic women's organisations, reflecting not only the growing consciousness of professional women (as expressed in newly-formed organisations of women cinema-workers, journalists and writers, and of women artists and academics) but of women workers and of mothers and grandmothers. Women have protested, and made gains, over conditions for women workers such as in the case of the nursery school workers forming their own strike committee to negotiate with the city council (Terekhina, 1990; Terekhina and Kozyreva, 1990). Women prostitutes in Moscow also threatened to withhold their services from CPSU members if no action was taken to protect their rights and fulfil their demands ('G.P.' [anon.], 1990). Women have been active in their capacity as mothers and grandmothers: they have expressed their anger over the needless infection of new-born babies with HIV, over the continuing effects of Chernobyl and other ecological disasters, and they have organised to fight compulsory conscription and bullying (*dedovshchina*) in the armed forces. Indeed women have even united in the public sphere to call for their own exclusion from it. The recently registered Christian-Democratic League of Women of Moldavia, for example, declared itself to be 'a mass, voluntary, independent, democratic organisation which aims to attract women (regardless of nationality and religion) to activity directed towards the spiritual revival (*vozrozhdenie*) and democratisation of society with the aim of ensuring their natural functions and guaranteed rights' ('Zhenskaia partiia?', 1990). Most recently, the Independent Women's Democratic Initiative (*NeZhDI*) emerged with a programme which takes up directly the reformist rhetoric of the redefinition of the relationship between state and 'individual'. *NeZhDI*, organising under the slogan 'Democracy without women is not democracy', accuses the government of consciously excluding women from the new public sphere and calls for women to organise their own initiatives to counter-act government policy. The *NeZhDI* alerts women to the fact that although the relationship between state and individual in Soviet society is up for renegotiation, that between public and private is not: the nature of women makes them primarily suited to the latter sphere.

FROM THE PATERNAL TO THE PATRIARCHAL STATE

How has it come about that, after seventy years of equal political rights and active participation in the sphere of social production, Soviet women are today being asked to consent to relocating themselves in the private sphere?

The first answer must be that although women have enjoyed political and economic 'equality' for seventy years, they have experienced this equality not as liberation but as dual oppression. The significant changes in the relations of production brought about by the Bolshevik revolution never entailed any similar disruption of the dominant gender relations: what emerged was an alternative form of patriarchy based on the equal mobilisation of women and men into the public sphere, while retaining the private sphere as the responsibility of women. There is no reason to expect, therefore, that the open attempts of Gorbachev to draw up a new social contract based on the increased role of the individual acting in an expanding space between the individual and the state should challenge the 'natural inequality' pertaining in the private sphere. Furthermore, since women's experience of their participation in social production has been such an unhappy one, many are willing to consent to their 'return to the home'. The gendered segregation of the labour market has unequally positioned women in manual labour, low-prestige and low-pay sectors of the economy where working conditions are worse than elsewhere. The vertical structuring of the labour market by gender also means that women, although starting off better qualified, end up at the bottom of the occupational ladder. As a result, women have negative images of themselves as workers and associate the private sphere, the home and the role of mother rather than worker, as the sphere in which self-expression might be achieved. Soviet women's distorted experience of 'equality' has thus meant that for many women a return to the private sphere (or at least the choice to do so) is seen as progressive.

The second answer must be sought at a more abstract level: the (re)location of women in the private sphere is an essential component of modern patriarchy. Current debates in the Soviet Union, concerning both the role of civil society and the position of women within it, appear to draw directly from liberal critiques of the absolutist state which was also posited as hindering the emergence of a truly modern society. However, the raising of the role of the individual and the challenge this presents to the rule of the father – enshrined in the paternal state – need not present more than a limited challenge to patriarchy. The withdrawal of the paternal state creates a division between the public (state) and the private (institutions of civil society), with the latter becoming a space in which individuals can exercise their rights *vis-à-vis* the state. As Pateman argues, this ignores a second division within civil society, which is related to the division between the private world of the family and the public world of civil society. The modern patriarchal order is constructed as a society which is

presented as divided into two spheres: civil society or the universal sphere of freedom, equality, individualism, reason, contract and impartial law – the realm of men or 'individuals'; and the private world of particularity, natural subjection, ties of blood, emotion, love and sexual passion – the world of women, in which men also rule.

(Pateman, 1989: 43)

Liberal democratic discourse focusing on the rights of the individual *vis-à-vis* the state, therefore, may challenge the right of the father, but need not challenge the right of the husband. This can be seen in the thinking of early proponents of women's rights. John Locke, for example, denied women's subjection to an authoritarian patriarchal father as something natural and inevitable, yet he retained a belief in the foundation in nature of women's subordination to men, who were the 'abler and the stronger', within marriage (Elshtain, 1981: 124–5). John Stuart Mill also sought a democratic, liberating family yet wished to retain those characteristics of family life tied to women's domestication and men's assumption of public responsibilities. In 'On marriage and divorce' he declared, 'The great occupation of woman should be to beautify life: to cultivate, for her own sake and of those who surround her, all her faculties of mind, soul, and body; all powers of enjoyment, and powers of giving enjoyment; and to diffuse beauty, elegance, and grace, everywhere' (Elshtain, 1981: 145).

In the Soviet context, the direct link between the end of the paternal state and the emancipation of the female individual is even less apparent. The paternal state has played a significant role in providing women with access to the basic material prerequisites for establishing oneself as a free and independent agent, and thus becoming eligible for participation in the public sphere (that is, access to paid employment, availability of birth control, child-care facilities, etc.). Nevertheless, liberal feminism and the notion of 'equality through difference' has found favour among some women in the Soviet Union. Filippova, for example, argues that, 'The love for the close, natural wiseness, a sensitivity to beauty, self-sacrifice in the name of creation – these are all primordial female characteristics which are particulary valuable in our cruel, breaking time' (Filippova, 1990: 4). In the final instance, such a position, like Gorbachev's, retains the division between the private and public spheres and, although citizenship is put formally above this division, the unrestructured nature of that citizenship makes it practically realisable only through the former, male-controlled public sphere.

THE CULTURAL CONTEXT

The 'equality through difference' argument illustrates an important point: the recognition of a division between public and private does not in itself entail the subordination of the private to the public; this is culturally specific. Pateman uses the notion of the 'fraternal social contract' to explain this structural subordination in societies based on the European liberal democratic tradition. This contract is an agreement via which the brothers inherit their patriarchal sex right and legitimise their claim over women's bodies and ability to give birth. In modern societies, Pateman argues, this is embodied in civil law, which is based on a reasoned agreement that it is to the rational mutual advantage of the participants in the contract to constrain their inter-actions and desires through such a law. This law necessarily excludes women, for women's passions render them incapable of making such a reasoned agreement. Thus the separation of civil society from the familial sphere is also a division between men's reason and women's bodies (Pateman, 1989: 51).

But how applicable is Pateman's argument in the cultural context of the Soviet Union? The novelist Tat'iana Tolstaia argues that it is barely applicable at all since Russian culture requires a new conceptualisation of power in relations between the sexes. This, she argues, is because Russianness itself is expressed in the subculture of emotion (commonly referred to as the 'Russian soul') and thus engenders a much stronger image of woman than that typical of western, enlightenment culture. This leads Tolstaia to the conclusion that there is no inequality of power between the public and the private spheres, and women are more likely to choose to stay at home than to follow a career, since careers are pursued primarily for power rather than money and that women have enough power as it is:

> Why should she want some kind of intangible political power over abstract people who don't want to submit, when right within her grasp is a full-fledged, seductive, constant, palpable power over the members of her family, over every object, chair, bed, broom, curtain, pot or pan, keys, the dog, the schedule and menu?
>
> (Tolstaia, 1990: 6)

This power over the home, hearth, household, children, birth etc., Tolstaia argues, at times extends to tyranny and thus it would be naive to claim that women are subordinated to men. Moreover, she argues, women's exclusion from the public sphere has been a privilege rather than a site of oppression since the 'public world' has been rendered devoid of any authentic worth; it is a world of meaningless parades, endless meetings, and lying speeches. In similar vein, Valentin Rasputin suggests that traditional Russian cultural norms should be revived, since although woman's role was not a 'civic' one it was nevertheless considered a significant one. Today, he argues, 'Woman has been led astray [*sic*] by public significance and emancipated . . . from her eternal and quiet duty of the cultural acceleration of the people; she has replaced spirituality with socialness, gentleness and female insight with categoricalness, femininity with effemininity, motherhood with painful child-bearing . . . familyness with unstable relations' (Rasputin, 1990: 171–2).

Although the culturalist approach does allow us to see the way in which women are involved in crucial areas of decision-making outside the public sphere, it does not help us evaluate how important these areas have been – that is, it allows us to see women as having a separate sphere of power from men, but it does not say anything about the relative nature of that power. Tolstaia does away with the public/private issue by simply declaring the two spheres to be of equal worth without entering into any discussion of why women's power should be exclusively in the private sphere and men's in the public, or of the nature of power within each sphere. Furthermore the images presented of the role of the mother are hard to square with the daily experience of most women. Both Tolstaia and Rasputin look back to a golden era of the Russian family in which the mother was a spiritual leader. In fact, of course, this form of family life existed only for a small minority of women and any return of women to the home today would be a return not as the bearers of spiritual authority, but as unpaid, domestic workers (Voronina, 1990). Moreover, even if in pre-revolutionary Russian society women did have equal but different power, there is no reason to think that this can be transposed to the modern, urban-based private sphere. The 'dominance' of women in the current family sphere may be less to do with the retention of their traditional sphere of influence than with the weakening of the traditional male role associated with the devaluing of the political and economic sphere referred to by Tolstaia herself. This weakening of the male role, moreover, has not led to more egalitarian relations between women and men but to a conservative retrenchment in which women take on many of the roles previously ascribed to men while espousing a desire to be more 'feminine', and men fail to pull their weight in the family while complaining that their wives are 'domineering' and 'unfeminine'.

The cultural specificity of notions of 'reason' and 'emotion', however, does not render irrelevant the core of Pateman's argument. The key element is that patriarchalism cannot be identified with paternal rule but has two dimensions: the paternal (father/son) and the masculine (husband/wife) (Pateman, 1989: 37). The social contract is, therefore, simultaneously a sexual contract: 'The social contract is the point of origin, or birth, of civil society and simultaneously its separation from the (private) sphere of real birth and the disorder of women' (Pateman, 1989: 45). The experience of Soviet women illustrates, however, a theoretical criticism levelled against Pateman's argument. It is that the sex-right of men over women cannot be explained by the fraternal social contract since it pre-dates the formulation of the liberal social contract. But this need not make Pateman's reading redundant if, as Diana Coole suggests, Pateman's general claim that modern patriarchy is contractual is replaced by the notion that contractarianism functions as an ideology, serving to legitimate, and to disguise, patriarchal relations that in fact rest on quite other foundations (Coole, 1990: 26).

These 'other foundations' lie outside the sphere of the contract and are sited in the construction of sexual identities as oppositions of male reason and female desire, of masculine sexual dominance and female submission. If we are properly to assess the prospects for real change in sexual relations in a restructured Soviet society, therefore, it is to the sphere of the formation of sexual identities which we must turn, for it is upon these that the 'fraternal social contract' and the exclusion of women from the public sphere rests. In the following section, therefore, an analysis of the construction of gendered identities in the youth cultural sphere will be undertaken. This will allow us to assess whether or not the new space in Soviet society is acting as a space for the creative construction of liberated gender identities (that is, liberated from masculine dominance and female submission) or whether it merely serves to maintain the hegemony of heterosexual masculinity.

POLITICS, IDENTITY AND MEANINGFUL ACTIVITY

Such a gendered reading of the youth cultural sphere is rendered all the more important by the fact that most interpretations of the Soviet youth cultural scene have been oriented towards classifying groups according to their political persuasion or social role.[3] It is only a very small proportion of non-formal activity, however, which is conducted on a socio-political level and in a goal-oriented form. It is estimated that 90 per cent of the *neformaly* are young people involved in their own horizontal groupings based on common residence, interests and places of study or work. These groups do not articulate defined platforms or goals as the socio-political organisations do; it is the process of grouping itself which is meaningful.

The analysis to be undertaken here will focus on the 'meaning' created by young people via youth cultural activity. The premise is that the youth cultural sphere provides young people with a space in which to explore an identity which is separate from the roles and expectations imposed by family, work and school: it offers a collective identity and reference group from which youth can develop an individual identity (Brake, 1985). This does not necessarily mean that young people's activity is apolitical, or devoid of political meaning, but it does suggest that young people in the Soviet Union, as in the west, are rejecting alienated forms of organised politics in favour of a new style of personal politics centred on issues of sexuality and pleasure (Cohen, 1986). The focus of the discussion which follows, therefore, will be not on the political orientations of Soviet youth but on the role of sexuality in the construction of the identity of individuals and groups in the youth cultural sphere. This will make visible the 'other foundations' of the fraternal social contract and allow us to assess whether the sphere of youth culture remains constrained by patriarchal notions of male domination and female submission or whether this new space also gives young people new freedom to construct alternative, more egalitarian gender identities.

SUBCULTURES: EXPLORATIONS OF MASCULINE IDENTITY?

Traditional preoccupations of male researchers with juvenile delinquency and, subsequently, with working-class (male) subcultures has meant that young women have been seen as, at worst, absent and, at best, peripheral to subcultural activity. Typically the presence of women has been recognised, but seen as contingent upon their romantic or sexual relationships with male members, and of no intrinsic value. Even in the light of feminist interventions in subcultural theory, gender awareness has led only to 'confirmation' that youth cultures and subcultures are 'masculinist', that is, they are some form of exploration of masculinity (Brake, 1985: ix). The first problem with which we are faced in exploring the capacity of young people to construct non-traditional gender identities in the youth cultural sphere, therefore, is lack of source material or gender-blind interpretations of such material.

Soviet discussions of youth cultural activity have either ignored women's presence altogether or have recognised their existence only in relation to the sexual activity of the male members of the group. In Fain's otherwise noteworthy discussion of subcultural groups (based, unusually, on participant observation work), women become no more than objects of the sexual attitudes of men. In the case of the biker subculture (*rokery*), he recognises the existence of female bikers (*rokershi*), but refers to them only as the girlfriends of male bikers who 'accompany' their men on the rear seat of the bike and are quickly drawn into sexual relations with them because of the night hours spent together (Fain, 1990: 28). In other subcultural groups, sexual relations with male members are portrayed not only as characterising the role of the girls in the group, but also as constituting their means of gaining access to the group in the first place. Fain notes that those girls involved in the *mazhory*[4] often become involved in prostitution in order to afford the high-life followed by the group. Indeed, others have argued that the association of money and sex for young women is a long-established one and has its roots in the common teenage games of 'spin the bottle' and 'daisy[5] (Chernyshkova, 1989). By their mid-teens, Chernyshkova argues, girls are used to expecting money for rendering trivial favours such as watching videos and going for car rides with men and it is only a short step from there on to the street.

When women are recognised as present in the youth cultural sphere, their activity is seen as wholly sexual: women are either the perpetrators of sexual deviancy or the victims of sexual exploitation.

The debate about young women's sexual deviancy centres on discussions of juvenile prostitution. It could be argued, of course, that the dominant interpretation of the growth of prostitution in Soviet society has been associated with strategies of young women for positive gender identity construction. Many images of the young female prostitute suggest that young women are rejecting the coarseness, hardness and masculinity of their mothers' generation and desire a more glamorous and feminine identity. Since the Soviet state has failed to provide them with fashionable clothes, cosmetics and elegant life-styles – through the consumption of which positive feminine identity is apparently constructed – young women turn to prostitution in order to achieve the image they desire (Waters, 1989). Clearly this provides a very circumscribed notion of femininity and one which is wholly related to the satisfaction of male desire. Furthermore, this is not the only image of the young female prostitute. Prostitution is also portrayed as a peculiarly female form of juvenile delinquency, and one which is particularly morally reprehensible. The juvenile prostitute is described as having lost all feminine identity, being 'barely distinguishable from a boy', as showing, 'a strange mix of womanly experience and childish lack of confidence in oneself' and of having 'much which is "masculine" in her behaviour' (Borshchevskaia, 1988). This clearly suggests that juvenile prostitutes show an abnormal development of gender identity and the task of social psychologists is posited as the 'normalisation' of such behaviour. In a similar way, although female members of the *mazhory* may use prostitution as the means by which they gain the material prerequisites for entrance into the group, it also ensures their ultimate exclusion. Such girls are looked down upon by the male *mazhory*, who will seek 'steady relationships' outside the group in order to avoid sexually-transmitted disease (Fain, 1990: 27).

Although in many of these cases there is a fine line between the women's sexual 'deviancy' and their sexual exploitation, a separate discourse about women as victims of the sexual regulation of men has developed primarily in relation to another form of youth cultural activity, the *dvor* groups.[6] In Kazan' it was reported that when the warring youth gangs which had been terrorising the city wanted to show their ultimate control, the means adopted was that of showing their ability to control the sexuality of women. The groups declared a temporary truce in order that a 'month of love' be instituted, during which the gangs declared their intention to make Kazan' 'a city without virgins' (Shchekochikhin, 1988). Subsequently there were repeated scares about 'love months' and 'love days' in cities such as Cheboksary, Ioshkar Ola, Izhevsk, Gorkii, Naberezhnie Chelny (Pankratov, 1990; Orlov, 1990). Within the groups themselves, girls are also used to negotiate power relations between the lads. There has been considerable discussion of the institution in groups of *obshchie devushki* (girls for common sexual 'use'). With these girls sexual relations are entered into not as a result of genuine attraction but as 'a means of socialisation, a way of "registering" lads in the group' (Yeremin, 1989; Pankratov, 1990). But this type of social control of young women is not restricted to the 'extreme model' of Kazan' described by Shchekochikhin, nor even to isolated, deviant subcultures. A male reader from Odessa, writing to the youth journal *Sobesednik* in 1988, described the common practice in schools of *pristavaniia* (pesterings). This involved groups of boys 'tricking' girls into accompanying them to secluded places where they were forced to undress or were undressed by force. In some cases photographs were taken of the naked girls ('"Foto" na pamyat'?', 1988).

When treated seriously, the recognition of this phenomenon raises important questions of gender relations not yet addressed in Soviet social science. Igor' Kon, for example, notes that 40–75 per cent of rapes are committed in groups, by people known to the victim and that, far from involving any sexual motivation, rape generally serves as a means of proving one's masculinity, that is, as a kind of test allowing one the right to occupy a certain position in the group (Kon, 1989). Often, however, the issue is reduced to a symbolic analysis. In a whole spate of youth films, pivotal scenes have centred on rape or attempted rape of girls in youth groups. Such films include *My Name Is Harlequin, Dear Elena Sergeevna, Tragedy in the Style of Rock, Little Vera,* and (most recently) *Avariia – the Cop's Daughter*. The rape is often seen more through the suffering of the male whose 'girl' is being raped (her boyfriend in *My Name is Harlequin*, her brother in *Tragedy in the Style of Rock* and her father in *Avariia – the Cop's Daughter*) and neither the implications for the young women nor the power relations at work in the committing of the rape are explored. The rape, therefore, remains an essentially symbolic event, designed to show the moral depths to which society has sunk and thus becomes a concrete enactment of Marx and Feuerbach's claim that the state of relations between men and women are indicative of relations within society as whole, an epiphenomenal reflection of the real relations within male society. Since such films reach a far wider audience than the writings of academics like Kon, it must be anticipated that the latter attitude – rape as the violation of the established sex-right of men – is the most widespread interpretation of rape.

For Soviet commentators, the very fact that the girls involve themselves in such groups in the first place suggests, at best, frivolous (*legkomyslennii*) behaviour and, at worst, their own complicity in the act. Put another way, the women who are the victims of the superior sexual strength and appetite of the male are no more than the mirror image of the women who are direct perpetrators of sexual deviancy themselves. This is reflected in the ambivalent position of one journalist, noted for her outspokenly pro-*glasnost'* position; when discussing the trial of ten young men charged and later convicted of repeatedly beating and sexually coercing girls known to them in a sadistic ritual, she said ,'Let us recall that both morality and the law forbid the coercion of girls, regardless of whether their behaviour is good, dubious or the sort that leaves no room for doubt. In this instance, we are dealing with the third type' (Lesoto, 1985).

TOWARDS A GENDERED READING OF YOUTH CULTURAL ACTIVITY

If we are to use academic and journalistic material in order to explore the subcultural activity of young women, therefore, we need to arrive at some kind of explanation, firstly, of women's invisibility, and, secondly, of the sexualisation of any activity which is recognised. One of the most important explanations of women's apparent invisibility in subcultural activity lies in the fact that there are real structural constraints on girls' participation since girls are controlled to a greater degree than boys in their leisure, their behaviour (especially sexual) and their labour. Girls rarely spend time just hanging out on the street and when they do go out, it is with a group of friends, or boyfriend, and they are expected back afterwards. Girls are also often required to devote a great deal of time helping out at home, so they simply have less free time in many cases (Nava, 1984: 11).

Apart from their subjection to greater parental control, girls are socially constrained by a serious dislocation between the discourses of adolescence and femininity (Hudson, 1984). The images associated with adolescence – the images of 'restless, searching youth' – are essentially masculine images, and thus when behavioural traits associated with adolescence are displayed by girls, they suggest not only lack of maturity but also lack of femininity. Such behaviour disrupts first and foremost not public order but, more importantly, the gender-specific norms upon which society is based. Consequently, while the Soviet press suggests that 'every boy's fate includes fights – if it does not then it is a product of an unnatural "tender" upbringing' (Kashirskaia, 1985), growth in the incidence of fights between girls leads to calls for the immediate control of young women since fighting amongst girls constitutes 'a gross misunderstanding of equal rights' and necessitates the creation of a 'cult of feminine charm' which should include 'tenderness, kindness and . . . chastity' (Rudenko, 1978).

A second explanation of the invisibility of young women has emerged from feminist interventions in subcultural theory. Blindness to women's presence and activity, it is suggested, was a result of the focus on male-dominated areas of activity, above all on 'the street', while young women's activities had a different site – the home. The 'teeny-bopper' or 'bedroom culture' was posited as a distinctly feminine form of subcultural resistance, consisting of the devising of fantasy relationships with pop idols within an all-female environment of 'best friends' (McRobbie and Garber, 1976). Soviet sociology has no such concept; although a brief discussion of the phenomenon of teen idols did appear in *Komsomol'skaia Pravda* in 1989, it consisted of little more than scornful references to the feelings girls express towards their idols and the conclusion that such behaviour represents the 'mass psychosis' of the twentieth century (Zaiarnaia, 1989). Indeed to some extent the feminist intervention appropriate to the west cannot be expected to satisfy the needs of any analysis of Soviet youth culture. The teeny-bopper culture, for example, assumes the possibility of a private space in the home available to teenage girls and the proliferation of pop artefacts via the consumption of which girls can express their fantasised romance. Clearly this does not reflect the cultural context Soviet teenagers find themselves in.

Despite the different socio-cultural context, however, the basic principle that subcultural forms are likely to be gendered – since the experience of becoming adult is determined not only by class and race, but also by sex – is a crucial one. Mica Nava argues that in patriarchal societies, manhood (defined in relation to women, to children and to labour) is significantly marked off from boyhood, but boundaries between girlhood and womanhood are far less accentuated. Thus, young men are likely to recognise the provisional nature of their subordination as youth and to struggle against it (through subcultural activity). Most women, however, never really acquire 'adult' status and the social power that accompanies it and thus girls neither recognise nor struggle against a 'transient' subordination as youth. Where girls do rebel against the confines of girlhood, therefore, their resistance is likely to take the form of the overt expression of sexuality, since this subverts the adult control of sexuality while remaining a feminine strategy (Nava, 1984: 14–16).

Such an understanding also helps explain why girls' youth cultural activity is seen as primarily sexual; sexuality need not be young women's downfall but might provide a strategy for affirmative action. This is important since, if we are to provide a 'gendered' reading of the youth cultural space, it is vital not to 'desexualise' women's activity but highlight the centrality of sexuality and gender in all subcultural activity. Such a reading is attempted below, through an examination of the subcultural activity of two – essentially 'masculinist' – groups active in Moscow in the period 1988–9.

BODY POLITICS: THE *LIUBERY* AND OTHERS

The term *Liubery*[7] originally referred to various groups of lads from the town of Liubertsy who caused a 'moral panic' in Moscow between 1986 and 1988 when numerous incidents of attacks by groups from Liubertsy on Moscow youth were recorded. The particular targets of the *Liubery* were those young people who could be outwardly identified as *neformaly*, although it soon became obvious that their much publicised 'ideological' mission to cleanse Russian society of western imitators (Iakovlev, 1987) often amounted to little more than the stealing of badges, jewelry and expensive items of clothing which were later sold on the black market. Indeed, evidence quickly emerged to show that the activity of the *Liubery* was not peculiar to Moscow but had been witnessed in many provincial towns on the periphery of large cities (Kupriianov, 1987).[8] By 1988 even the targeted Moscow *neformaly* themselves were referring not to the *Liuber* as such but to groups and individuals who were '*tipa Liubera*' ('*Liuber* types'). It is their understanding of the term which is adopted here. The term *Liubery* is used as a short-hand to describe almost any working-class, provincial young male, since what is being classified is neither socio-economic position nor territorial origin, but a strategy employed by young provincial males for dealing with the problems posed by adolescence in contemporary Soviet society.

This becomes more apparent if we focus not on the form of *Liuber* activity (their espousals of neo-Stalinist ideology) but on its substance, the cult of strength. The material aspect of this is the *Liuber* obsession with muscular strength and the secret body-building dens (*kachalki*) established by them in order to train. This strength is then exerted over other males – through their penchant for beating up members of subcultural groups (especially hippies and heavy metal fans), and over women via the 'snatching' of Moscow girls from discos and cafés and taking them back to Liubertsy. Such activity requires no political or ideological interpretation; body-building and muscular strength is a common craze across the spectrum of young Soviet men and is one expression of the struggle of teenage males to establish a secure sense of their own masculinity. As Rutherford suggests, 'The dominant meanings of masculinity in our [Christian] culture are about producing our bodies as instruments to our wills . . . our struggle for self-control is acted out as mastery over others' (Rutherford, 1988).

Here it is important to remember that hegemonic masculinity is secured through the subordination not only of femininity but also of other masculinities (Connell, 1987: 183). It is not surprising, therefore, that it was those who seemed to conform to an alternative masculinity who were singled out as the targets of *Liuber* aggression, the hippies with their long hair and pacifism being the most obvious case. In this respect, the *Liuber* strategy might be compared to what has been termed the 'skinhead solution', which involves a neo-proletarian, hard style and tendency to espouse traditional conservative values, hard work, patriotism and defence of local territory. This strategy rests on the construction of what Cohen refers to as 'a "biological" community of labour whose territories are then staked out through a more or less violent body politics on the streets of the working class city' and has also led to attacks on hippies, gays and other minorities in western societies (Cohen, 1986: 64). This is not to suggest that the essence of masculinity is any 'natural aggression', but that, in order to form a secure gender identity, young men have to negotiate survival in a street environment which is already violent.

A little considered, although integral, aspect of *Liuber* activity is their snatching of Moscow girls from discos. The invasions of territory made by the *Liubery* in Moscow are primarily into the spaces where they may gain access to women: cafés, discos and clubs. The importance of this lies in the deliberate violation by the *Liubery* of the norms regulating the control of access to girls. Such transgressions have a long history and have required societies to develop social organisations to deal with the problem. In pre-revolutionary Russian society, as in other pre-industrial or industrialising European societies, youth communities were entrusted with ensuring that social and moral norms were adhered to. In the Russian case this peer-group took the form of the *khorovod* (a youth grouping of the village with its own internal life and involving not only round-dancing but a whole complex of activities) whose main function was to exert control over the process of courting (Gromyko, 1986: 161–221). The strict rules governing the establishing of 'courting couples', however, effectively constituted a secure mechanism of controlling the sexuality of women. The breaking of these rules would lead to friction between groups of lads from different villages and disputes were often settled in a physical way. The connection here to the fights between groups of Muscovites and 'out-of-towners' at Moscow discos is obvious.

WHAT DO WOMEN DO?

The masculinist nature of subcultural activity, however, does not mean that young women are reduced to the objects of the mediation of relations between men. On the contrary, young women are able, through subcultural activity, to find some space in which creative gender construction can take place. One form this has taken is highlighted here via reference to a second subcultural group, the *Stiliagi*.[9]

Like their predecessors of the 1950s, revivalist *Stiliagi* define themselves as lovers of rock'n'roll music. Their major *tusovki*[10] (gatherings) take place at concerts of their favourite groups, discos where there are rock'n'roll nights, in parks, or even metro stations, where they can play their music. The public nature of the *tusovki* suggests that the group is a typical masculinist subculture (as opposed to a female 'teeny-bopper' subculture). What is unusual about the group, however, is that many of its members (both male and female) came to it via the *Bravisty*, the fans of the Soviet rock group Bravo. Until recently Bravo was led by the dynamic female singer Zhanna Aguzarova whose distinctive style – black suit, white shirt, narrow tie and patent leather shoes – was painstakingly followed by both girls and boys. Although subsequently many of the girls again followed Zhanna in her switch to more traditionally feminine styles of the 1950s, none the less, at least during the winter months (for practical reasons) the girls continued to dress in a masculine style.

The importance of the fact that it was Zhanna's 'style' which was followed cannot be underestimated, since it is style (*stil'*) which lies at the heart of the group identity of the *Stiliagi*. Authority within the group was also determined by how well and for how long you had been dressing in 'style', and this is important for understanding the role of the girls in the group. The male members of the group tended to be younger and less permanent members than the girls, since at 17 or 18 the boys would be conscripted into the army for two years and usually did not return to the *tusovka* afterwards. Consequently, the girls were largely responsible for keeping the *tusovka* alive and introducing new members to the rules of what constituted correct 'style'. The creation of their 'style' also gave the girls a focus for the positive construction of their own femininity. The girls took a conscious pride in the fact that their particular style meant that they could avoid the constant search for western, fashionable, yet affordable clothes and records which takes up most of the time and money of young Soviet citizens. Furthermore, the centrality of rock'n'roll also shaped the group's priorities; the girls' concerns were much more with what concert was coming up and what item of clothing they were sewing or 'obtaining' than with boyfriends, husbands or families. Indeed, even when pressed to speculate on a future life outside the group, the girls rather reluctantly admitted that pressures of work and family would eventually force them out of their present life-style, but remained confident that this would not change their value-orientations.

Perhaps the key to the 'subject position' of the *Stiliagi* girls lies in the fact that young women participating in the activities of the group do so on their own terms. None of the women interviewed had gained access to the group via their romantic attachment to a male member of the group but had become involved either through chance encounters at concerts or through female friends already involved. Moreover, the image being identified with was that of a strikingly non-traditional woman. But the girls' apparent lack of concern with romance and willingness to brave the derision of adults for their masculine dress is mixed with seemingly stereotyped views on gender-roles. When asked about relations between the girls and boys in the group, one of the girls in the group stated,

> They make me feel like a girl, a real girl . . . our lads always get out of the bus first and offer us their hand, so that the girls can get out and

through the crowd ... it shocks everybody. It's really nice for us – we walk with a look on our faces, as if to say, 'go ahead, laugh at us, at how we look, but look how we are treated, just look ...'

(Interview with members and ex-members of the *Stiliagi*, Moscow, 15 April 1990)

The key point here, however, is that for the *Stiliagi* girls this was an act not of conformity, but of resistance. Just as women who have taken their demands to be allowed 'to return to the role of wife and mother' into the political sphere, these girls saw the way they were treated by the boys as a rejection of the general disrespect accorded to women in adult society. In the same interview the girls said they felt sorry for those girls who had left the *Stiliagi* to join the *Rokabilly* who, according to them, treated the girls disrespectfully.

CONCLUSION

Youth no longer believes in the paternalistic declarational-conde-scending character of relations to it by the state. It is prepared to take the weight of responsibility for the country's affairs on its own shoulders.

(Tsybukh, 1990)

With these words Viktor Tsybukh, president of the youth affairs committee of the USSR Supreme Soviet, acknowledged that in the current stage of the development of Soviet society there is a new negotiation of the relationship between state and individual. Young people, who have in the past been turned into dependent objects of state policy, are being called upon to throw off the chains of the old paternal state and emerge as active citizens of society, as the real 'subjects' of social relations. What Tsybukh fails to recognise, however, is that the subjects he refers to are gendered subjects and their ability to act – to rise up and throw off the chains of the paternal state – is unleashed or constrained by the prevailing social relations governing the space in which their subjectivity is formed. By focusing on the activity of women in the youth cultural sphere, we can see how the new space opening up between state and individual is already imbued with notions of male dominance (men as subjects) and female submission (women as objects of male sexuality). This may not be caused by the 'fraternal social contract' which is emerging to replace the 'paternal' relationship between state and individual in Soviet society, but it is articulated in its rhetoric of 'equality through difference' and the pseudo-universalism of the public realm. This, from the outset, limits the 'youth rebellion' heralded by *glasnost'*, to the overthrow of the fathers by the sons. If male colonisation of the new space is to be halted, therefore, there must be a radical restructuring of gender identities. By looking to the youth cultural sphere, we can gain some insight into the process by which such identities are constructed and how they might be radically restructured. Although work in this area has barely begun, we can already at least point to the fact that no single definition of femininity or masculinity is passively accepted by young Soviet women and men: such identities involve constant reconstruction and negotiation within and between youth worlds. These identities – both individual and group – will increasingly define young people's experiences of 'de-socialising' societies and will determine the scope of the democratisation under way. At the current stage we can posit only two things. First, democratisation has revealed the space in which such identities are constructed and this space appears firmly located in the political discourse of men. But second, and more important, this monopolisation of the new space has not gone uncontested and women have not yet given up their claims on it.

NOTES

I would like to thank Chris Corrin, Annie Phizacklea, Shirin Rai and Nick Lampert for their comments on earlier drafts of this chapter.

1 Although the *neformaly* are usually referred to in English as 'informal groups', they are not so much informal as non-formal, that is what makes them beyond 'the formal' is not their aims, organisation or activities but their relationship to authority structures. Non-formal groups are spontaneously-forming groups of people desiring inter-personal communication beyond the private sphere but (consciously) wishing to remain outside the established state, party, public or voluntary structures.
2 Although I accept the broad definition of 'civil society' suggested in the introductory chapter to this book, I employ the term primarily to refer to one of its discourses, that is civil society as the locus of political right in an emerging liberal-democratic state. This draws on classic social contract theories of the seventeenth and eighteenth centuries and is singled out here because of the attention being paid to this discourse in discussion of the current renegotiation of relations between the state and individual in Soviet society.
3 Soviet research often refers to 'socially positive' and 'socially negative' groups while western research often tries to place groups on a familiar left–right continuum represented by classifications of groups as 'neo-fascists', 'neo-Stalinists', 'muscular socialists', etc.
4 The term *mazhory* is applied to those young people perceived by 'ordinary kids' to be from privileged backgrounds. *Mazhory* tend to dress in imported, high-quality clothes and follow western trends in fashion and music.
5 Daisy (*romashka*) is often cited by Soviet writers as a typical 'sexual game' played by teenagers. It consists of the girls in the group lying in a circle – thus

forming the shape of a daisy – while the boys work their way round the group having sexual intercourse with each of the girls.

6 These groups are usually referred to not as *neformaly* but as *gruppirovki*, thus locating them in the juvenile delinquency discourse rather than the development of civil society discourse. The groups are formed on a territorial basis most often around the *dvor* (courtyard). The intra-group fighting and the highly territorial nature of the groups make their nearest equivalent the urban gangs of American cities. The groups have gained particular notoriety in the Volga cities, especially Kazan' and Cheboksary.

7 I use the plural form *Liubery* since this is most often adopted in secondary literature, although *Liubery* and other *neformaly* themselves tend to use the plural form *Liubera*.

8 Iakovlev's article described the *Liubery* in great detail, including their characteristic checked trousers, white shirts and narrow black ties, their typical gait, their developed muscles from weight-training and their abstinence from smoking, drinking and use of drugs. Above all, the article claimed that the *Liubery* had a defined philosophy of cleansing the city of hippies, punks and heavy metal fans who, according to them, disgraced the Soviet way of life. It was claimed that they had a hymn and symbol calling for Liubertsy to be made the capital of Russia and that they were organised by older hardened criminals. Kupriianov's article in *Sobesednik* was crucial in deflating the myth of the *Liubery*. Kupriianov argued that the *Liubery* were little more than uncoordinated groups of suburban teenagers whose trips to Moscow were inspired by boredom in Liubertsy, which was poorly provided for in terms of leisure and entertainment. He also suggested that the *Liubery* united only in reaction to specific incidents, such as not being allowed into city centre cafés or discos.

9 The *Stiliagi* emerged in the 1950s and are generally considered to be the first youth cultural group in the Soviet Union. In the early 1980s there was a significant revival of the group and at the height of this new wave (in the mid-1980s) there were an estimated 200–300 *Stiliagi* active in the Moscow area.

10 The *tusovka* is a basic unit of Moscow youth culture and is used to identify both one's own (e.g. 'she was in our crowd': *ona byla v nashei tusovke*) and where the crowd hangs out (e.g. 'the punks used to hang out on Pushkin Square': *panki ran'she tusovalis' na Pushke*).

REFERENCES

Beliaeva, N. (1988) 'The basis of publicly-run society', *XX Century and Peace*, no. 6: 18–25.

Bessolova, O. (1989) 'Women's movement must not be reduced to women's councils', *Moscow News*, no. 29: 12.

Borshchevskaia, M. (1988) 'Dzhul'etty na "shchelchke" ', *Moskovskii Komsomolets*, 21 October: 2.

Brake, M. (1985) *Comparative Youth Culture*, Routledge & Kegan Paul, London.

Chernyshkova, T. (1989) 'Khau du iu du, interdevochki!', *Sobesednik*, August 35: 6.

Cohen, P. (1986) *Rethinking the Youth Question*, Post 16 Education Centre, Institute of Education, London.

Connell, R.W. (1987) *Gender and Power*, Polity Press, Cambridge.

Coole, D. (1990) 'Patriarchy and contract: reading Pateman', *Politics*, vol. 10, no. 1: 25–9.

Elshtain, J.B. (1981) *Public Man, Private Woman*, Princeton University Press, Princeton, NJ.

Fain, A. (1990) 'Specific features of informal youth associations in large cities', *Soviet Sociology*, vol. 29, no. 1: 19–42.

Filippova, N. (1990) 'Muzhchina i zhenshchina', *Komsomol'skaia Pravda*, 7 March: 4.

' "Foto" na pamyat'? (1988) *Sobesednik*, no. 47: 10.

Gorbachev, M. (1987) *Perestroika*, Collins, London.

Gorbachev, M. (1988a) 'O khode realisatsii reshenii XXVII S'ezda KPSS i zadachakh po uglubelniiu perestroiki', *XIX Vsesoiuznaia Konferentsiia KPSS: Stenograficheskii Otchet Tom 1.*, Politizdat, Moscow.

Gorbachev, M. (1988b) 'Demokratizatsiia – sut' perestroiki, sut' sotsializma', *Komsomol'skaia Pravda*, 13 January: 1–4.

Gorbachev, M. (1988c) 'Molodezh' – tvorcheskaya sila revoliutsionnogo obnovleniia', *Dokumenty i Materialy XX S'ezda VLKSM*, Molodaia Gvardiia, Moscow: 3–29.

Gorbachev, M. (1989) *Pravda*, 8 January: 1.

'G.P.' [anon.] (1990) ' "Seksual'nii pliuralizm" ', *Literaturnaia Rossiia*, 19 October.

Gromyko, M. (1986) *Traditsionnie Normy Povedeniia i Formy Obshcheniia Russkikh Krest'ian XIX Veka*, Nauka, Moscow.

Hosking, G. (1988) 'A great power in crisis', Reith Lecture no.1, *The Listener*, 10 November: 16–19.

Hudson, B. (1984) 'Femininity and adolescence', in A. McRobbie and M. Nava (eds) *Gender and Generation*, Macmillan, Basingstoke, 31–53.

Iakovlev, V. (1987) 'Kontora Liuberov', *Ogonek*, no. 5: 20–21.

Kashirskaia, V. (1985) 'Muzhchinu rastit boi', *Molodoi Kommunist*, no. 15: 11.

Kon, I. (1989) 'Proshcheniia net', *Nedelia*, no. 46: 10–11.

Kupriianov, A. (1987) 'Liubery – pri svete fonarei, ili pasynki stolitsy', *Sobesednik*, no. 7: 10–15.

Lesoto, E. (1985) 'Some thoughts about a trial', *Komsomol'skaia Pravda*, 17 September: 2, translated in *Current Digest of the Soviet Press*, vol. 37, no. 38: 13–14.

McRobbie, A. and Garber, J. (1976) 'Girls and subcultures', in S. Hall and T. Jefferson (eds) *Resistance Through Rituals*, Hutchinson, London, 209–22.

Migranian, A. (1989) 'Democratisation processes in socialist society', *Social Sciences*, no. 1: 105–20.

Migranian, A. (1990) 'For the USSR authoritarianism is a dream', *Telos*, no. 85: 125–31.

Millar, J. (1985) 'The little deal: Brezhnev's contribution to acquisitive socialism', *Slavic Review*, Winter: 694–706.

Nava, M. (1984) 'Youth service provision, social order and the question of girls', in A. McRobbie and M. Nava (eds) *Gender and Generation*, Macmillan, Basingstoke, 1–30.

Orlov, A. (1990) ' "Sku-u-chno, patsany ..." ', *Komsomol'skaia Pravda*, 21 March: 2.

Pankratov, A. (1990) 'Kazan'-nostra', *Komsomol'skaia Pravda*, 17 January: 3.
Pateman, C. (1989) 'The fraternal social contract', in *The Disorder of Women*, Polity Press, Cambridge.
Rasputin, V. (1990) 'Cherchez la femme', *Nash Sovremennik*, no. 3: 169–72.
Rudenko, I. (1978) 'One time, after a dance', *Komsomol'skaia Pravda*, 14 May: 2, translated in *Current Digest of the Soviet Press*, vol. 30, no. 42: 6.
Rutherford, J. (1988) 'Who's that man?', in R. Chapman, and J. Rutherford, *Male Order: Unwrapping Masculinity*, Lawrence & Wishart, London.
Scanlan, J. (1988) 'Reforms and civil society in the USSR', *Problems of Communism*, vol. 37, no. 2: 41–6.
Shchekochikhin, Iu. (1988) 'Ekstremal'naia Model'', *Literaturnaia Gazeta*, no. 41: 13.
Startseva, S. (1990) 'Women in society: the right to choose', *Soviet Union*, no. 5: 6–7.
Terekhina, V. (1990) 'Bastuet detsad!', *Komsomol'skaia Pravda*, 3 April: 1.
Terekhina, V. and Kozyreva, Iu. (1990) 'Surovii ponedel'nik', *Komsomol'skaia Pravda*, 11 May: 2.
Tolstaia, T. (1990) 'Notes from the underground', *New York Review of Books*, vol. 37, no. 9: 3–7.
Tsybukh, V. (1990) 'Zavtra budet pozdno', *Pravda*, 9 April: 2.
Voronina O. (1990) 'Chto takoe feminizm?', *Moskovskaia Pravda*, 13 May: 2.
Waters, E. (1989) 'Restructuring the 'woman question': perestroika and prostitution', *Feminist Review*, no. 33: 3–19.
Yeremin, V. (1989) 'Podval', *Ogonek*, no. 8: 10.
Zaiarnaia, O. (1989) 'Alen Delon govorit po-frantsuzski', *Komsomol'skaia Pravda*, 10 December: 4.
Zhenshchiny v SSSR (1981) Finansy i Statistika, Moscow.
'Zhenskaia partiia?' (1990) *Sovetskaia Moldaviia*, 30 May: 1–2.

7 Sexual revolution or 'sexploitation'?

The pornography and erotica debate in the Soviet Union

Rosamund Shreeves

INTRODUCTION

Five years ago, sex was virtually absent from public life in the Soviet Union, both in terms of discussion and visual and literary represent-ation. However, despite official assertions that 'permissiveness has nothing in common with *perestroika*',[1] the past five years have been marked by the sudden explosion of sexually explicit material in art, cinema, theatre, lit-erature and the press in the Soviet Union. Soviet films such as *Little Vera* have broken previous taboos on the representation of sex, while western erotic films dominate the programmes of the 'video salons' which have begun to spring up in towns and cities across the Soviet Union.[2] What have generally been referred to as erotic theatre and erotic shows are being staged, and even shown on Central Television.[3] A number of newspapers and magazines have begun to feature photographs of topless and semi-naked women, and erotic magazines have begun to make an appearance, often as joint ventures with western companies. Co-operatives openly selling erotic photographs have emerged, while on street corners and in the underground, stalls sell 'sex-digests, sex education brochures, sex anecdotes, dubious newspapers and calendars of naked women' (Lapin, 1990: 4). *Perestroika*, it would seem, has brought a liberating sexual revolution to a repressive and repressed Soviet society. Yet in what sense might this be considered a sexual revolution? The sudden mushrooming of sexual images has led to a deep sense of confusion over definitions of pornography and erotica in Soviet society, which has resulted in fierce public debate. On the one hand, this debate involves the redefinition of the permissible limits of the depiction of sex. On the other, it is intertwined with a fundamental renegotiation of sexual morality and sexual behaviour. Thus the pornography debate which has emerged since 1985 provides a window through which to examine the ways in which sexuality is being constructed under *perestroika*.

Significantly, most of the material which has appeared to date depicts nude women and is directed primarily towards a male audience. Women's sexuality and non-heterosexuality have as yet found little expression. In the light of this, it must be asked whether the appearance of representations of sexuality constitutes a positive relaxation of restrictive taboos or a negative portent of the beginnings of commercial exploitation and commodification of women's sexuality.

Western experience suggests the complexity of the pornography issue for women. Caught between a liberal, non-evaluative discourse on pornography and a repressive discourse from the moral right, which has sought to suppress not only the representation of sexuality, but also sexual practice which falls outside the bounds of heterosexual sex within marriage, the feminist movement has attempted to construct a gendered position on pornography and sexual liberation. Feminist critiques have focused on the nature of images of women in pornography, its construction of women as ever-available objects of male desire.

However, beyond this critique of sexist images a fierce controversy has arisen within the feminist movement itself. Since the 1970s, radical feminists have increasingly focused on pornography as the root of male oppression and violence against women, and have called for increased censorship. An alternative strand of feminist critique asserts that this approach threatens to play into the hands of the moral right, putting at risk women's exploration of their own sexuality and pleasure. From this perspective, pornography can be either repressive or liberating. Although the present images of women in pornography do little to help women to construct a positive sexual identity, what is needed is more rather than less sexually explicit material, produced by and for women, along with wider debate on the economic, social and political roots of women's oppression.[4]

Debates over pornography, censorship and erotica in the west have touched on some of the basic questions of women's liberation, the place of sexuality in both our oppression and project for liberation, and the ways in which men, patriarchy, capitalism and the state are responsible for the sexual oppression of women (Valverde, 1989: 237). The aim of this chapter, then, is to examine the debate which has emerged around pornography and erotica in the Soviet press since 1985. What does it tell us about the way female sexuality is being constructed under *perestroika* and the opportunities for women's sexual liberation?

DISCOURSE AND SILENCE: POST-REVOLUTIONARY CONSTRUCTIONS OF SEXUALITY IN THE SOVIET UNION

The western media has seen the appearance of sexually explicit material as representative of a broader pattern of sexual liberation, brought about by *perestroika*. In the Soviet Union also, hopes have been expressed that *perestroika* will lead to a revaluing of sex in Soviet society.[5] This suggests that the construction of sexuality in the Soviet period might be seen in terms of liberation and repression, related to revolution and counter-revolution in the political sphere.

The post-revolutionary sexual revolution

The early post-revolutionary years were marked not only by radical changes in the economic and political spheres, but also by radical changes in the sexual sphere. The new Bolshevik government proposed a transformation of the pre-revolutionary sexual culture, challenging the hypocrisy of bourgeois sexual morality and religious prejudice, and stressing the need for equality in sexual relations between men and women. As early as December 1917 laws on marriage and divorce were introduced which deprived husbands of patriarchal rights within the family and gave women the right to economic and sexual self-determination (Reich, 1972: 166). Old sexual mores were also challenged from below. With the upheavals of revolution and civil war many men and women were torn away from traditional marriage and entered into other forms of sexual relationship. Between 1917 and 1923, spontaneous demonstrations (often nude) calling for free love took place on the streets of cities such as Petrograd, Moscow, Odessa and Saratov. 'Free love societies' sprang up in the Ukraine, and free love was openly discussed in youth newspapers such as *Komsomol'skaia Pravda* (Stern, 1981: 23). This period of revolutionary transition was marked by open, pluralistic debate on sex and sexuality, as people sought to renegotiate the boundaries of sexual morality in the new society and the place it should occupy in the life of the citizen.

The Stalinist counter-revolution

The debate on sex and sexuality was one of the first casualties of the onset of the more authoritarian political climate which announced the Stalin era. Through legislation and the imposition of a strict moral code, individual sexual behaviour became subject to state interference and control. As the reactionary theorist Zalkind stated in 1925:

Our point of view can only be revolutionary and proletarian and strictly practical. If any sexual activity contributes to the isolation of a person from his class ... deprives him of his energy at work ... diminishes his fighting qualities, he must put a stop to it. Sexual choice ought to operate according to class criteria; the class (i.e. the Communist Party) has the right to intervene in the sex life of its members.

(Stern, 1981: 35)

The new morality was centred on a suspicion of sex as a wasteful consumer of energies better devoted to the building of Communism. In line with the re-emphasis on the family as the basis of societal stability, it presented disciplined, heterosexual sex within marriage as the only true model of Communist sexuality. Deviation from this 'moral norm' could be interpreted as a political offence, and used as evidence of political deviance or 'anti-Soviet' behaviour (Suvorova and Geiges, 1990: 12; Stern 1981: 150).

In effect, sex became an absence at the heart of Communist discourse, yet this very silence disguised the centrality of sex to social control, since it masked an overt politicisation of sexuality and the negation of sexual pluralism.

The post-Stalin era

With the end of the Stalin era, the silence on sexual matters was partially lifted, and articles began to appear once again in the press. Studying how articles on sex are broached in the Soviet media reveals a marked change in tone over time: 1966 'Filth'; 1967 'Grammar of love'; 1968 'Pedagogy and intimate matters'; 1969 'Let us speak out on intimate matters' (Stern, 1981: 110). However, articles continued to take the form of attacks on deviance from official morality, rather than pluralistic discussions of sexuality (Heitlinger, 1979: 21; Kollontai, 1977: 25).

Yet beneath the single, rigid model of offical morality an evolution in sexual morals was taking place, particularly amongst the young (Stern, 1981: 90). An alternative discourse on sexuality was coming into confrontation with offical discourse, revealing an ever greater disparity between the real life of the population, its fierce desire for change, and a morality in which it no longer believed.

So, *perestroika* might be seen in terms of a further 'liberation' of sexuality, with the new policy of *glasnost'* making possible the emergence of pluralistic discourse previously suppressed and submerged under a monopolistic official morality. However, the simple equation of the opening of discourse and sexual liberation must be qualified. On the one hand, those whose sexuality has been most oppressed clearly have the most to gain from the opening of public debate on sexual relations. In terms of women's sexuality, as Ellis, O'Dair and Tallmer suggest, the more sexual expression is confined to the private sphere, the more vulnerable women become to sexist practices, particularly within a society which is hostile to the development of women's autonomy and self-expression (Ellis *et al.*, 1990: 17). However, the mere fact of sexuality being 'put into discourse' does not necessarily indicate a loosening of repression (Foucault, 1984). Indeed, even the most apparently open and explicit detailing of sex may construct sexuality in relation to gender and power relations in society (Coward, 1985: 183).

To turn again to the 'sexual revolution' of the 1920s, it is clear that the opening of pluralistic discourse was problematic for women. On the one hand, the limitations of Bolshevik theory, which paid little attention to the links between sexual relations and women's position in society, or to the need to eliminate prejudices on a psychological level, hampered attempts to formulate a woman-centred definition of sexual freedom. Alexandra Kollontai was alone amongst the Bolshevik leadership in trying to construct a discourse on sexuality which would enable women to define a new and positive sexual identity. On the other hand, in the prevailing cultural and economic climate, the 'sexual revolution' had very different implications for men and women. The more liberal marriage and divorce laws led to the abandonment of women and children on a large scale, and 'sexual freedom' essentially meant the possibility for sexual licence without responsibity for men. In the light of this, Kollontai's attempt to define a new kind of 'free love' fell victim to the struggle between left and right within the party, and her insights into the question of gender, sexuality and power relations were dismissed. The sexual question was resolved in the direction of 'protecting' women from sexual abuse, a discourse which, as we have seen, introduced this 'protection' at the price of repression.

Soviet women in the current period are heirs to two similar repressive discourses. Throughout the 1970s and early 1980s, official discourse on sexuality continued to propagate a morality which subjected women's sexuality to heightened social control and which reinforced existing patriarchal relations. Official models of sexual behaviour prioritised male pleasure, stating that the ideal duration of the sexual act was two minutes, while a man who delayed ejaculation for the enjoyment of his partner was doing something 'terribly harmful' that could lead to 'impotence, neuroses and psychoses' (Stern, 1981: 115). Moreover, official discourse on sexuality was situated within an ideology which emphasised essentialist gender roles, and which stressed the desirability of female passivity. Girls were informed that 'lack of modesty' could bring about a 'total fiasco in intimate relations', and were exhorted to 'learn self-respect' so that there would be 'no need to pass a law prohibiting hugging and kissing in public' (Heitlinger, 1979: 21). Cast in the role of protectors of morality, women were denied access to their own pleasure.[6]

The 'underground' dissolution of official morality was also problematic for Soviet women. In the absence of sex education and contraception, the result of this 'liberalisation' of sexuality amongst the young was a rocketing abortion rate and growing numbers of illegitimate births (Kon, 1987). Moreover, although sexology has barely existed as an academic discipline, and no comprehensive surveys of sexual mores have been carried out, the findings of Kon and others such as Dr Mikhail Stern suggest that this underground sexual revolution took a form which reflected wider negative social attitudes towards women. Making the linguistic connection with the use of the slang word *trakhnut* (to beat), a common expression for sexual intercourse, Stern suggests that Soviet men have increasingly come to see sex as a demonstration of power over women (Stern, 1981: 69–71). The brutalisation of sexual relations has been graphically described in novels such as Julia Vosnesenskaia's *The Women's Decameron*, and has also become a topic of debate in the official press since 1985 (Nosova, 1990a). Perhaps unsurprisingly, in a recent poll carried out among young Muscovites aged 18 to 28, a third of the female respondents stated that they suffered from anorgasm (Geiges, 1990: 48). So, if sexuality continued to be repressed in general in the Soviet Union, it could be argued that women's sexuality was doubly repressed.

The limitations of sexual *glasnost'*

Since 1985, discourse has no longer been confined to restatements of official morality. The media, particularly youth papers and weeklies and women's magazines, have serialised books on sex and have carried articles and regular columns dealing with all kinds of issues about sex and sexuality. These have addressed amongst other issues, different attitudes to sex between men and women, orgasm and anorgasm, and lesbianism.

The new possibilities for pluralistic debate have given women the opportunity to speak out on their concerns and desires, and to work towards a new woman-defined construction of female sexuality. A flood of letters to the press have spoken out against the lack of contraception and the degradation which women face in maternity hospitals and abortion wards and have linked this with negative attitudes to female sexuality in Soviet society (Nikolaeva, 1989: 10). A few women have pointed directly towards the importance of addressing the connection between sexual relations and the oppression of women. Feminists such as Larisa Kuznetsova have taken up many of Kollontai's ideas, calling on women to recognise that 'models of sexual behaviour have an impact on all areas of men and women's behaviour' and to get rid of the 'virus of slavery that has been inside them for too long' (Kuznetsova, 1990; Porter, 1980: 142). As part of a resurgence of women's activism, young women in particular are striving towards definitions of female sexuality and female identity which do not prioritise marriage and motherhood. In the article 'Olia i Iulia' a bewildered journalist reports on a small group of young women who have united in opposition to men and marriage, which they see as oppressive and destructive of women's individuality. It is hinted that they have sought to define a lesbian sexuality (Toktalieva, 1989: 11). Although this article refers only to a small group of women, grass-roots activity has also been reflected in the recent emergence of the Libertarian Party, which has made the question of changing repressive attitudes to sexuality central to political change.[7]

However, much of the discourse on sexuality, and particularly female sexuality, reflects conservative attitudes. This is particularly true of the state programme of 'sex education' brought into schools in 1985. The course on the 'ethics and psychology of family life' is based on a pedagogical theory which stresses the need to combat the perceived 'masculinisation' of women and 'feminisation' of men. It focuses not on sex education, but on the inculcation of traditional gender roles (Atwood, 1987).

In the press, a number of 'experts' such as the regular *Rabotnitsa* columnist, Dr Grishin, construct sexuality through a 'scientific' discourse of norm and pathology, stressing prohibitions and the need to avoid 'sexual deviance' (Grishin, 1989, 1990b). Grishin's advice to women is laced with traditional moral invocations towards female chastity. The mother of a 14-year-old girl is advised to tell her daughter that an interest in sex is natural, but that early sexual experience can be physically and psychologically damaging and causes 'moral discomfort'; that the first pregnancy is especially hard for young girls and that abortion can lead to infertility; that there is a grave danger of venereal disease; that the sexual demands of boys develop before those of girls and that girls therefore need to know how to refuse (Grishin, 1990a: 31).

However justified these concerns about early sexual activity might be, the call for girls to learn how to refuse rather than for boys to learn self-control shows the prevalence of a moral double standard, which permeates the current debate on sexuality. Sex continues to be presented in essentialist terms as a male drive or desire, while female sexuality is presented as innately passive, and related to women's 'great mission' as producers of the new generation (Nosova, 1990a: 28). Women's sexuality is presented not as a matter of articulating their own desire, but as a matter of predicting and regulating male desire, from which they must learn to protect themselves.[8]

So, although *glasnost'* is to some extent enabling women to challenge previous constructions of female sexuality, it seems that little has changed since the beginning of 1989, when an article in the academic journal *Sotsiologicheskie Issledovaniia* stated that most sex education was inadequate and unlikely to help young women's sexual orientation and development (Borisov, 1989: 81–4). In a controversial statement, the article suggested that this might be better served by reading erotic literature. Might the current mushrooming of erotica be considered a positive development for Soviet women? Or does it serve to undercut still further the strand of positive discourse on female sexuality which has emerged? In the next section I shall turn to an analysis of the pornography and erotica debate, looking particularly at what it reveals about public attitudes towards female sexuality.

THE SOVIET PORNOGRAPHY AND EROTICA DEBATE UNDER *PERESTROIKA*: THE POLITICAL APPROACH TO PORNOGRAPHY

Perhaps the most striking feature of the pornography debate which has emerged since 1985 is its overt politicisation. From the outset, approaches to pornography have been determined and constrained by a political framework, as both left and right have taken up the issue as a symbol for wider debates over individual freedom and state control.

This politicisation can be partly explained by the previous position of pornography in Soviet law. Under article 228 of the Criminal Code, pornography is defined as 'the preparation, propagation or publicising of pornographic writings, images or other objects of pornographic character'. In the light of this tautological definition, the term 'pornography' has remained open to both the broadest and narrowest interpretations, according to political rather than legal criteria. The purely political character of the law is evident in the dramatic decrease in prosecutions under article 228 since 1985, which reflected the relaxation of state control over individual expression permitted by *glasnost'* rather than any legal change.[9]

In reaction to the state's politicisation of pornography, an opposing strand of argument emerged within the dissident movement of the 1960s and 1970s, which equated the production and consumption of *samizdat* (underground) pornographic material with political subversion. This approach was adopted by underground groups such as 'Progressive Political Pornography' in Kiev, one of whose manuscripts stated, 'In reading these pages, you become an internal saboteur of the system' (Stern, 1981: 159). Octabriana, the heroine of their works, was portrayed not only as a symbol of eroticism, but also as a symbol of political revolution.

The politicisation of pornography within the dissident movement has some significance for the position adopted by anti-conservatives in the current period. Reformers have continued to equate the right to depict sexuality with liberalisation in the political sphere. From this perspective, pornography is presented as the literal embodiment of a radical challenge to authoritarian and conservative political structures. In his analysis of 'Sex and perestroika', the writer Viktor Erofeev, for example, contrasts the 'erotic self-expressiveness' of the radical, younger generation with the conservatism of those 'still very influential people in the Soviet Union who not only long to forbid everything, but long to punish those guilty of pornography as severely as possible' (Erofeev, 1990: 17). The desire to control the representation of sexuality is interpreted as symptomatic of an authoritarian desire to maintain state control over autonomous individual expression. In contrast, the representation of sexuality is often presented as a 'democratic' act.

Conservatives have cast their arguments against the representation of sexuality in terms of the need to limit individual freedom of expression in the interests of society. From this perspective, it is essential to impose control from above on harmful individualistic expression, of which pornography is a prime example.

From both perspectives, any critique of the nature of representations of sexuality and their relationship to actual sexual freedom remains subordinate to a political position. This is evident from a continued confusion on the level of discourse. Adherents of both positions often make interchangeable use of the terms 'erotic' and 'pornographic', either in a positive or pejorative sense. Equally, from both perspectives, the fact that most of the images under discussion are of women is discussed in primarily symbolic terms. There has been little space for a considered gendered analysis of images of sexuality and the implications of permissiveness or control for women in the Soviet Union. The position of the 'democrats' is particularly interesting in this respect. A key issue for them has been the 'de-sexing' or 'defeminisation' of women under the Soviet system, and the opportunities for women to 'rediscover' their sexuality under *perestroika*.

> Beauty contests strike a blow at the traditional 'Soviet' image of woman ... a Communist Stakhanovite in overalls whose principal virtue was her modesty. In today's image there is emphasis on the erotic element, on physical beauty, on initiative, cleverness, elegance and efficiency.
>
> (Erofeev, 1990: 17)

However, this concern for the liberation of women's sexuality is essentially male-defined, and often carries a misogynist sub-text. The sexism is implicit: women's sexuality is to be 'liberated', but in terms of the male viewer–definer–judge and the female viewed–defined. An alternative male view asserts that pornography makes men behave more tenderly towards women and leads to healthier relations between the sexes. Yet this justification of pornography is accompanied by a virulent attack on Soviet women, who, it is argued, would do well to shed some of their aggressiveness and rudeness towards men and emulate the 'kindness' and 'understanding' of the women in erotic photographs (Baskov, 1990: 26). This approach lays the blame for the appearance of pornography and men's need of it on Soviet women themselves who, it is argued, have lost their 'femininity' through too much emancipation and a lack of proper beauty aids.

Sexism is also embodied in the way in which 'radical' journals and newspapers have couched their discourse on sexuality, often undercutting debate on sexual relations with images of naked women for male consumption. In many cases, images have taken the place of analysis altogether, as a 'short-hand' way of indicating a 'democratic' outlook. Both reformist and conservative rhetoric on pornography continues to reflect prevalent patriarchal prejudices against women in Soviet society.

The aesthetic approach to pornography

The pornography debate as a whole has been shaped and dominated by this political framework. Within this constraint, however, it has ramified into a number of sub-debates, revolving primarily around the questions of artistic freedom as against aesthetics and morality.

As the first beneficiary of the relaxation of state control, the arts were not slow to adopt a 'democratic' perspective, or to adopt nudity as a symbol of change and artistic freedom. Debate about this sudden ubiquity of images of sexuality, again primarily naked women, has been framed mostly in terms of its effect on Soviet culture rather than its meaning for gender relations.

One aspect of the debate has been the issue of socialist realism and artistic freedom. While some argue that the appearance of erotica is symptomatic of a break from socialist realism with its hypocrisy and taboos about sexual relations, others claim that it is part of a trend to show only the darkest side of Soviet reality. Such art, they claim, has lost sight of its main role: to uplift (Kichin, 1989: 8).

This question is linked to the issue of the benefits or drawbacks of the introduction of self-financing for the arts. While some assert that self-financing is the basis of independence from state censorship, others argue that it has served only to debase culture by forcing it into commercialism. In this context, nudity and erotica are interpreted either as evidence of new-found freedom or as a means of cheap titillation, a substitute for real artistic content in films devoid of artistic merit (Kichin, 1989: 8). This approach draws on the traditional debate between westernisers and Slavophiles over Soviet culture and western mass or 'pseudo' culture.

The majority of those taking an aesthetic approach draw some lines between the pornographic and the erotic. However, most distinctions have been based on purely aesthetic criteria. Some attempt has been made to distinguish between 'positive erotica' which has aesthetic value and which contributes to the 'meaning' of a work of art, and 'negative pornographic' images included for purely sensationalist or commercial reasons (Maksimov, 1990: 13). Nevertheless, it is clear that arbitration based on 'good taste' is intensely subjective, and that it is not hard to find 'artistic' justifications for the inclusion of 'erotic' images. An extract from de Sade proclaiming the desirability of the sexual emancipation of women for the delight of men, accompanied by engravings of naked women tied to the rack, is prefaced by an introduction which describes de Sade's work in terms of 'art for art's sake' (Karabutenko, 1990: 12). So, although this aesthetic approach occasionally touches on issues such as the brutality or 'visual sadism' implicit in many representations of sexuality[10] it absolves the critic from the need to examine power and gender relationships within these images in more depth.

The moral approach to pornography

While reformers have based their arguments primarily on artistic freedom, conservatives have countered with a rationale stressing the need to uphold moral values and to safeguard society from permissiveness and chaos.

Central to this approach is the assumption that there is a direct, causal link between the appearance of sexual images and wider patterns of social and moral 'degradation', particularly amongst young people.[11]

Letters to the press declaim against the 'enforced embedding in mass consciousness of erotica and open pornography' whose consequence, 'visible to the naked eye', is to 'incite and provoke young people to commit sexual crimes' (Shtyriakov, 1990: 4). 'Can we really be surprised that young boys are going to "serve" foreign homosexuals, that young people are playing sex games like "Daisy", that sixteen-year-old boys are selling their female class-mates to foreigners?' the writer asks, and 'Why do we allow such vulgar pluralism in the question of showing sex, if it is obvious that it leads to the arousal of sexual passions, the growth of sexual crime and falling morals?' (*ibid.*).

The implications of this approach for women are problematic. On the one hand, the desire to 'protect' women from abuse and exploitation is often cited as a prime reason for the censorship of sexual images. 'How can they speak from the podium about raising the role of women, mothers in society, and simultaneously facilitate their transformation into objects of sollicitation?' one letter asks. This signals, at least, a recognition of the problems of sexual exploitation and violence against women, glibly dismissed by some defenders of pornography.[12]

On the other hand, like the western moral right, their approach hides a sub-text which is diametrically opposed to the sexual autonomy of women. As many letters to the press reveal, the concept of upholding moral values often implies a suspicion of all discourse on sexuality:

> When culture turns into ersatz culture, 'sex' (aerobics, athletics, etc) is not slow to appear. What's more, I've heard that they are going to print a translation of a sexual encyclopedia for adolescents. That's enough brother Slavs! Don't deform the souls of those who will form our nation. . . . It's disgusting when even the main newspapers discuss the problem (?!) of the shortage of contraceptives in our country. I could go on.
>
> (Yurii Shupik, quoted in Shreeves, 1990: 6)

The use of moral arguments against the 'sexploitation' of women is based on a definition of 'deviant' sexuality as any form of sexual practice or sexual fantasy which does not conform to the traditional model of procreative sexual intercourse: sanctified within marriage, with the man on top. Moreover, one particularly striking feature of the 'moral' outrage over pornography is its virulent criticism of any expression of active female sexuality. The mere portrayal of the heroine of the film *Little Vera* lying on top of her lover was enough to call down an avalanche of outraged moral protest.[13] So, while the 'moral approach' has recognised some of the dangers of pornography, it suggests a return to an image of sexless moral purity and to the stricter moral policing of women.[14] In light of the resurgence of religion, particularly the orthodox tradition, the influence of this moral approach nevertheless seems set to grow.

A gendered approach?

Several of the approaches towards pornography in the emerging debate have made use of the rhetoric of a gendered approach as a sub-text in their support for or criticism of the appearance of sexually explicit material. However, the use of this rhetoric has been primarily symbolic rather than constitutive of genuine attempts either to analyse the specific sexual oppression of women or to give women the opportunity to express their own desires and needs. The entire debate has been constrained within a male-defined political discourse which sees pornography as a barometer either of political disorder or political freedom. Within this paradigm, images of women are seen as symbols either of the degeneration or the liberation of Soviet society. By implication, women are either to be 're-sexed' on men's terms, the burden of 'beauty' added to the already considerable double burden of work in the private and public spheres, or to be 'protected' from the dangers of this 'sexual revolution' at the cost of their own sexual autonomy.

So far, I have spoken of the pornography debate as though it is being constructed without the participation of Soviet women. Clearly they are faced with the extreme difficulty of negotiating a space between these two dominant male-defined discourses to express their own perspectives and needs. This difficulty is heightened by their under-representation in political and economic power structures in general and in the media in particular. However, women have been vocal in their response to the appearance of sexual images. Essentially, two distinct strands of dis-course can be defined, which bear some ressemblance to the pleasure/danger controversy in the western feminist movement outlined above, although most women have raised the issue of pornography in moral terms far removed from feminist formulations.

The majority of women writing in the press, particularly older women, are profoundly uncomfortable with the current representation of sexuality. Many stress the need to protect women from pornography, posing a rhetoric of love against the rhetoric of sexual liberation, and presenting the family as a refuge for women.[15] Kapitolina Koksheneva, writing in *Sovetskaia Zhenshchina*, notes the interest of young people in love and sex and agrees with the necessity for sex education. However, she decries what she terms a 'false conception of freedom' which presents sexuality in terms of 'bare physiological facts' and the female body as a kind of 'erotic dessert' (Koksheneva, 1990: 18–19). Tatiana Okulova points to the objectivisation of women, stating that *perestroika* has led not to the destruction of stereotypes and the freeing of the individual, but to the exchange of old stereotypes for new ones (Okulova, 1990). She argues that fidelity, maternity and the family are being undermined by the pornography industry and criticises the propagation of films that show sex without love. She also calls for the creation of special censorship bodies to protect young people from 'unsuitable' films and for the setting up of a branch of the police to deal with 'morality'. Clearly, in the current climate, such calls for the censorship of sexually explicit material and moral policing can be easily turned against women. In Riga, for instance, the morals police set up to combat prostitution have arrested women merely for socialising with foreign men or for 'possession of items of feminine hygiene' (Fast, 1990: 11). Okulova's critique, which makes direct (though selective) allusions to western feminist responses to pornography, rests on the continued categorisation of 'good' and 'bad' women according to their sexual 'purity'. 'It is clear that in the 1990s, those women who have not lost the ability to blush will have to be put on the endangered species list' (Okulova, 1990: 173–87).

A minority of women have attempted to move away from this position and to reappropriate and redefine pornography for women. An article asserting a positive self-identification and self-affirmation of lesbian identity specifically links the discussion of sexuality and sexual practice with a challenge to patriarchy. Stating that sexual relations between women can be endowed with all the love, friendship and pleasure of which women are capable, the writer asserts women's right to active sexual pleasure, and access to a woman-defined erotica:

> They may watch erotic images and video films together, play sex games or simply sleep together. In contrast to heterosexual relations, the sex life of lesbians is not determined by fixed rules. There are no 'right' or 'wrong' ways to have sex.
>
> ('Edgar' 1990: 18)[16]

This approach, however, remains the exception.

CONCLUSION

We could see *perestroika* on the one hand as the possibility of the opening of new explorations of sexuality and pleasure for Soviet women, and on the other as representing new threats in the form of the commercial exploitation of women's sexuality. The potentially radical discourse on 'sexual revolution' under *perestroika* is being constructed primarily through an explosion of sexual images which portray Soviet women as sex objects for male consumption. Control of these images may be achieved only at the price of greater censorship and the curtailing of debate, along with the curtailing of women's search for a new sexual identity. The pornography and erotica debate exemplifies the difficulties faced by Soviet women in attempting to define their identity and to construct an alternative gendered discourse on *perestroika*.

NOTES

1 Statement made by the Head of the State Committee for Cinematography, reported by Reuters, 5 May 1988.
2 See, for example A. Lapin, 'Sekstrasensy', *Komsomol'skaia Pravda*, 28 October 1990, p. 4, and E. Zarutskaia, 'Samii strashnii uzhas: Seks-tragediia s epizodami nasiliia i grabezha', *Sovetskaia Latvia*, 20 October 1989, p. 4 for a description of the programmes of some of these video salons.
3 The most famous or infamous case occurred in 1988, when the popular programme 'Before and after midnight' showed scenes of a naked woman being covered in whipped cream from an 'erotic show' on Vorovsky Street in Moscow. For a report on this and the public reaction to it see Kuznetsov, 1989. The first Soviet 'Festival of Erotica' was held in Sochi in July 1990. See *Sobesednik*, no. 28, 1990, pp. 8–9.
4 For a more detailed outline of current western feminist debates over pornography see *Feminist Review*, no. 36, 1990.
5 See the interview with the Soviet sexologist Igor Kon in T. Suvorova and A. Geiges, 'Liubov' vne plana', *Sobesednik*, no. 1, 1990, p. 12.
6 This approach coincided with fears about a growing demographic crisis, and increasing stress on the importance of maternity which dominated official ideology on the 'woman question' during the 1970s and early 1980s. See, for example, M. Buckley, 'Soviet interpretations of the woman question', in B. Holland (ed.) *Soviet Sisterhood*, Fourth Estate, London, 1985, pp. 45–50.
7 See Radio Liberty Monitoring, *Soviet Media News and Features Digest*, no. 523, 1990, p. 33; Kalinin, 1990; Debrianskaia, 1990; 'Seksual'nii pliuralizm', *Literaturnaia Rossiia*, no. 42, 1990.
8 Speaking of defence against rape, for example, an article addressed towards young women cites an excerpt from a 'helpful' Polish novel: 'Some are fated by nature to rouse cruelty in men, either by being too naive or too daring. The victim is nearly always guilty in some respect.' Men are not urged to respect women's consent or non-consent. Rather, women are urged to be aware of and play by men's rules (Nosova, 1990b: p. 48).
9 Despite an obvious increase in the open showing of sexually explicit material since 1985, Vadim Medvedev reported at the 28th CPSU Congress in 1990 that only 86 people were sentenced in 1989 for screening 'pornographic and violent' western videotapes, as opposed to 300–400 in the mid-1980s. See Special Report on the Congress, Radio Free Europe/Radio Liberty 9 July 1990. A new pornography law is under deliberation.
10 See, for example, Kichin's argument, as cited above.
11 The inter-relationship of images and social trends has been the subject of fierce controversy in the west. See for example, Segal, 1990: pp. 29–41.

12 Valentin Baskov, for example, dismisses any possible link between pornography and sexual violence against women, addressing the question of rape with the comment that 'It is on the whole extremely difficult to rape a Soviet woman. They are fairly strong since it seems that almost half of them are engaged in heavy manual labour.' See 'Golaia zhenshchina', in *Gorizont*, no. 4, 1990, pp. 19–26, on p. 20.

13 See the selection of letters in Maria Khmelik, *Little Vera*, Bloomsbury, London, 1990; also V. Garov, 'Podrugi "malen'koi Very" ', *Trud*, 27 September 1989, p. 3.

14 See for example Valentin Rasputin, 'Cherchez la femme', *Nash Sovremmenik*, no. 3, 1990, pp. 168–72.

15 This might be compared with the construction of female sexuality advanced by women in the 19th-century social purity movements. See for example Bland, 1984, and Hunt, 1990.

16 It seems clear from the article that the writer, named only as 'Edgar', has some knowledge of debates within the lesbian movement in the west. The 'Libertarian Party' also has close links with western groups and is affiliated to the International Lesbian and Gay Association.

REFERENCES

Atwood, L., (1987) 'Gender and Soviet pedagogy', in G. Avis (ed.) *The Making of the Soviet Citizen*, Croom Helm, London.

Averina, N. (1990) 'Gorkii khleb sladkoi zhizni', *Pravda*, 5 August: 8.

Baskov, V. (1990) 'Golaia zhenshchina', *Gorizont*, no. 4: 19–26.

Bejin, A. (1985) 'The influence of the sexologists and sexual democracy', in *Western Sexuality*, P. Aries and A. Bejin (eds), Blackwell.

Bland, L. (1984) 'Purity, motherhood, pleasure or threat? Definitions of female sexuality 1900–1970s', in S. Cartledge and J. Ryan, (eds) *Sex and Love: New Thoughts on Old Contradictions*, Women's Press, London.

Borisov, S.B. (1989) 'Eroticheskie teksty kak istochnik seksual'nogo samoobrazovaniia', *Sotsiologicheskie Issledovaniia*, no. 1: 81–4.

Chester, G. and Dickey, J. (eds) (1988) *Feminism and Censorship: The Current Debate*, Prism, Bridport.

Coward, R. (1984) *Female Desire*, Paladin, London.

Debrianskaia, E. (1990) 'Partiia neogranichenoi svobodu', *Baltiiskoe Vremia*, no. 26.

'Edgar' (1990) 'Lesbiianki: ikh zhizn' i vzaimootnosheniia', *Baltiia*, no. 5: 18.

Ellis, K., O'Dair, B. and Tallmer, A. (1990) 'Feminism and pornography', *Feminist Review*, no. 36: 15–18.

Erofeev, V. (1990) 'Sex and perestroika', *Liber*, no. 1: 17.

Fast, T. (1990) 'Devochki–90: kak ikh opekaet rizhskaia militsiia nravov', *Literaturnaia Gazeta*, 1 January: 11.

Foucault, M. (1984) *Histoire de la Sexualité*, Gallimard, Paris.

Garov, V. (1989) 'Podrugi "malen'koi Very" ', *Trud*, 27 September: 3.

Geiges, A. (1990) 'Seks posle nochnoi smeny', *Novoe Vremva*, no. 26: 48.

Grishin, A. (1989) 'Razgovor dlia dvoikh', *Rabotnitsa*, no. 11: 25–6.

Grishin, A. (1990a) 'Razgovor dlia dvoikh', *Rabotnitsa*, no. 3: 31.

Grishin, A. (1990b) 'Razgovor dlia dvoikh', *Rabotnitsa*, no. 11: 26.

Heitlinger, A. (1979) *Women and State Socialism*, Macmillan, London.

Hunt, M. (1990) 'The de-eroticisation of women's liberation: social purity movements and the revolutionary feminism of Sheila Jeffreys', *Feminist Review*, no. 34: 23–46.

Kalinin, R. (1990) 'Ia ne stal by spat' s Mikhailom Gorbachevim', *Baltiiskoe Vremia*, no. 26.

Karabutenko, I. (1990) 'V sadu markiza de Sada', *Sobesednik*, no. 13: 12–13.

Kichin, V. (1989) 'Kuda ty denesh'sia bez nebol'shogo rasputstva?', *Literaturnaia Gazeta*, no. 42: 8.

Koksheneva, K. (1990) 'Est' li vybor?', *Sovetskaia Zhenshchina*, no. 6: 18–19.

Kollontai, A. (1977) *Selected Writings*, ed. A. Holt, Allison & Busby, London.

Kon, I. (1987) 'Otkrovenno o zapretom', *Ogonek*, no. 28.

Kon, I. (1989) 'Proshcheniia net', *Nedelia*, no. 46.

Kuznetsov, V. (1989) 'Koe-chto ob "eroticheskom eksperimente" ', *Zhurnalist*, no. 2: 38–9.

Kuznetsova, L. (1990) 'Razgovor pered zerkalom?', *Rabotnitsa*, no. 3.

Lapin, A. (1990) 'Sekstrasensy', *Komsomol'skaia Pravda*, 28 October: 4.

Maksimov, A. (1990) 'Pravo byt' razdetim', *Sobesednik*, no. 4: 13.

Nikolaev, V. (1991) 'Mezhdu erotikoi i pornografiei', *Argumenty i faktv*, no. 2: 6–7.

Nikolaeva, E. (1989) 'Ne khochu zhalet' chto ia zhenshchina', *Moskovskie Novosti*, no. 4: 10.

Nosova, N. (1990a) 'Uroki Ol'gi i Tat'iany – Seks v shkole shkola seksa?', *Komsomol'skaia Zhizn'*, no. 13–14: 25–8.

Nosova, N. (1990b) 'Uroki Ol'gi i Tat'iany – Kak izbezhat' iznasilovaniia?', *Komsomol'skaia Zhizn'*, no. 21–22: 44–8.

Okulova, T. (1990) 'Nam dobrie zheny i dobrie materi nuzhny – razmyshleniia o zhenshchine i "zhenskoi teme" v sovremennoi masskul'ture', *Nash Sovremennik*, no. 3: 173–87.

Phillips, E. (ed.) (1983) *The Left and the Erotic*, Lawrence & Wishart, London.

Porter, C. (1980) *Alexandra Kollontai: A Biography*, Virago, London.

Reich, W. (1972) *The Sexual Revolution*, Vision Press, London.

Rodgerson, G. and Semple, L. (1990) 'Who watches the watchwomen?: feminists against censorship', *Feminist Review*, no. 36: 19–28.

Segal, S. (1990) 'Pornography and violence: what the "experts" really say', *Feminist Review*, no. 36: 29–41.

Shreeves, R. (1990) 'Sexual revolution or sexploitation?', *Radio Liberty Report on the USSR*, vol. 2, no. 31: 4–8.

Shtyriakov, V.A. (1990) 'Erotikha – to zhe oruzhie', *Komsomol'skaia Pravda*, 12 May.

Stern, M. (1981) *Sex in the Soviet Union*, W.H. Allen, London.

Stites, R. (1978) *The Women's Liberation Movement in Russia*, Princeton University Press, Princeton, N.J.

Suvorova, T. and Geiges, A. (1990) 'Liubov vne plana', *Sobesednik*, nos. 1–13.

Toktalieva, G. (1989) 'Olia i Iulia', *Sobesednik*, no. 46: 11.

'Umrem bez seksa' (1989) *Sotsiologicheskaia Industriia*, no. 39: 8.

Valverde, M. (1989) 'Beyond gender dangers and private pleasures: theory and ethics in the sex debates', *Feminist Studies*, vol. 15, no. 2: 237–54.

Wood, N. (1985) 'Foucault on the history of sexuality: an introduction', in V. Beechey and J. Donald (eds) *Subjectivity and Social Relations*, Open University Press, Milton Keynes: 156–75.

Zarutskaya, E. (1989) 'Samii strashnii uzhas', *Sovetskaia Latvia*, 20 October: 4.

8 Monogamy and female sexuality in the People's Republic of China

Harriet Evans

Since the earliest stages of its approach to 'woman-work', the Chinese Communist Party (CCP) has consistently upheld monogamy as a socialist principle of marriage.[1] It has been represented in different forms and with different emphases, following the changing priorities of party and state policy. However, whether in discussions about courtship and marriage, the family and child-care, or marital friction and divorce, it has been accorded a kind of inviolable superiority in the social and moral hierarchy of sexual relations. While day-to-day practice and individual experience of sexual and gender relations have been subject to momentous changes in China, particularly under the effects of the economic reforms introduced since the early 1980s, the notion of monogamy has been retained in the official discourse about women and marriage as a concept and practice consistent with standards of 'socialist morality'. The following discussion seeks to examine the meanings signified by the model of monogamy as a normative expectation of sexual behaviour, and the nature of the interests served by its inclusion in the official discourse of sexuality.[2]

The following discussion uses the term monogamy to refer not to rules of inheritance or of family structure but to a standard of sexual and gender relations. In legal terms, the 'monogamous system of marriage' (*yi fu yi qi zhi*) refers to both male and female behaviour. The inclusion of monogamy in the first clause of the 1950 Marriage Law of the People's Republic of China was to provide the legal basis for the elimination of the 'feudal system of bigamy and concubinage', which had for centuries perpetuated women's subordination – in economic, social, political as well as sexual terms – to patriarchal authority.[3] In gender terms, its initial purpose after 1949 was to protect women's right to choose their own marriage partner, and simultaneously to eradicate patriarchal control over marriage arrangements. The reiteration of the legal requirement to uphold the legally registered monogamous tie in the second Marriage Law, passed in 1980, indicated recognition that venal marriage practices had by no means been eradicated, despite the achievements of the first law. By implication, male interests in controlling marriage negotiations and the consequent injustices against women were still the principal target of the law.

Central aspects of the post-1949 official discourse of sexuality, however, represent the monogamous union as a predominantly female standard of marital conduct. Whether in the 1950s, when the major concerns of the official discourse of sexuality were first established, or in the radically different socio-economic context of the early 1980s, examples of monogamous conduct have consistently invoked women's behaviour as the principal standard of sexual and marital morality. Constant attention is drawn to expectations of female behaviour within the monogamous context. Images of conjugal contentment hold out promises of happiness to those who respect the norms of 'socialist morality'. Descriptions of misery and suffering accompany images of women who violate the discourse's values. In contrast with the prevalence of female exemplars in women's and youth journals, male conduct is notable principally for its absence, except in extreme cases where a man's failure to respect the monogamous requirements of the law has led to criminal action. The prevalent representations of female fidelity, self-sacrifice and self-denial in the marital context would suggest that, as a discursive practice rather than a legal requirement, monogamous responsibilities are primarily associated with female conduct. Female conformity to the sexual and gender principles associated with monogamous marriage is projected as the principal agent of marital and familial stability.

MARRIAGE REFORM AND MONOGAMY IN HISTORICAL CONTEXT

Ever since the years of intellectual discovery and cultural renaissance known as the May Fourth Movement (1915–21), when marriage and family reform was put high on the agenda of the burgeoning women's movement, free-choice monogamous marriage was identified as the indispensable first step towards eradicating patriarchal authority over women, both by the Nationalist Party (KMT) and the Communist Party. In the nationalist government's Civil Code of 1930, penalties for adultery and bigamy established monogamy as the normative practice, despite the fact that concubines were not mentioned.[4] Article 237 of the government's Criminal Code of 1935 further laid down that all marriages were to be strictly monogamous. Similarly, article 1 of the

Jiangxi Soviet's Marriage Regulations, passed by the CCP on 1 December 1931, linked the principle of freedom of marriage with the 'abolition of the feudal marriage system', and article 2 prohibited polygamy and 'enforced' monogamy. The 1934 Marriage Law of the Jiangxi Soviet Republic included the same provisions, as did the 1944 regulations of the CCP's Shaanxi-Gansu-Ningxia Border Area. While certain differences between these laws over the interpretation of *de facto* marriage and cohabitation meant that monogamous relationships did not necessarily have to be legally registered, it was assumed that male and female monogamy represented the structural form of sexual and marital relations most appropriate to the 'cause of the revolution'.

While there is virtually no evidence to show how people reacted to these regulations, or how they were applied, the projection of monogamy as an indispensable component of a progressive solution to the 'feudal marriage system' was clear. The ideological message accompanying the regulations was that monogamy represented an historic advance on the feudal system of marriage, in that it attacked customary practices of 'male power' (*fuquan*) in perpetuating patriarchal authority over matrimonial and familial affairs. The contradictory aspects of monogamous marriage, noted by Marx and Engels, were omitted from Chinese discussions about family and marriage reform in this period; its progressive contribution to extending freedom of individual choice to both sexes dominated all other possible representations.

Given the lack of information about the characteristics of the debate informing the CCP's marriage regulations before 1949, it is difficult to draw any conclusions about the implied meanings of monogamy during this period. To what extent was it coterminous with the indissolubility of marriage, for example? Or coterminous with pre-marital chastity and sexual exclusivity? On the basis of the CCP's insistence that free-choice marriage did not signify either free love or the abolition of the family, it may be assumed that monogamy was associated with aims to stabilise a reformed family unit beneficial to the cause of revolution, rather than to form the foundation for experimentation in gender and familial relations. In a CCP document drawn up by the Special Committee for Northern Jiangxi of the Central Committee entitled 'Plan for work among the women', the following was stated:

We must not only refrain from imposing limitations on the freedom of marriage, since this would be contrary to Bolshevik principles, but we must resolutely oppose the idea of absolute freedom in marriage as it creates chaotic conditions in society and antagonises the peasants and the Red Army. We must make it clear that the Central

Committee never maintained absolute freedom of divorce either, because it would be an anarchistic practice.[5]

The conservative orientation of this approach to the potentially experimental aspects of the new regulations conformed to CCP interests in maximising support for its programme of social revolution, rather than for the more specific issues associated with woman-work. It also indicated the fundamentally conservative interests which informed subsequent approaches to the issue of monogamous marriage.

MONOGAMY AND THE 1950 MARRIAGE LAW

The 1950 Marriage Law continued to uphold the legally registered monogamous union as a progressive contribution to women's emancipation. As the necessary concomitant of the free-choice principle, it would protect women's new rights of sexual equality in the 'new democratic family system'. In contrast to the history of marriage reform in Russia, where monogamy had briefly come under fire from sections of the Bolshevik movement in favour of a more experimental, possibly libertarian approach to marital and sexual issues, its parameters were tightly drawn in China. Under the terms of the new law as projected in the official discourse on sexuality and marriage, legally registered monogamous marriage acquired a series of meanings which consolidated its status as the single acceptable model of sexual relations. As a form of sexual and gender relations, it was given an almost absolute validity, which as one commentator explained, was 'dictated not only by the physiological differences of the sexes, but also by the perpetuation of the race'.[6] As a sexual relationship, monogamy was therefore projected as rooted in nature. As a social relationship it was defined as the foundation of the new socialist family, and therefore of the basic unit of society, for as the same commentator noted, 'Even in Communist society, we cannot conceive of any objective basis or necessity for eliminating the family.' By extension, it became a synonym for normative sexual relations according to which, as sexual partners, a man and a woman were bound to each other for life. In the terms of the 1950s official discourse, the monogamous union thus acquired the connotation of an exclusive and indissoluble tie, which as this study shows had particular significance for women.

Between 1949 and 1953 the thrust of official concerns in implementing the new Marriage Law was to eradicate anomalies from the feudal past. It was also to protect women from the possibility of their husbands taking advantage of the legal abolition of feudal arrangements to abandon their former wives. Court cases brought against men who were initially married under parental arrangement and who then married a woman of their own choice, refusing to recognise this as a form of polygamy, invariably upheld the man's union with his first wife. Accompanied by free choice of partner, monogamy would bring with it a new respect for women and would erode the idea that women were the private property of men. Suggestions that it might reinforce the ownership of private property in the hands of the male were dismissed as characteristics of the bourgeois marriage system. Monogamous marriage in a socialist system was 'fundamentally different' from marriage under capitalism because it was 'no longer based on economic considerations ... nor on sexual attraction, but on absolute equality between the sexes and joint partici- pation in socialist labour.'[7] To emphasise the same point, the salacious connotations of marriage in American society were used to highlight the virtues of socialist monogamy.[8] Moreover, love which endured for a long time in marriage was the humanist (*rendaozhuyi*) expression of the individual's sense of social responsibility.[9]

After a series of month-long campaigns to publicise the Marriage Law came to an end in early 1953, the state's focus in implementing the law changed quite radically. It was recognised that the first three years of the law's implementation had resulted in enormous suffering, often ending in women's death by suicide or homicide.[10] It had notably failed to convince the rural population of the need or desirability of replacing traditional marital arrangements, given that the new law threatened to disrupt the 'patrilinean family structure on which the rural communities were based'.[11] At best, it had achieved only limited results in the urban areas. The intensified attempts to spread the message of the new law in the 1953 campaigns perhaps signified a last-ditch attempt to overcome resistance to it. In any event, the end of the campaigns ushered in a period of retrenchment from the more extreme potentialities of the free-choice model. The general tenor of publicity about marriage practices indicated a desire to build on the gains made rather than to strive for new ones. Divorce became more difficult to obtain than before, and claimants were often warned that 'liking the new and hating the old' (*xi xin yan jiu*) was not adequate grounds for separation. Mediation was frequently urged to patch up marital conflicts in the name of preserving family harmony.

The implications for women were striking. The change in orientation of the publicity accompanying the Marriage Law in effect signified that women's interests were no longer to be served by prioritising their new marital rights, but by making concessions to conservative opinion in order to preserve family and marital stability. This was accompanied by numerous articles encouraging women not to complain about their lot in life, to be caring wives and efficient domestic managers. Despite the many divorces and remarriages of women now freed from the Confucian yoke, one consequence of the new emphasis on monogamous marriage was to produce images and expectations of 'virtuous' women which were not far removed from traditional concerns.

To begin with, monogamy was no longer discussed with reference to precisely the same needs. Cases when the monogamous principle had been violated by male adultery were discussed no longer as examples of the need to eradicate the injustices of the feudal past, but much more as instances of the individualistic and corrupt ways of 'bourgeois behaviour'. This shift in target granted an ideological justification for extending the target of criticism. The male focus of the feudal label did not easily allow for criticism of female behaviour, given that women were seen as victims of an oppressive system. Discarding the notion that the feudal system was responsible for sexual misdemeanours, therefore, permitted identification of women's behaviour alongside men's as examples of sexual immorality. It also afforded an opportunity for bringing under discussion various practices and attitudes which did not conform to the revised model of monogamy and which could not be simply dismissed as remnants of the past. The meaning of monogamy as a discursive practice was extended to include what it was not; it served to identify positive forms of behaviour and simultaneously isolated as deviant or abnormal modes of conduct which could not be assimilated into the standards of the official discourse. Monogamy thus acquired the status of a moralising principle.

Central among the concerns related to the discourse's insistence on the unitary model of monogamy was women's pre-marital sexual behaviour. Considerable attention was paid in the official journals of the 1950s to the extent to which pre-marital experimentation with different partners should be permitted prior to the stage of 'consolidating the love relationship' (*jianli aiqing guanxi*), after which no turning back was countenanced. A number of articles indicated that while 'friendship' (*youyi*) should not be mistaken for 'love' (*aiqing*) because this would limit the individual's freedom of choice,[12] the notion of freedom of choice should not be interpreted as an invitation to irresponsible behaviour, as in the case of the Shanghai factory worker who had five or six boyfriends every year.[13] But still the question about pre-marital limits remained. Was it immoral to go back on an initial understanding to 'develop feeling' (*peiyang ganqing*) if things did not work out properly? The confusing dividing line between freedom of choice and 'fickleness' needed to be clarified, particularly since young girls were likely to be led astray by the advances of worldly men.[14] While such questions indicated that the new courtship practices publicised alongside the Marriage Law were subject to different interpretations, they were all indications of the state's interests in extending the sexual standards implied by the term monogamy to pre-marital practices. Girls who married the first and only man who had indicated his amorous intentions were praised for their steadfastness. Indeed, one such who was praised for deciding to marry her first love, despite his lower status and wealth, was in addition told that to embark on a love relationship with her second suitor would have created a triangular relationship which violated the monogamous requirements of the law.[15] Pre-marital fidelity was demanded of girls if their relationship with a man had continued for some time and had become 'more than a relationship between friends'.[16] Any indication that a pre-marital relationship had led to expectations of love on the part of one of the partners meant that marriage was the only option available. Love, or any behaviour indicative of amorous expectations, was thus treated as the first step to which the monogamous principle applied. After this stage was reached, no further development could take place until marriage – the public and legal commitment to respect the monogamous principle – had been finalised. 'The sex life of a couple begins after marriage', so the leading sexologist of the 1950s commented.[17] And thereafter, 'the inevitable result [would be] the establishment of a family' (*jianli jiating*).[18]

That a monogamous relationship demanded marital fidelity goes without saying, but here too women were thought to bear the main responsibility. Disruption of marriages because of the intrusion of a 'third one' (*disanzhe*) was described as 'invariably the fault of women'.[19] Women's violation of the principle of monogamy by committing adultery or interfering in a stable relationship could lead to dire consequences, and even to petty crime.[20] Even when violation of the monogamous principle was the man's just as much as the woman's responsibility, it was she who was censored. During the anti-rightist movement, for example, a student in Wuhan University sent a couple of photos to a girl with a letter declaring eternal love.[21] After their marriage, she was sent to Shanghai to work, and he was sent to a small town near Wuhan. In less than a year, he had got together with another girl, and despite criticisms from his workmates, he insisted on continuing his relationship with her. Eventually his wife got to hear of what was going on, and fell ill, whereupon he decided to go to Shanghai to see her. Unable to disguise his coldness towards her, he told his wife that he was in love with someone else and suggested divorce. She realised that all he was interested in was his own feelings, that he was nothing but 'selfish and hypocritical' (*zisi jia xuwei*). But at the end of the story, it was his girlfriend, not he, who was reproached. 'She, a certain Yang, already had a boyfriend, whom she had known for a long time, and had often bragged about (*kuayao*) to her fellow students. Their relationship had gone beyond one of ordinary friendship. So why did she have to fall in love (*biaoshi aiqing*) to a man who already had a wife?'

For women, monogamy thus emerged as a behavioural requirement that in some respects echoed the traditional norms of chastity. Monogamy was represented not only to demand marital fidelity, but also pre-marital abstinence. It was also accompanied by expectations that a wife support her husband's interests and service his needs, whether as his sexual partner or as the self-sacrificing manager of his domestic affairs. Some such images invoked conventional gender constructs. Others included a reference to some disability of the husband, as if to underline the need for the wife's care and attention. The corollary was that marital harmony and by extension family stability depended on female self-restraint for the sake of the dominant male other.

Insistence on conformity to the monogamous model could be presented as a positive move to protect women from male abuse. A less benign interpretation would suggest that as an exclusive tie covering pre-marital as well as marital behaviour, monogamy was demanded as a means of extending state control over intimate aspects of the lives of ordinary men and women. As such it signified the intervention of state interests in aspects of married life that could not be reached by concentrating on the productive and economic functions of marriage alone. Many negative images of conduct that transgressed the parameters of the official model suggested that any divergence from the discursive norm of the conjugal, and legally registered, couple would lead to unhappiness and pain. Not only was divorce seen as increasingly disruptive at a time when the state was attempting to encourage couples to put their energies into work and production, but the failure to marry, and therefore to have children, was also seen as an unacceptable rejection of the monogamous model. As one article put it, 'marriage is an individual's natural biological need; not to marry is abnormal (*bu zhengchang*) and does not have any physical benefit'.[22] Monogamy thus emerged as a social ordering principle, oriented to minimise friction and tension at a time when changing experiences and work threatened to disrupt many marriages. By warning particularly women of the dangers that would follow any failure to respect the established norms, the constructions associated with the official model of monogamy functioned to harness energies and behaviour to serve state interests.

MONOGAMY, FEMALE GENDER AND STATE POWER IN THE 1980s

Issues concerning women's marital and sexual responsibilities were effectively absent from the official discourse between the early 1960s and the late 1970s. Prominent areas of discrimination against women, over, for example, equal pay, labour, and political representation were briefly examined during the 'criticise Lin Biao, criticise Confucius' campaign of the early 1970s. However, it was not until after the Cultural Revolution, when journals such as *Chinese Youth* and *Chinese Women* started publication again after the years of enforced silence, that the topics of the 1950s were revived. It was immediately apparent that the 1950s discourse on sex and gender-related issues overdetermined important aspects of its successor; many of the themes explored in the 1980s were established and defined in the earlier period. However, the variety of the approaches the latter adopted suggested that the concern to promulgate a unitary set of sexual standards, applicable to all young men and women, whatever their socio-economic circumstance, was no longer shared. With the exception of brief periods – notably those of greater political constraints – the 1980s discourse was more open and enquiring, less insistent on achieving complete unanimity of opinion, and more removed from the unifying interests of the state than had previously been the case. New themes that responded to the changing aspirations of the younger generation emerged, such as how to behave in singles' dances, changing attitudes towards pre-marital sex, the pros and cons of responding to marriage bureau advertisements in the papers, and what to do on the night of the honeymoon. Questions about love, sex, virginity and contraception were addressed with a candour and flexibility that had often been absent from the more didactic and exhortatory tones of the 1950s materials. The debates of the 1980s showed more interest in examining the lessons to be learnt from individual experience, even when this diverged from the norms of 'socialist civilisation' (*shehuizhuyi wenming*). More diverse and explor- atory than its 1950s precursor, the 1980s discourse seemed to indicate a diminished interest in categorising and controlling modes of sexual and gender behaviour through didactic means.

Alongside the radical changes taking place in Chinese society, the diversity of the positions adopted since the 1980s in the official approaches to sex-related issues has in large part been in response to the emergence of other, informal and more popular discourses and practices of sexual gender relations. The increasing divorce rate would seem to suggest that the specific associations of monogamy are no longer the same as before; it now may mean little more than that a woman should have one husband at a time. One immediate result of the 1980 Marriage Law's new regulations permitting divorce on the grounds of 'alienation of affection' (*ganqing polie*) was that the divorce rate rose in several cities. In Shanghai, the number of divorce cases filed at the People's Court in 1981 represented a 53 per cent increase over 1980. They made up about a third of all cases handled by Chinese courts in 1986.[23] Another more brutal example of changing practices is the revival of 'feudal' customs; the sale of child brides and concubinage testify to the continuation of practices condemned by law. Popular magazines and comic books, widely available on street stalls, contain often sensationalist themes along the familiar lines of misogynist sex and violence. The statistical results of recent surveys of young people's attitudes towards pre-marital sex and marriage further testify to approaches which substantially differ from the values upheld by the official discourse. Various sources show that attitudes towards pre-marital sex have become much more permissive, to the extent that in a survey carried out among young people in Shanghai in 1986, 50 per cent saw nothing immoral in pre-marital sex.[24] An article in a popular journal further assumed that pre-marital sex between a couple before marriage was inevitable. [25]

However, the apparent autonomy of popular practices, and the emergence of new spaces facilitating the elaboration of discourses on sexuality removed from the controlling arm of state power have not eclipsed state interests in defining appropriate marital and sexual behaviour. For alongside the abundance of advice and information about sex-related matters, and despite the changes in the modality of the official discourse of sexuality, it is clear that much of it is, as in the 1950s, oriented towards channelling individual, and particularly female, behaviour in the service of social and moral order. More specifically, in the context of the present discussion, much of the discourse continues to identify the monogamous relationship as the site in which women's responsibilities to society are properly realised.

However, a look at the negative representations in the discourse of the consequences of a woman's failure to respect her monogamous responsibilities indicates that it is the method of argument and representation that has changed, and not the basic purpose. One prominent area in which this is apparent is in the representation of women who remain single, often categorised under the term the 'problem of the over-thirty-year-old old maids' – a specifically 1980s phenomenon. The continuing definition of marriage as a biologically natural bond automatically isolates women who reject it as deviants.

Female celibacy and the failure to produce children continue to be seen as signs of some irregularity, to be treated with suspicion. The appropriation of nature into the meaning of monogamy means that spinsterhood is not infrequently projected as a physiological abnormality. A woman's inability, reluctance or failure to marry can thus easily be constructed as a social problem, such that many women who claim to have voluntarily foregone marriage in order to devote themselves to work find themselves the butt of pity and mockery. Even in the survey of Beijing college and university students, only 8.93 per cent of the respondents indicated approval of marrying but refusing to have children. [26] Whether in advice to courting couples, or in warnings to young women about the pitfalls of cohabitation, the persistent assumption is that marriage and eventual childbirth are dictated by female nature. At most, the official discourse reluctantly acknowledges that while couples who decide not to have children might be subject to 'all sorts of gossip and comment' (*gezhong shengyin he yilun*), it is nevertheless possible for the individual to make such a choice.[27]

The following autobiographical account written in 1984 by Tang Liqin, a single woman, is a telling example of the difficulties encountered:

[People say that] I am too picky, that I have too pure a view of love and marriage.... People discuss me when they are passing the time of day. They feel sorry for me, casting curious glances my way. They say that I am a 'high-priced girl', that I am old, psychologically abnormal, physiologically incomplete, possessed of a shameful secret that cannot be told ...

Society can tolerate couple after couple who share the same bed while dreaming different dreams. It will conduct countless mediations for families in which the couple has just married and the relationship is verging on collapse. Faced with the grim reality of marriages made carelessly with no emotional basis, where each party takes what he or she needs, to the point where husband and wife divorce or a third party gets involved, society will go to great lengths to censure them in the 'court of morality' or punish them according to the law ...

There is no need to advocate being single. It should be like a religious belief – not promoted, but with freedom of belief [guaranteed]. If a person is willing to remain single, is it like graft or embezzlement, posing a potential social threat? And under the present national policy of fewer and better births, how does it impair the national economy? Looked at from this angle what is reproachable about not marrying unless one finds an ideal mate, remaining single all one's life? I go so far as to feel quite at ease about doing so. Perhaps this will be seen as the reflection of psychological abnormality, but I hope I can gain social recognition and support.[28]

If the personal anxiety experienced by single women were not adequate penalisation for their refusal to marry, discriminatory institutional and economic arrangements echo the values of the official discourse by making it almost impossible to sustain an acceptable livelihood as a single woman. Single women are given low priority in allocation of housing and are assigned unfavourable work schedules.[29] They are in general obliged to live in the crowded conditions of the dormitory attached to their work-place, or with their parents. The lack of physical privacy, and the continuing widespread view that sex outside marriage is immoral confront single women with the choice of either a life of sexual deprivation or one of marital monotony.

Another area of women's experience in which monogamy, as an exclusive and life-long tie, is projected as a social and moral barrier against chaos and suffering, concerns the increasing rate of sexual violence and crime. While very occasionally the increasing sex crime rate is used to support arguments in favour of extending sex education to eradicate sexual ignorance and fear among young people, it typically features in short stories and cautionary tales warning young women of the consequences of not sticking to one man.[30] For example, a recent article in *Zhongguo Funü* suggested that a woman might be inviting violent abuse if she agreed to sleep with a man outside wedlock.[31] Young girls who break off a relationship prior to marriage, women who seek divorce against their husband's wishes, or who sleep with someone before marrying, are invariably portrayed as responsible for their own unhappy fate; it would be unrealistic of them not to expect a life of suffering and hardship. Any woman who is not safely protected by her pre-marital chastity and marital fidelity is generally represented either as the innocent victim of unscrupulous male design, or as the immoral and selfish perpetrator of her own suffering. The woman who does not respect the moral and sexual obligations of the monogamous tie has only herself to blame for her anguish.

The following two cases, typical of many published during the 1980s, illustrate this point from different angles. The first described the confusion of a student at a technical school in Changsha who was courted by three men.[32] One, the son of an important local government official, said that if she married him his father would arrange for her to stay in Changsha after graduating. The second was a cadre in the factory attached to her school and was responsible for having brought her to the school from the mountain district where she was brought up. He was nine years older than she, but promised to find her a job in his factory if she married him. The third, whom she liked the best, was a worker in a small factory in her home town. The opinions which followed the publication of the girl's initial letter seeking advice from the editorial of *Zhongguo qingnian bao* contained different suggestions about which of the three she should choose, but none of them indicated that she was wrong in entertaining ideas about all three men, because she hadn't 'affirmed a love relationship' (*kending aiqing guanxi*) with any one of them. The monogamous principle was respected as long as experimentation was not accompanied by signs and declarations of love.

The response to a second case was very different, and the girl in question was castigated for the emotional anguish she felt when confronted with the need to make a choice.[33] A girl fell in love with a classmate at her college. But since it was not considered a good idea for university students to have love affairs, neither she nor her boyfriend did anything about it. After graduating, the man was assigned a job far away from Shanghai, and since the two decided that they had no hope of ever living in the same place, they decided not to pursue the romance. At her parents' behest, the girl was then introduced to another man, and although she was not totally happy about the prospect of marrying him, they quickly registered their marriage so that they could apply for housing. At this point, to her delight and dismay, her first love returned to Shanghai. She wanted to break off her first marriage, and her friends advised her that it was all right to do so since she had not yet lived with her legally registered husband. She would not therefore require a real divorce. The editorial replies to the girl's letter asking if it were possible to rescind her marriage suggested that she 'had handled this business in a rash manner', and that it was not possible to break off her marriage without obtaining a divorce. Editorial policy thus implied that she had two choices: either to stick with her first love and resign herself to seeing him only twice a year, or to find someone more convenient to marry and then set about the business of developing 'mutual affection'.

Pressure to conform to the sexual requirements of monogamous marriage has been maintained by constructing and controlling sexual behaviour in the interests of state power and social stability. Just as in the 1950s, women are informed that failure to uphold the marital and monogamous duties expected of a wife will have a negative impact on the children, and that non-marital sexual activity threatens the very fabric of society. The monogamous model of marriage constructed by the official discourse thus appears as standard of moral and social order upheld by the agency of female conduct. However, the 1980s discourse was not a mere repetition of that of the 1950s, and the young people who in recent years have constituted the major target of writings about sex-related matters are very different from their forebears in the 1950s. The focus on the monogamous relationship as a mediator of women's social responsibilities, and by extension as a principal site of the construction of female gender, must therefore respond to forces and pressures that are radically different from those of the earlier period.

At the risk of extreme generalisation, these could be summed up under what has been called the 'refamilisation' of society: the process by which, under the combined effect of economic, social and demographic interests, the family-household has been confirmed as a key unit of economic, social and moral importance.[34] Within the family, it is the conjugal couple that is the fulcrum of order; and within this relationship, it is women who are asked to bear the major responsibility for domestic affairs, whether as the main consumer of labour-saving devices within the household, or as the bearer and nurturer of children. The obligation to uphold the monogamous tie, through sexual fidelity and marital service, is women's. It is thus through the construction of women's responsibilities and functions within the monogamous relationship that female gender emerges as a moralising force. It could further be argued that it is because of women's responsibility as the protagonist of monogamy that monogamy itself acquires the status of a moralising principle.

Monogamy in post-nineteenth-century European history has often been discussed as an aspect of pro-natalist policies. In China, the reverse has been the case. For women, monogamy is associated both with sexual fidelity and with fertility control, failure to exercise which may be severely penalised.[35] Women's monogamous responsibilities therefore include accepting a series of physical, sexual, psychological and even medical constraints, some of which may cause extreme anxiety and suffering. Tang Min, a writer from Xiamen, has also pointed to the anxiety and misery that women are subjected to as a consequence of the dual burden to marry and to have only one child.[36] In the passage quoted above, Tang Liqin alluded to the inconsistency between the state's interests in limiting population growth and the representation of 'normal' (*zhengchang*) women as those who marry and bear children. In view of this contradiction, the suggestion that monogamous marriage, with its connotations of wifely service, sexual fidelity and reproduction, is upheld because of its utility as a moralising and ordering agent, is strengthened. Monogamy, as the foundation of the family and household unit, functions as an apparently natural authority patrolling behaviour and expectations in the service of social stability and morality. Within the terms of the current context, the recurring glorification of women's domestic role since 1978, at a time when women would seem to be freer than ever before to embark on activities and experiences outside the domestic sphere, is just another facet of the same construction.

Ever since the 1950 Marriage Law, the conjugal relationship has been defined as the core unit of the socialist family. The official discourse of the 1950s privileged the young urban woman who was engaged in social labour, was mother of a healthy child and was satisfactorily married, over other women, and hence relegated the domestic housewife, the uneducated granny and the hard-working farmer's daughter to a subsidiary position in the hierarchy of gender images. Whatever the imputed status, however, it was through the conjugal relationship that the state constructed women's primary and 'natural' responsibilities to society. Between 1950 and 1953 the 'new democratic' image of the monogamous relationship held out to young people the promise of a future built on a truly companionate basis. After 1953 this progressive tone became partially eclipsed by another more conservative one, which emphasised the importance of women's contribution to family stability, and therefore of respecting the sexual and gender requirements of monogamy. Many women trying to obtain a divorce were told not to be 'frivolous' and not to disrupt the harmony of the 'socialist household'. During the 1955 'prettification' campaign, the attempt to persuade women that their first duty to society lay in being good housewives and mothers was accompanied by encouragement to dress prettily for their husbands. The monogamous marriage therefore represented a social and moral obligation on women to behave in ways that served more the interests of the state than their own. Monogamy signified a process of self-denial in the name of the husband and state. By the 1980s, writings about women, sexuality and marriage had departed from the unitary concerns of the 1950s. Monogamous marriage was represented in more diverse and varied forms, in response to the changes affecting Chinese society. However, the greater detail, the apparent flexibility and the more permissive tones of the 1980s discourse did not obscure the continuing insistence on conformity to the monogamous model. In its extended meanings of pre-marital abstinence, and virginity on marriage, what was upheld in the name of sexual equality and women's emancipation continued to function as a new constraint on women's sexual and gender conduct. The model of monogamous marriage was constructed to channel the choices women might make concerning life-style, relationships, marriage and motherhood into one basic model. Monogamous marriage represented a sexual, moral and social obligation on women to behave in ways that perpetuated their function as agents of social and moral order, in the service of interests defined by the state. The 'feudal' system of patriarchal authority has been effectively replaced by a new series of constraints which deny women the possibility of giving autonomous expression to their own interests and aspirations in marriage.

NOTES

1 See Delia Davin, *Woman-Work*, Oxford University Press, Oxford, 1976, p. 17, for an explanation of the term *funü gongzuo*, to refer to 'all sorts of activities among women, including mobilising them for revolutionary struggle, production, literacy and hygiene campaigns, social reform, and so on'.

2 The notion of an 'official discourse of sexuality' does not seek to elaborate a theory, but refers to the texts, themes and representational practices through which knowledge about sex-related issues was disseminated in the officially controlled press.

3 See the *Marriage Law of the People's Republic of China* (1950), Foreign Languages Press, Beijing, 1973.

4 For discussion about the KMT and CCP approaches to marriage prior to 1949 see M.J. Meijer, *Marriage Law and Policy in the People's Republic of China*, Hong Kong University Press, Hong Kong, 1972.

5 ibid., p. 39.

6 Chen Jianwei, 'Lun fengjian jiazhangzhi de pochu' ('On the breaking down of the system of feudal patriarchy'), *Hebei ribao*, 8 April 1959, p. 3.

7 Deng Yingchao, 'Xuexi Sulian renmin chongggao de gongchanzhuyi daode pinzhi' ('Study the lofty qualities of Communist morality of the Soviet people'), in *Lun shehuizhuyi shehui de aiqing, hunyin he jiating (On Love, Marriage and the Family in Socialist Society)*, Qingnian chubanshe, Beijing, 1953, p. 3.

8 Li Wei, 'Cong Meiguo fulu shang kan "Meiguo shenghuo fangshi" ' ('Looking at "the American life style" as seen in American prisoners'), *ZGQN* 10, 16 June 1952, pp. 32–3.

9 Deng Yingchao, 1953, p. 4.

10 A government report of 1953 estimated that 70,000 to 80,000 women per year died in this way; see *Guanche hunyinfa yundong de zhongyao wenjian (Important documents in implementing the Marriage Law campaign)*, Renmin chubanshe, Beijing, 1953, p. 12.

11 Kay Ann Johnson, *Women, the Family and Peasant Revolution in China*, University of Chicago Press, Chicago, 1983, p. 147. The difficulties in implementing the new law in the countryside were also the result of the lack of any economic incentive to rural households to radically alter the traditional arrangements underwriting marital and family structure; see Elisabeth Croll, *The Politics of Marriage in Contemporary China*, Cambridge University Press, Cambridge, 1981, pp. 163–4.

12 Wu Jiu, 'Qingnian nan nü zhijian de youyi he aiqing' ('Friendship and love between young men and women'), *ZGQN* 8, 16 April 1955, pp. 22–3.

13 'Zunzhong aiqing shenghuo zhong de ziyuan yuanze' ('Respect the principle of voluntary choice in love life'), *ZGQN* 10, 16 May 1956, pp. 36–7.

14 Xu Hua, 'Bu yao zhao nianling tai xiao de zhongxuesheng tan lian'ai' ('Don't have love affairs with middle school students who are too young'), *ZGQN* 22, 16 November 1956, p. 26.

15 Wei Hua, 'Aiqing' ('Love'), *ZGFN* 7, 1958, pp. 18–19.
16 Xu Hua, 1956.
17 Wang Wenbin, *Xing de zhishi (Knowledge about Sex)*, Renmin weisheng chubanshe, Beijing, 1956, p. 40.
18 ibid., p. 26.
19 *ZGQN* 9, 1956, p. 38.
20 Liu Lequn, 'Women fufu guanxi weishenmo polie?' ('Why did our marriage break down?'), *ZGFN* 11, 1955, pp. 6–7.
21 Lai Gen, 'Xidi yixia ba, liangxin zhanmanle wugou de ren' ('Have a wash, filthy people, and let your conscience wash you clean'), *ZGQN* 22, 16 November 1957, pp. 31–2.
22 Zhang Xijun, 'Cong shenglixue jiaodu tan hunling wenti' ('Talking about the age of marriage from a physiological perspective'), *ZGQN* 6, 16 March 1957, p. 34.
23 For figures about divorce in the 1980s, see Emily Honig and Gail Hershatter, *Personal Voices: Chinese Women in the 1980s*, Stanford University Press, Stanford, Calif., 1988, p. 210, and Elisabeth Croll, *Chinese Women Since Mao*, Zed Books, London, 1983, pp. 82–5.
24 Published in *Zhengming*, no. 4, April 1986, pp. 38–9.
25 Zhang Lang, 'Bu yuan jiehun de guniang' ('The girl who did not want to marry'), *Jiating Yisheng (Family Doctor)*, no. 8, 1 August 1986, pp. 32–3.
26 See Tong Zhiqi, 'The new tide of reform and female college students today', in *Chinese Education: A Journal of Translation*, Summer, 1989, p. 104.
27 Huo Gang, 'Dui jiating jiegou de xin xuanze' ('New choices in family structure'), *ZGFN* 10, 2 October 1990, p. 34.
28 Tang Liqin, 'Yi wei da guniang de dubai' ('Soliloquy of an old maid'), *Shehui* no. 4, August 1984, pp. 47–9, quoted in Honig and Hershatter, 1988, pp. 107–8.
29 For the difficulties confronting single women, see Honig and Hershatter, 1988, p. 107.
30 The view of sex education as indispensable to transforming fundamentally misogynist attitudes and practices is in, for example, Liu Dalin, 'Xingkexue yu funü jiefang' ('Sexology and women's liberation'), *Shehuikexue zhanxian (Front Line in the Social Sciences)*, no. 1, January 1987, pp. 120–5.
31 Li Honglin, 'Tan zhencao' ('On virginity'), *ZGFN* 4, 2 April 1989, pp 20–1.
32 *Zhongguo qingnian bao (China Youth News)*, 12 February 1981, p. 3.
33 *Zhongguo qingnian bao*, 5 September 1982, p. 8.
34 For further discussion about the changing function of the family-household in post-Mao China, see Jean Robinson, 'Of women and washing machines: employment, housework and the reproduction of motherhood in socialist China', *China Quarterly*, no. 101, March 1985, pp. 32–5. See also Elisabeth Croll, 'New Peasant Family Forms in Rural China', *The Journal of Peasant Studies*, July 1987, pp. 469–99.
35 For discussion about the penalties imposed for failure to observe the single-child policy, see Elisabeth Croll, Delia Davin and Penny Kane, *China's One-Child Family Policy*, Macmillan, London, 1985.
36 Tang Min, formerly an editor of Xiamen Literature, acquired notoriety for her provocative writings about contemporary Chinese society. These included a number of short stories about the contemporary conditions of abuse and oppression, such as enforced abortion, that women in Chinese society have to live with. For more about Tang Min and her work, see David Kellogg, *In Search of China*, Hilary Shipman, London 1989.

Part III

Towards a woman's consciousness?

9 Gendered identities
Women's experience of change in Hungary

Chris Corrin

INTRODUCTION

My concern in this study is with the ways in which Hungarian women have been able to construct their identities within society and how 'state'[1] and societal forces have intervened and shaped this process. I am very much aware that in a study of this length points can only be touched upon rather than fully explored (for more detailed consideration see Corrin, 1992). In the so-called 'socialist' period the Hungarian state authorities and policy makers intervened directly in the process of basic material provision, allowing women access to the fundamental pre-conditions for entry into the public sphere. Such interventions were concerned primarily with the introduction of large numbers of women into waged employment and measures aimed at easing women's paid work by providing contraception and child-care services. Essentially there are three or four central areas in which women are vitally involved and where feelings of pride, self-respect, well-being, humiliation, guilt, anxiety, and fear of failure arise. Women as paid workers, domestic workers, child-bearers and child-carers are at the heart of social relations, yet as far as decision-making in all its spheres is concerned women are seen to have a less than central part. In this chapter aspects of women's activities in childbirth and controlling child-bearing are considered in addition to issues concerning the duality of the mother–worker role under which all Hungarian women have laboured for at least the forty years from 1948 to 1988. A key focus will be the duality of state and society pressures upon women and the ways in which the statist policies of the modern Hungarian authorities attempted to shape women's expectations and thereby their lives. Hungarian women have recognised these pressures yet until the political changes of 1988/9 they had little opportunity to try to change their situation and redress the balance in their lives. In considering women's activities towards change in the recent period it is possible to assess something of the consequences of the political changes for women, at the levels of attitudes, legislation and everyday reality, to gauge how much real space has been opened up for women's activities.

'STATE' AND SOCIETY: RELEVANT ACTORS IN SHAPING WOMEN'S LIVES

I would argue that the Hungarian state forces in a similar but different way from the Italian state forces 'played a key role both in shaping a female political subject and in laying the bases for the quandaries concerning women's identity which have permeated feminist debate' (Ergas, 1986: 301–2). By similar but different I mean that although in many aspects of policy and debate the Hungarian state has acted within the same overarching framework as the Italian state power, the rhetoric and thereby some of the consequences of policies, intended and unintended, differ in both content and form. My primary concern here is less with women as 'political subjects' than with the complex and contradictory expectations placed upon women.

The terms 'state' and 'society' are used to relate to changing conceptions of political participation and social interaction. Definitions of the state usually include aspects of the monopoly of the legitimate use of force. Who defines which forces are legitimate? Generally not women. Some theorists have viewed the state as a neutral instrument of public policy, such as equal employment. For many feminist theorists the state is actually a combination of forces, the strongest being male dominance. [2] Here we see again the differences between the so-called liberal strategies of women's emancipation concerned with adaptation, women gaining individual rights as they are already defined within society, and the more radical efforts towards liberation concerned with redefining the whole arena of human needs.[3] For women in Hungary the fusion of rights and duties by the statist powers meant that women always lost out. Conceptions of citizenship were pivotally tied to duties, and women's duties were so all-encompassing that they were oppressed under their weight. For many men in this situation their so-called rights and duties were not only compatible but complementary. For women, though, their 'right' to work conflicted with their 'duty' as mothers. In addition women's duties have always been more emotive and stressful than those of men, because men constantly distance themselves from the domestic sphere. Although many aspects of the domestic world are not only undervalued but culturally downgraded, women are often made to feel failures if all does not run smoothly in this area. Women are caught in the double bind that their domestic responsibilities are not as important as men's worldly ones, yet men are allowed to countenance failure without being devalued personally. If any aspect of domestic life fails to live up to often idealised assumptions, it generally happens that women are held personally responsible and women caught in such situations feel guilty about whatever it is that has not met expectations. Examples of these situations range from men choosing to take lovers and making their wives feel it is their own unattractiveness or lack of 'caring' that has forced them to seek comfort elsewhere, or children not doing so well at school; because helping with schoolwork is seen to fall within the domestic sphere and therefore women's responsibility, not doing well is obviously the mother's fault.

STATE POLICY ON LIBERATING WOMEN THROUGH PAID WORK

It is now recognised that the total form of state within Hungary during the 'state socialist' period was one that placed economics first; all other issues, including welfare and social policy matters, were measured in importance against the economic imperatives. This approach, coupled with state rhetoric of women's equal place in society, lead the way to the 'double burden' which women in Hungary and similar Soviet-type societies suffered. Women were free to work eight hours each day at the public, paid work-places and then come home to another four hours or so in their private, unpaid work-places. The psychological strain of this is well summed up by María Márkus when she writes of women having to 'explain' their behaviour constantly in terms of the worker–mother duality:

> In the case where she is trying to fulfil both functions she may have a sense of bad conscience about not being a good mother (when she is at work) and not being a good worker (when she is at home – e.g. with an ill child). The existence of this 'bad conscience' can be verified in almost all sociological investigations dealing with the problem of motivation to work, and life satisfaction.
>
> (Márkus, 1973: 32)

These psychological stresses were not broadened out on to a group level as they might have been in some social situations, but remained at a personal level for the great majority of Hungarian women. Many of the women with whom I spoke at length during the 1980s stressed the fact that the children were definitely *their* responsibility, and that they felt guilty if things did not run smoothly in the home, even if the reasons for problems lay beyond their control. The space for women to *be women* did not seem to exist, except perhaps for very short periods before women prepared for marriage, so that women were always viewed, and generally viewed themselves, in relation to others. Women were often regarded in relation to men primarily as wives and domestic workers, and to children as mothers and carers, as well nurses, teachers, and providers. In addition women's identities were shaped by their lives as daughters and grand-daughters, as well as daughters-in-law, and the strain of attempting to be or become 'all capable' for those needing care or attention was an enormous one. The joy and increased horizons that can come with becoming a mother or being a daughter tended to become overshadowed in that the time which women were able to spend with children or parents became so telescoped that practical, often physical needs were prioritised over the no-less-important aspects – the emotional and enjoyable sides of developing close relationships.

Having someone to talk with in such situations becomes vital, but building support networks was often not straightforward either in terms of attitudes or opportunities. One support group started by mothers in a housing estate on the outskirts of Budapest in 1986 was a good example of differing needs and expectations amongst women. The mother who related it to me was seen to be an 'intellectual'[4] and 'middle class' and she said there was a definite division between those mothers who were 'intellectuals' and those who were not. These divisions expressed themselves within this group through attitudes towards home care, principally environment, play and food. The 'working-class' women or those who were not 'intellectuals' believed that the homes of the other women were too untidy, and not always suitable for children to play in. In addition, rather than giving the children a game or taking them to the park, the 'intellectual' women often seemed to allow the children do whatever they chose. So far as food was concerned, the 'working-class' mothers argued that the other mothers did not give the children 'proper home-cooked food' but were content to let the children eat 'snack-type' foods with less nutritional value. These disagreements in the way houses were kept, how children played and what they ate were enough to lead to a breakdown in the co-operation within the group, even though all the women concerned still needed to find shared care for their children.

My own feeling on this was that in many countries of the world such differences exist between how women live and bring up their children, but the specific point of this within Hungarian society was that the women had few experiences to enable them to criticise constructively or to be able to agree to differ. Trust is all important in all human relations and there seemed a lack of trust between women, and no framework or space within which to secure an environment and relationships to give and gain others trust. Women badly felt the lack of this in their everyday lives. The inability to have their group 'recognised' externally, in that none other than the official women's council was recognised for funding or resource provision, also added to this loss.

Two structural factors are important to emphasise within the Hungarian 'double burden–shift–day' context – about women's guilt feelings and the psychological pressures suffered by Hungarian women. One is undoubtedly the sustained rhetoric of the Hungarian authorities about the 'facts' of Hungarian women's emancipation, stressing how many women work and have child-care and benefits provided, coupled with a concerted effort on the part of the state forces of propaganda actively to discredit women's power in other parts of the world – be it western feminism, African women producers' achievements or women's successes elsewhere. Tiers of cultural superiority seem to be built into most European societies, generally placing their own at the top! In this way Hungarian authorities follow long traditions.

A second factor concerns the major differences in attitude toward social and 'state' divisions, primarily in so far as family groupings are concerned. In much the same way that many black families in Britain would hesitate before calling in the state, in the form of the police, to sort out a violent dispute, so people in Hungarian families strictly avoid any entry by state officials into their domestic lives. This was true not just in the case of police or state officials in situations of domestic violence, but also when criticising or problematising conflicts within families and domestic life, even in considering the oppressive nature of women's private, unpaid, domestic work. Why should the burden fall on women and what was to be done about it, were questions that Hungarian women considered, but invariably answers such as the one given to me by Ilona were the most common:

> We [women] are not prepared to make our family life even harder by causing strains between ourselves and our husbands. Things are difficult enough in Hungary in these times. It is natural that women take on the majority of the work in the home, after all men work so hard in the outside world. In Hungary you know, our family life is important to us, especially to us women.
>
> (Corrin, 1992)

Ilona and other women talked a good deal on this theme and it became clear to me that two factors played equally decisive parts during the 1980s in confirming women's responsibility for home work and their desire for 'smooth' family lives. The state–society divide was probably the major factor in women's desire not to problematise their extra work in the home – the domestic division of labour. Most women considered that their lives were hard enough, and their partners also worked very hard often in second and third jobs within the second economy, so that it did seem reasonable to them to carry out their own second or third job in the home and caring for children.

There is ample evidence to show the rising prospects for earning within the second economy in Hungary from the late 1960s. Yet the structure of second economy work, coupled with women's unpaid working responsibilities, meant that very few working women could participate in it. In contrast, some intellectual women, such as language teachers, could participate. This economic activity generally gave status and respect to those engaged in it. In couples where both men and women worked at more than one job it remained the case that the women did the majority of housework, and all of the child-care. When men did share some responsibility for domestic work it was viewed as 'helping' women. This view of men 'helping' women combines both the factors that are important for Hungarian women: the difficulties of everyday life in Hungary and the expectations which the state authorities place on women within their 'emancipated' lives. The latter I can only call the 'natural' or 'propaganda' factor which comes out clearly in the anti-equality debate.

The state encroachment into almost every sphere of women's lives was underlined by the activities of the Hungarian Women's Organisation (Magyar Nök Tanacs Országos). This was not an autonomous movement but was virtually a branch of the Communist Party, which women saw primarily as a 'paper organisation'. Women from this organisation went to international conferences 'representing' Hungarian women but their contact with most women's everyday lives was non-existent. This is another example of party or state intrusion into public, collective spheres – the fact that a so-called women's organisation existed meant that no groups of Hungarian women could gather together *legally*, as there was no 'real need' with the official organisation to represent them.

WOMEN, CHILDBIRTH AND CARE

Several women with whom I spoke in Hungary had a very negative image of the process they underwent when giving birth to their children. Generally these women felt that the care that they received during pregnancy was sufficient, but several felt that they did not have enough information about what they could expect when the baby was being born. Recent research into women's experience has shown that women have many fears surrounding childbirth.[5] Some survey questions related to such fears, grouping them around six reasons: fear of the possibility of injury to the new-born baby; fear of complications; fear of being at the mercy of the staff; fear of the delivery process; fear of losing self-control; and fear of the unknown. Such fears may well be shared with women in many countries, but what is unusual about the Hungarian case is that women have to choose whether, and if so how much, to pay their doctors. Although in theory the health service is free to all, in practice a 'tipping' system has been in place for many years in which there is a 'going rate' for operations and treatments. The 'going rate' in March 1991 for childbirth was anywhere between 5,000 and 8,000 forints (the exchange rate was approximately 120 forints to £1 sterling). The recent survey showed that women felt that it was good to pay, but that this was more for peace of mind before the child was born, as it turned out that during the childbirth process they had little control or access to information, or no more than did women who were unable to pay.

Childbirth in Hungary, as elsewhere, has become an area monopolised by professional men in which the women are generally thought of as having no competence to assess the situation. In Hungary, unlike Britain, there are no 'radical midwives' offering full, supportive care for women before and after the births, which can often take place in the home, rather than on a metal table under bright spotlights. Discussions are now being initiated in which women will have not only more choice, about birthing stools and differing birthing methods, but also about control for women, so that they do not feel so vulnerable under the authority of 'professional men' but can enter into some form of dialogue about their needs and wishes.

A common experience in the late 1980s was that the environments and situations in which women gave birth were hostile:

> Zoltan was a very big child and it was a dangerous birth. His life was in danger when he was born. He was 4 kilos which was big in comparison to me, not on his own. Zoltan was born with the care of a man who didn't know much about birth and pain. He was quite rude and yelling at me when I said I was in pain. This was a doctor who we had asked to work for us and we paid him too.
>
> (Corrin, 1986)

In such a situation a woman's self-image can be almost destroyed when she is informed by professional men that she is weak and making a fuss about a bit of 'natural' pain. At the time when women are creating new lives they need support, as the first few weeks after a child's birth is an exhausting time for mothers. In theory mothers are respected within

Hungarian society, and certainly people seem generally more tolerant and open towards children than in societies such as Britain. The pro-natalist policies of successive administrations in Hungary point to the government emphasis on raising the low birth-rate. Yet in practice many women are humiliated in more ways than when under medical care. When in humiliating situations women sometimes internalise a feeling of guilt and believe that they are not living up to the idealised, non-existent versions of women who give birth one day and are rushing around the home caring for everything and everyone the next. It is important to note here something of what women face in trying to control their bodies in terms of conception and child-bearing.

Inexpensive and generally available contraception in Hungary is relatively recent. The condoms which were on the market from the 1960s were often poorly made and people did not 'trust' them. It was not until the 1970s that oral contraceptives were made easily accessible for all women. The methods used by couples to avoid conception vary across generations and between rural and urban women, with contraceptive pills being the most common. Natural rhythm methods were very popular until the 1970s in many rural areas and amongst older couples. It was initially a source of wonder to me that vasectomy was rarely discussed by Hungarian couples. It is not promoted by the medical profession because sterilisation for men and women is viewed as a very drastic measure for totally restricting births. The whole area of population policy legislation is certainly an instructive one within the Hungarian context (see Corrin, 1992). One aspect of governmental policy concerning population measures has recently raised the level of debate concerning abortion within society. This was the question of whether or not to alter the existing abortion law.

Within the new circumstances of more 'open' government it became clear that the politicians were content to let the two 'sides' in this debate – the Church and anti-abortion groups, and the feminist network and pro-choice groups – publicly raise the subject, whilst they seemed to 'wait and see'. When collecting signatures for a petition initiated by the feminist network, which called for no change in the present law and for choice for women, in August 1990, I and two members of the network had some fascinating conversations with women about the proposed changes, the need for abortion to remain relatively freely available to women[6] and we could see for ourselves the generational differences amongst women on this subject. At first we thought that perhaps the younger women would be less interested in signing because the issue of abortion was not one that personally affected them as yet. On discussing this with some of them though, it became clear that they did not want to lead the same lives that their mothers had led, having to work so hard and to put their children in child-care institutions. Essentially, what the young women were saying was that they wanted to create different futures for themselves. How they would attempt to do this was not clear. [7]

WOMEN THEMSELVES

From Virginia Woolf's 'I' to Simone de Beauvoir's 'What is a woman?' women have persistently sought answers to the question 'Who or what is a woman?'.[8] There was ample evidence in my discussions with women, and in Hungarian writings concerning women that many women felt that forces beyond their control were often shaping their own images of themselves, and at the most extreme end these were images of failure. Such negative stereotypes of women often engendered guilt, failure and lack of pride, which in turn could lead to depression and even alcoholism. In her work on women and alcoholism Zsuzsa Valkai tries to outline which factors seem important in motivating women towards alcoholism and a lack of self-esteem is certainly a major one:

> We all have critical or heavy times, mainly when things do not happen as we would like them to. None the less it is possible that we women doubt a lot in ourselves, we blame ourselves because of being unlucky, more times than men do, because we are expected to have a sexual role by our cultural traditions, a woman can only feel herself fully well not when she is a self-developed independent being, but when she lives with a man in a relationship of dependency.
>
> (Valkai, 1986: 131)

These sentiments speak volumes about the hidden pressures under which women in Hungary, and elsewhere in the world, live.

This notion of a 'sexual role' is by no means a new one, yet has always escaped definition and generally discussion. It certainly relates to the 'otherness' of women in a male-defined world. Women are seen to have a 'sexual role' or a 'maternal role' or a 'family role' or a 'something-else role' whereas men just are, or so it seems. Men living alone do so through choice or strength, or disappointment with their previous partner. Women living alone in Hungary and many other countries of the world, are often pitied. Such women who have chosen to live independently from men, sometimes with other women and children, sometimes alone, have, it seems, often been feared by men and as such are then reviled. Sexual relationships outside marriage are not as socially unacceptable now in Hungary as they would have been in the recent past, but the desperate housing shortage does create all sorts of practical difficulties. By relationships outside marriage I am referring to couples 'living together' rather than married people involved in extra-marital affairs.

The high divorce rate in Hungary has shown that with many women sueing for divorce on the grounds of alcoholism or cruelty from husbands, the situation is far from rosy. Whilst breakdowns of sexual relationship within marriage are not generally discussed, this does not necessarily mean that such reasons for couples parting do not exist. In schools, sexual education either does not occur, or is veiled in embarrassment on the part of the teachers and pupils. In magazines, such as *The Communist Youth Paper*, when sexuality was discussed, it was generally written about in fairly crude terms and rarely in terms of emotional and physical satisfaction.

For lesbians things are very difficult in Hungary, as in many other parts of the world. Certainly, if sex is viewed as primarily to create children and 'families' then lesbian sex would seem either irrelevant or unhealthily sensuous or selfish. Homosexuals do not fit into the hard workers and good mother roles that the Hungarian state has long expounded for Hungarian women. Homosexual acts for certain men are still illegal as 'offences against the family and youth'. There is only one publicly-known homosexual rights group in Hungary at present, the National Gay Council, which has featured in the Alliance of Young Democrats' (FIDESZ)[9] magazine *Magyar Narancs* (*Hungarian Orange*). This group set up in 1990, keeps a relatively low profile owing to the persisting open hostility to homosexuals (see Corrin, 1992). There are a few gay men's bars in Budapest, the popular 'Egyetem' having long been established as a meeting place for men, but there are no such places for lesbians to meet as yet. Women still gather in underground Metro stations, and some other 'known' places. I was given to understand that in the past few decades gay men and lesbians married each other because of strong social and state pressures. As marital status was quite often considered crucial to some jobs, such marriages helped the people concerned to get some form of apartment – eventually. Still, very few people discuss homosexuality and even the most open-minded people in Hungary still seem to view homosexuality at best 'a bit unnatural'.

One expression that became widespread within Hungary during the late 1970s and early 1980s, which I think was unique to Hungary, was the 'child-care syndrome', or 'GYES' disease. In her book *From the child-care allowance to the child-care benefit* (*A Gyestöl a Gyedig*) Dr Erika Sándorné Horváth writes of the trade union research on women claiming the allowance; it shows that a significant proportion of them are suffering from 'neurotic illnesses'.[10] Some women who are at home alone all day, often with a partner who has a second or third job for most of the evening, and who live in a very small flat with young children, are driven to taking sedatives, to unlimited smoking and often to drinking alcohol. The trade union research cites women in the cities, and gave as the primary reasons the lack of any company, the narrowing of living possibilities and wanting a job. Among villagers these symptoms were not as apparent because the living conditions differed. The extended family network amongst women is more apparent in the countryside, as there is more female unemployment; housing conditions, whilst often poor, are not generally as cramped as in the high-rise estates in cities. Possibilities for having more than one job are somewhat more limited in villages.

Dr András Veer wrote a series in the *Women's Journal* (*Nök Lapja*) entitle d 'Disease that has a manifold face' ('Betegseg, amelynek szaz arca van'), where he argued that caring for a young child is a critical time in a woman's life. She is taken out of her regular environment, the rhythm of her life, and often isolated in a way that she can scarcely bear. For Dr Mária Szilagyi, a psychologist working with neurosis patients in the VIIIth district of Budapest, many of the women with whom she talked 'are not alcoholics, they only congregate together, they get nervous because they cannot fulfill the desired purpose for which they get the allowance' (Horváth, 1986: 62). Of course such situations were not formed purely on the basis of women being at home on the allowance. Whilst this is often the primary reason they gave, other secondary reasons included growing up with negative identifications with images of motherhood, or feeling a less feminine quality or 'role'. Feeling alone, uncared for and with nobody to share experiences with was certainly a common feeling.

These women's relationship to motherhood, fulfilling certain expected 'roles' within the home – or not feeling able to do so – were central. Women apparently felt something of a 'superwomen complex', in terms of believing (whether or not their husbands, families, friends did so) that they should be wonderful mothers, cooks and cleaners all day, and adorable sex creatures at night. This theme – just how much is expected of women, especially 'sucessful' women – crops up again and again in many different ways.

For those young women who definitely do want something different from their mothers' lives, from rushing from work to home, paid work to unpaid work, with little free time for themselves or their children, the future may at this point seem brighter. Yet perhaps the evidence of this 'child-care sydrome' is something to be considered. These women were caring for children under the old system. Some of the current nostalgia for spending time within the home overlooks sheer economic necessities and the possible lack of future opportunities for women within the more differentiated market-oriented conditions developing in Hungary today.

ANTI-EQUALITY DEBATE AND FEMINISM

That there has been no actual feminist debate or dialogue within Hungary until 1990 or 1991 is a measure of how controlled discussions were concerning women's identity. An unusual and very destructive situation arose in the early 1980s in Hungary – mainly within intellectual circles in Budapest but there was a 'ripple out' effect – concerning a 'men's rebellion'. Katalin Hanak noted that the western neo-conservative attack in the early 1980s considered the women's movement one of their targets. The so-called 'silent majority' in the USA condemned the legal possibility of abortion based on individual decision: 'According to other conservative trends, the preference given to minorities in a disadvantaged position and to women in the labour market was interpreted as a discrimination against whites and men' (Hanak, 1984: 160). The speeding up of legal, economic, cultural and family equality for women caused a form of anti-women campaign, open or concealed, in everyday political and academic life. Hanak viewed this anti-women lobby as primarily concerned with the interests and existence of life (that is, the primary interests) of men. This debate in Hungary was accelerated in 1982 with several dramatic writings (Biró). These authors argued that the situation of men was worse than that of women and attempted to prove this by instancing an increasing trend: middle-aged men were dying in higher numbers than women in Hungary and at a younger age. The responsibility for this worsening situation was to a small extent placed within society (environmental damage and overworking) but the primary blame was attached to women. Women, it was claimed, over-used and abused their emancipation, using it only for having children, after which they left the men. Such women knew only rights, they did not know duties.[11] Rather than trying to reach an understanding these men searched for a scapegoat, making a basic problem of society into a fault in the personal lives of women. It is possible that within some of these writings there was also an intention to shock.[12]

Rather than this work being dismissed as narrow-minded and prejudiced, it was recognised in Hungary that it must point, even indirectly, to the belief that men's rights have been injured by women's liberation. Within all this debate, in terms of whether the positive effects for women and men have still resulted in imbalanced relationships, there are very mixed impressions and beliefs about feminism. In her work Judit Sas argues that the 'blind feminism' which turns against men did not take men's problems into consideration at all, nor the identity problems which derive from the fact that they themselves tended to live through the situation 'like losers'. This probably hindered men in forming new roles. Yet it was recognised that the men's rebellion is similarly short-sighted in that it is unable to recognise that women's liberation is not only of interest to women but it has great advantages from the men's point of view. Sadly, the swing toward biological explanations by the anti-equality group had important repercussions within Hungarian society, especially within the context of the very controlled, if not overtly biased, media representation of women's movements, feminist and otherwise. Feminism was portrayed within the Hungarian media as something unnatural and very selfish, certainly not something to which Hungarian women would wish to relate. When asked her opinion of women's movements' demands that men share all housework, one middle-aged mother of two explained,

> No. It isn't natural in Hungary. I could follow the lifestyle of couples where the woman is too manlike, too strong and who wants to divide all the work 50: 50. These marriages after a time break down. . . . It is too much for our culture that women are so strong and so equal because changes here in Hungary in all areas are *very* slow. Traditions are very deep.
>
> (Corrin, 1992)

The persuader word 'natural' is certainly much (ab)used in the debates about women's equality, and it is something which the media has had a hand in emphasising – that Hungarian women are 'naturally' kind, gentle, loving mothers and wives and not hard-hearted, selfish, grasping, 'feminist-type women', like certain feminists elsewhere. This has its effect. When asked if she knew much of the women's movements elsewhere, one young woman who was very well read and had an intellectual job which enabled her to travel occasionally to western Europe replied,

> No, very little. Only from gossip – very funny or strange things. For example, that they hate men, or they want men to bear children, etc. They make it all seem ridiculous here.
>
> (Corrin, 1992)

This was not an uncommon response; many women believed that, on the basis of what they knew of the women's liberation movements in, say, western Europe, they would not wish to be associated with it. They stated that problems between men and women should be sorted out within the family, and all stressed the need for more communication, more face-to-face talking between men and women.

Some students were interviewed on this subject by their lecturer, Pál Tamás, in 1987; he notes that: 'for the boys this is a rather dangerous and hardly conceivable women's aspiration for power', whereas the young women, whilst not identifying themselves as feminist ('this would mean something unwomanly'), were of the opinion that feminism is not an aggressive phenomenon. Overall though, in their opinion, the successful woman and the feminist are at opposite poles. Tamás noted that:

> According to 9 out of 10 recently interviewed professional women, the feminist has in some way become disappointed in the other sex. This disappointment is transferred into an ideology.
>
> (Tamás, 1987: 5)

Yet this debate is certainly not currently considered to be of much importance within Hungarian society.

Such attitudes against 'feminisms' were apparent in the recent experiences of the Feminista Hálózat (Feminist Network) in Hungary, in that there was doubt whether the network should be called 'feminist', as many women in Hungary still view feminism as a negative, somewhat embittered movement, rather than as a positive force for change and development.

In the present political climate, though, it is useful to note here the complex arguments which tend to separate certain beliefs about 'rights'. The old distinction of socialist rights has come to be challenged by different groups within Hungary. The Hungarian socialist right to free medical treatment now entails very poor medical treatment, regardless of the tipping system, because of the inadequate infrastructure of the health service generally, within a crisis-stricken economy. For women the right to work lost all meaning over the years as it was associated with the total exhaustion of working all day in paid work and most evenings and weekends at home. So women's right to choose with reference to abortion may not be the first argument that will be taken up by most Hungarian women. Yet women's right to control their child-bearing is viewed as a necessity by many Hungarian women. Women writing as 'concerned citizens' in reply to a letter in a newspaper in 1990 calling for restrictions on abortion helped to regenerate women's activism in defence of their rights.

ATTITUDES REGARDING WOMEN AND WOMEN'S POLITICS

When considering how state forces and societal developments interact in the Hungarian context, women's perceptions of and involvement in this interaction are often either ignored or seriously undervalued. Here the concept of citizenship is crucial to understanding. It has long been argued that the concept of citizenship brings with it notions of inequality. In western market-oriented systems status and social class are often contradictory forces within citizenship claims. Whilst certain state structures attempted to guarantee equality of status in society, social-class barriers perpetuated inequality. In the so-called 'state socialist' countries such as Hungary social-class barriers had supposedly been cleared away and indeed were certainly blurred under the Kádárist compromise. But issues of status remained very obviously on the societal agenda. Status was very often measured in economic terms in Hungary as well as by influence. Being a party member brought with it a kind of status, certainly in so far as bureaucrats were able to set the agenda for economically-generated differentiation within Hungarian society. Party members also reaped financial rewards through a variety of accepted practices, some corrupt. Yet, within other areas of Hungarian life being an oppositionist also brought with it some status, in the form of dignity – a concept often used within Hungary today.

It is important to consider the 'equalising' effect of citizenship in terms of how the state forces viewed women as a collective entity in Hungary. From 1948 Hungarian state forces seemed to play a large role in constructing and shaping this collective identity. The adoption of Soviet-styled Marxist-Leninist ideology had its effects within Hungarian life. The *modus vivendi* reached under Kádár's government was one in which lip-service was still paid to state-generated equality (See Szelényi, 1983 on inequalities). Women's 'emancipation' was ensured and women were considered to have achieved, or more often to have been awarded, 'equality'. As noted earlier the concept of equality often confuses more than it clarifies. With whom were Hungarian women supposed to be equal and within which categories? Were working-class Hungarian women, or poor women, equal with poor men? Were poor Romany women on equal terms with poor Hungarian women? Were intellectual women supposedly equal with less educated women or men, or with intellectual men? There are many and varied elements to the different groupings within societies. There were of course party women, rich women, poor women, and their concerns remained nuanced and various. Yet it is essential to stress that the Hungarian state systematically produced policies based on a specific collective identity – 'women' – which cut across traditional social and economic divisions.

Women have never been and indeed cannot become one 'category'. They do make up half of the world and so are involved in many different arenas of life. Despite the fact that around 98 per cent of Hungarians are of Magyar origin, cultural and ethnic diversity amongst women in Hungary exists. These are most marked for those women of Romany origin, with other differences for rural Slavic women and women of German descent, and the ethnic Hungarians from Romania. Of course fundamental differences exist in economic activities, household patterns and life-styles amongst Hungarian women and the urban/rural divide is a very important one. As noted when considering citizenship, the issues of class and status often outweigh sex in making up women's perceptions of themselves.[13] But, and it is a big but, reasons for considering women as a collective entity include:

1 the fact that Hungarian policy makers and scholars consider women as an entity in policy-making and sociological study;
2 the fact that women suffer inequalities because of their ability to give birth to children and thereby are ascribed gender attributes which are socially and often officially constructed. Many such expectations placed upon women result in their direct and indirect oppression *as women*.

It is relevant to note that one of the letters which sparked off women's activity countering the anti-abortion groups such as *Igen* (Yes) was a letter written to a newspaper by two women who signed themselves 'concerned citizens'. This is a new departure in political activity – that women feel able to voice concerns as citizens rather than by seeing women's rights within the statist categorical mould. That citizens are concerned about abortion rights as a *social* issue rather than women being concerning about abortion rights as a *women's* issue is a step forward. Women's (and men's) activity as citizens on social issues is the site of the 'great debate' about the existence of an active 'civil society'.

Citizenship is clearly not a universal concept so that issues of class, ethnicity, and status are often held, sometimes in contradiction within each citizen. For women especially, careful and nuanced considerations of relationships to citizenship rights, notions and claims are required. Certain rights and claims are negotiable and it seems that at least a start is being made in this direction in Hungary today. It is to be hoped that women's voices can be heard in the coming years, putting questions within the various debates about the future directions of Hungarian society.

NOTE ON METHODOLOGY

The origins of this work stretch back to 1982 when I first discovered Hungarian sociological writings. My first visit to Hungary was in 1984 when I had overcome some of my worries about 'researching women's experience', given the current debates about women objectifying others in their work or making careers 'off women's backs'. My aim was to privilege women's experience of change, and with close contact with many women in Hungary over the last seven years I am now pleased to be writing about these interpretations so that they can feed back into some of the debates now developing within Hungary. My way of working was ethnographic in that I spent as much time as I could with women, discussing everyday concerns and particular aspects of their lives, such as work, child-care, money, personal identity and sexuality, hopes and dreams and political change. Sometimes I taped more formal 'interviews' which were always open-ended and included exchanges of information from me about 'western' women and feminism in all manner of different aspects. I also transcribed documentary and other material written by Hungarian sociologists and interviewed people in Hungary who had worked on 'the woman question'. It was relatively easy to spend time with women from various backgrounds and age groups in Budapest, but less easy because of time, money and access, to get to know women elsewhere. This study is to some extent Budapest-focused, but many women now living in Budapest spoke of their lives elsewhere and some women's experience is included from Debrecen, Pécs and Györ as well as surrounding areas of Budapest.

NOTES

1 I use 'state' as a useful shorthand description of the structures and duties of those involved in the various bureaucracies, governmental organisations and decision-making circles.

2 Elizabeth Wilson in her book *Women and the Welfare State*, London, Tavistock, 1977 argues that the state not only tries to define women but also regulates their sexuality.

3 Parallels have been made between feminist arguments concerning women's liberation and similar issues for many ethnic and nationalist movements. This issue is also pivotal for lesbians and gay men. What is involved is not just a radical redefinition of 'rights' but the valuing of the right to non-assimilation, that is, the right to be different. Being different should not mean having to assume a lesser social status.

4 I use quotation marks here since definitions of what is 'intellectual', 'middle class' or 'working class' vary widely. The conversations regarding the group took place in English and so the words used roughly correspond in general terms but the whole issue of class in Hungary is something still to be fully considered.

5 This was noted by Antal Lászlo in his paper 'Natural Birth in Hungary: The Obstacles to the Changes in Obstetrics', a paper given at the 1991 Annual Convention, Hungarian Sociological Association 24–28 June 1991, Budapest.

6 Limitations were placed on induced abortions in 1974 but these were lifted in 1989. Extreme anti-abortion groups would prefer abortion to be banned outright whilst others would allow it if the mother's health is endangered.

7 Many women fear that if abortion restrictions were replaced, or indeed if it was outlawed altogether, women's lives would again be at risk because of back-street or illegal abortions. Given the high incidence of teenage sex in Hungary and the lack of cheap contraception for girls under 18, these young women could be badly affected by legal changes.

8 For a detailed discussion of this subject look initially at Ergas 1986: 299–313.

9 FIDESZ is the Youth Party in Hungary with representatives in Parliament. When members reach the age of 35 they must leave the Party.

10 There is ample literature of criticisms concerning how diagnoses are made against women, sometimes in terms of male (and even female) doctors not listening, believing and taking seriously women's health complaints and needs.

11 An aspect of this rebellion was maintenance payments – many men believed it was contemptible to make contributions (voluntary or forced) to their ex-wives who were looking after the children. As custody tends to be awarded to mothers, they in turn remain in the marital home, so that with the housing shortage in Hungary men do in practice lose a home of their own.

12 It was unfortunate, in so far as it added weight to the anti-equality group, that Biró was interviewed on television on New Year's Eve 1982 by a woman who was to an extent aggressive in her style of questioning. Biró was literally only able to get a few (incoherent) words in here and there, so appeared in a strange way vindicated in maintaining his stand about the misuse of women's liberation.

13 This distinction between women's ideas about identity and the statist notions of women as a category clearly point up the differences which cross-cut the outcomes – often unintended – of certain policy decisions. Sex and gender are factors amongst others in building up women's identity, yet for the state authorities gender often becomes not only the major defining characteristic for all women but an elastic conception which serves to blur all other divisions.

REFERENCES

Hungarian sources

Biró, Dávid (1982) 'A "teremtés koronái" es a "gyengébb nem"' ('The "masterpiece of creation" and the "weaker sex"') *Valóság* no. 9, 1982.

Hanak, Katalin (1984) 'Fantasticality – Reality – Fantasy', in *Jel Kép (Symbol)*, Special edition, Mass Communications Research Centre, Budapest.

Sándorné, Horváth Erika (1986) *A Gyestöl a Gyedig (From the Child Care Allowance to the Child Care Benefit)*, Kossuth Könyvkiadó, Budapest.

Tamás, Pál (1987) 'Hova Létt a Magyar Féminizmus?' ('Where has Hungarian feminism gone?') *Élet és Irodalom (Life and Literature)* 1 May: 5.

Valkai, Zsuzsa (1986) *Miért Isznak a Nök? (Why do women drink?)* Magvetö Kiadó, Budapest.

English sources

Corrin, Chris (ed.) (1992a) *Superwomen and the Double Burden: Women's Experience of Change in Central and Eastern Europe and the Former Soviet Union*, Scarlet Press, London.

Corrin, Chris (1992b) *Magyar Women: Hungarian Women's Lives from the 1940s to the 1990s*, Macmillan Educational.

Eberhardt, Eva (1991) *Women of Hungary*, Women of Europe Supplement, Commission of the European Communities, no. 32, January, Brussels.

Ergas, Yasmine (1986) 'Convergencies and tension between collective identity and social citizenship rights: Italian women in the seventies', in Friedlander, Cook, Kessler-Harris and Smith-Rosenburg (eds) *Women in Culture and Politics: A Century of Change*, Indiana University Press, Bloomington.

Fehér, Ferenc, Heller, Agnes and Márkus György (1983) *Dictatorship over Needs: An Analysis of Soviet Societies*, Basil Blackwell, Oxford.

Ferge, Zsuzsa (1979) *A Society in the Making: Hungarian Social and Societal Policy 1945–79*, Penguin, Harmondsworth.

Hann, C.M. (1980) *Tazlar: a Village in Hungary*, Cambridge University Press, Cambridge.

Konrád, György and Szelényi, Iván (1979) *The Intellectuals on the Road to Class Power*, Harvester, Brighton.

Márkus, Mária (1973) 'Factors influencing the fertility of women: the case of Hungary', *International Journal of Sociology of the Family*, no. 2.

Márkus, Mária (1975) 'Change in the function of socialization and models of the family', *International Review of Sociology*, no. 3.

Rakovski, Marc (1978) *Towards an East European Marxism*, Allison & Busby, London.

Rich, Adrienne (1972) *Of Woman Born: Motherhood as Experience and Institution*, Virago, London.

Rowbotham, Sheila (1973) *Woman's Consciousness, Man's World*, Penguin, Harmondsworth.

Scott, Hilda (1982) *Sweden's Right to be Human: Sex Role Equality, the Goal and the Reality*, Allison & Busby, London.

Sharpe, Sue (1984) *Double Identity: the Lives of Working Mothers*, Penguin, Harmondsworth.

Szelényi, Iván (1983) *Urban Inequalities under State Socialism*, Oxford University Press, Oxford.

Wilson, Elizabeth (1977) *Women and the Welfare State*, Tavistock, London.

10 Feminism and Bolshevism

Two worlds, two ideologies

Marina Malysheva
Translated by Hilary Pilkington

Even the most inveterate sceptics and pessimists, who are prepared to deny there have been any real changes in recent years in the Soviet Union, are forced to concede one thing: that our awareness and understanding of the past has changed to such a degree that even if a volte-face were to occur, people could not return to their former way of thinking. The history of Bolshevism has been substantially reinterpreted and the path to socialism re-evaluated. The only subject as yet to receive virtually no discussion is the emergence and defeat of the women's movement in Russia, and the place and role of feminism in social development. These are subjects which remain shrouded in silence: a silence which has resounded for so long that, by now, it screams from the depths of our existence, 'Why?'. This chapter sets out to answer this question by re-evaluating Bolshevik ideology through the prism of feminism. Such a re-evaluation requires a reconsideration of the history of the pre-revolutionary Russian women's movement, including an assessment of its level and form of development within the broader spectrum of nineteenth-century European women's movements. In the light of this, the impact of Bolshevism on the women's movement and the experience of Russian women under Soviet rule will be considered. Such a reassessment of Russian women's history is vital for an understanding of the current emergent women's movements in Soviet Russia – a subject which is taken up in the next chapter by Valentina Konstantinova.

THE WOMEN'S MOVEMENT BEFORE THE REVOLUTION

The origins of feminism the world over, I would contend, are in 'good deeds' (*blagodeianie*), taking the concrete form of organisations to help those in need.[1] 'Good deeds' is defined here not as 'charity', but in the Christian sense of the word, which retains a wider and deeper meaning.

Feminism in Russia, as elsewhere, began with such good deeds and its first concrete manifestation was the founding in 1812 of the St Petersburg 'Society of Patriotic Ladies' which declared its main task to be the easing of the burden of widows, orphans and other helpless people. At the end of that year, the society was renamed the 'St Petersburg Women's Patriotic Society'. Although such societies may appear to be a long way from contemporary feminist movements, which focus on the demand for equal rights for both sexes, their importance lies in the fact that charitable work provided women with their first common experience of social activity. This need not be explained by patriarchal, conservative, or biologically essentialist notions that charity and caring for the suffering is closer to female nature: the fact that women's activity was of a 'caring' nature has its roots in socio-economic circumstances, namely the absence of women from highly-educated professions and administrative work. At the beginning of the nineteenth century, the majority of women were without even an elementary education and to raise the question of the admission of women to higher education was considered extremely seditious. For this reason, women had to begin by being active in the spheres to which they had access: they made use of what space they had within their patriarchally delimited education and daily life.

This activity naturally led women to begin to work towards achieving the right to education, without which the recognition of their individual and human rights was inconceivable. By 1816 there appeared, under the jurisdiction of the aforementioned society, a women's educational institution: the House of Diligence (*Dom Trudoliubiia*), which later became the Elizabeth School (*Elizavetinskoe Uchilishche*). These schools, which became widely known as the private schools of the St Petersburg Women's Patriotic Society, were ostensibly founded to care for homeless children. Later the society was transferred to the department of institutions of the Empress Maria and bore the name 'The Imperial Society of the Women of St Petersburg'. By the end of the century (1895) it had seven boarding schools and eight non-residential schools under its jurisdiction. By 1840 the total number of female educational establishments in the country had risen to twenty. Institutes had been opened in Odessa, Astrakhan, Kiev, Belostok, Kazan', Warsaw, Saratov, Irkutsk, and Tiflis, using money donated by the local nobility. In 1845 the Central Council of Women's Educational Institutes was established and societies to promote individual branches of women's education began to spring up everywhere.

In contrast to other European women's organisations, it was this movement for the right to education which was to become the most defining feature of the women's movement in Russia. During the 1860s, the movement for the education of women was definitively formed and threw up its own ideologues who subsequently became ardent fighters for the rights of women. In March and May 1868 requests from 400 women were sent to the rector of St Petersburg University, asking for the setting up of 'lectures or courses for women'. Among the petitioners were about a hundred women of the highest social circle, many of whose names were to become part of the history and cultural heritage of the nineteenth century: E.I. Konradi, N.V. Stasova, V.P. Tarnovskaia, E.N. Voronina, O.A. Mordvinova, A.P. Filosofova and M.V. Trubnikova to name but a few. A key task of a women's history of Russia must be to return to and reread the great and varied work of these women. But the 1860s should not only be remembered as the time when the question of the admission of women to higher education was finally raised, for this decade also marked the greatest wave of the Russian democratic movement of which feminism was an integral part. In this period, 'feminism' was seen not as a destructive, isolationist or bourgeois movement but as a philosophy and ideology which appeared in the philosophical and journalistic works of the most democratically and progressively minded people, regardless of their sex.

Indeed, in Russia, it was a man, N.I. Pirogov, who was to become the chief ideologue of the women's movement. This should not surprise us since it is not uncharacteristic of the experience of other European countries. Men such as John Stuart Mill in Britain and Von Hippel in Germany were at the forefront of feminism as a brand of social thought. It is also worth noting that although Mary Wollstonecraft's *A Vindication of the Rights of Women* was published long before J.S. Mill's *On the Subjection of Women*, Wollstonecraft had been strongly influenced by another man – Condorcet – and, in France, Olympe de Gouges formulated her *Declaration of the Rights of Woman* as an analogy to the *Declaration of the Rights of Man*. Pirogov's importance was that his work *Pedagogical Tasks* started a sharp polemic in Russia about the place and role of women in society, a polemic in which all the serious socio-political and literary journals enthusiastically participated. These journals included the journal *Rassvet* (*Dawn*), which had published the remarkable work of the Russian pedagogue, V.Ia. Stoiunin, 'Something on our contemporary woman'; the journal *Istoricheskii Vestnik* (*Historical Herald*), which, in 1885, published Stoiunin's answer to Pirogov's *Pedagogical Tasks*; the journal *Vestnik Evropy* (*Courier of Europe*), in which S.T. Aksakov edited a section called 'Family chronicle'; the weekly journal of culture and politics *Voprosy Zhizni* (*Questions of Life*); the journals *Russkaia Mysl'* (*Russian Thought*), *Nash*

Sovremennik (Our Contemporary), not to mention the journal *Zhenskoe Obrazovanie (Women's Education)*. From 1869, the journal *Otechestvennie Zapiski (Notes from the Fatherland)* ran a monthly chronicle under the heading 'News on women's affairs' and by the mid-1880s, the volume of literature on the 'woman question' had grown so much that in 1887 *Severnii Vestnik (Northern Herald)* had to publish a special bibliographical index.

Evidence suggests, therefore, that Russian women in the last century were no worse, and perhaps even better educated than in many Western European countries. In Paris, Russian women gained access to education before French women themselves. Before the 1880s there were no women's gymnasia in France at all and the 'Society for the dissemination of education among women' built a closed secondary educational institution, the 'École normale', primarily catering for foreign women. In Russia at that time there were not only women's gymnasia but also higher educational courses in Petrograd – courses at the Medical Academy – from which several women doctors who took part in the 1878 war had graduated. The standards set in women's secondary educational institutions abroad, moreover, appear to have been lower than those in Russia. 'As regards our secondary educational institutions . . .', wrote E. Likhacheva, 'at the beginning of the eighties, the course of study offered was better than that offered at similar institutions in Europe, and the same can be said of the pedagogical education of our women. It was wider than that given abroad' (Likhacheva, 1901: 646). Catherine Ilmen, from Britain, agreed with this. Writing in the journal *Review of Reviews* in May 1904, she reported with admiration that,

> The education of Russian girls shows considerable similarity to that of English-speaking girls, although differentiated by greater freedom. If a Russian girl does not so wish, she is not tied to the kitchen or the nappies. She has an unquenchable striving for knowledge, systematisation and activity. The Russian girl is an idealist and forgets herself. In trying to preserve her ideal, she completely ignores the practical side of life. The Russian girl studies a lot. She is the most educated of all European girls. She studies not only foreign languages but also foreign history and geography – she knows them like her own language. Without any exaggeration, one could say that the fifteen year-old Russian secondary-school girl (*gimnazistka* or *institutka*) can put a French girl who has completed a history course to shame.
> (Ilmen, 1904: 8)

Despite the vision portrayed in post-revolutionary history-books, therefore, Russian women were not an illiterate mass and their situation was enviable if viewed in the wider European context. In 1880 the number of women finishing secondary school was only slightly lower than the number of men. In 1916 the statutes of the Petrograd Polytechnical Institute were confirmed by the Minister of Public Education and marked the first women's polytechnical institute in the world; there was nothing of its kind in either Britain or America. This is not to suggest that we should laud the tsarist regime, or conclude that it was deeply concerned with the progress of women's education. However, evidence about some of the tsar's ministers might suggest that a rethinking of our views is warranted. The Russian Minister of Internal Affairs, Maliutin, for example, made great personal sacrifices to ensure that public courses for women could be set up. In January 1870 he and his wife opened up their own house in order that the courses might take place and, in 1872, it was he who secured the opening of higher educational courses for women in medicine at the Military Medical Academy.

In order to understand just how brave this was, one need only look at the note sent by Count Shuvalov, head of the Third Section of His Imperial Majesty's Chancellery, which claimed that among the signatories of the note received by St Petersburg University concerning the establishment of the courses were such individuals, 'whose participation in the establishment, and moreover in the influencing of the courses might lead to the closing of the institution and, ultimately, to various false interpretations and an unfavourable impression' (Likhacheva, 1901: 520). In the second year of the courses, moreover, the head of the St Petersburg police wrote,

> state and criminal law is being taught by two young professors, Gradovskii and Tagantsev, apparently because it is the fashion to do so.... They are preaching dangerous truths, in Gradovskii's case about state power and the form of government.
>
> ('Note from Trepor', cited in Likhacheva, 1901: 526)

Undoubtedly the spread of education among women was seen by the tsarist regime as a threat to the conservative structures of society, but the authorities already understood better than a decade earlier that prohibition was not the answer. The absence of their own universities had initiated a mass migration of women abroad. In 1873 more than a hundred Russian women were studying at Zurich University. By the mid-1870s there were even more, and the government was finally convinced of the necessity of rational measures to attract Russian women away from foreign universities. In 1875 a special governmental report was published on the provision for women in Russia of the opportunities in higher education which they were seeking abroad.

Thus there is every reason to suggest that the women's movement in Russia was adequately developed and that, at times, it was in advance of the movement of other countries with which it was inextricably linked. In 1878, when news emerged of the opening in St Petersburg of the higher education courses for women with their systematic, university-style teaching, the whole of Europe was excited. John Stuart Mill sent a letter to the founders of the higher educational courses for women in St Petersburg:

> It was with a sense of pleasure, mixed with admiration, that I learned of the enlightened and courageous women in Russia who had raised the question of the participation of their sex in various branches of higher education – history, philology and science, including medical practice – in order that the conspicuous forces of the academic world be turned to the benefit of higher education for women. This is what the educated nations elsewhere in Europe have been demanding for themselves with ever increasing determination, but without success. Thanks to you, dear ladies, Russia may achieve this goal before the others.
>
> (Likhacheva, 1901: 508)

Unrestricted travel abroad facilitated the dissemination among Russian women of new views and ideas about their intellectual capabilities and their social roles. Although the opening of the higher educational courses for women in St Petersburg in 1881 led to a fall in the number of Russian women studying abroad to nine, the closing of the courses in medicine increased the numbers once again to hundreds. Of 152 female students studying in Paris in 1889–90, only 24 were French, 8 were British and 107 were Russian; 123 of these students were studying in the faculty of medicine, of whom 92 were Russian. Subsequently many of these women became members of international women's organisations and formed various women's organisations in Russia. In 1904, for example, the journal *Zhenskii Vestnik* began to appear, edited by a talented and intellectual woman, M.I. Pokrovskaia, a doctor by education but also a brilliant polemicist. The journal carried monthly reports on the women's movement in Russia and abroad and on the activity of women's organisations, as well as reviews of books and brochures on the 'woman question'. The journal remained in existence until the Revolution, and in 1917 Pokrovskaia published two brilliantly perceptive articles – 'The Revolution and humanity' and 'Two documents of contemporary civilisation' – about the bloody nightmare that our people were experiencing. The real significance of what this courageous woman wrote is only now beginning to penetrate our consciousness, which has been blocked for so long by class barriers. Arguing with the author of an article, published in *Pravda* on 17 May 1917 and discussing the expectations of the Revolution held by workers and peasants, Pokrovskaia wrote,

> We do not agree with the author's suggestion that, for the masses, the revolution means bread, land, and economic improvements rather than electoral rights, freedom of speech and parliament. The Russian people values spiritual blessings – this is obvious from its strivings in the religious sphere. If we are able to explain the meaning of rights and freedoms to the people, then its better elements will become staunch champions of these rights. Emphasising that, if they participate, the revolution will reward the people with bread, leads to the recruitment of support from the worst sections of society when the stability of the new system is dependent on support of its best sections.
>
> (Pokrovskaia, 1917: 67)

THE REVOLUTION AND THE WOMEN'S MOVEMENT

Nevertheless, the advent of the Revolution meant that the class struggle was to harness the women's movement for its own purposes. The 'Union of Women's Equality' was the first political organisation of Russian women in which two tendencies – the feminist and the social-democratic – were locked in struggle and, at the First All-Russian Women's Congress in December 1908, the Union split. This confrontation along party and class lines, which was being experienced throughout the country at that time, was inevitable. For the ideologues of Bolshevism the split was viewed as a great blessing, but for those who thought differently, it signified the great tragedy of a people who had been drawn into irreconcilable enmity. The journal *Zhenskaia Mysl'*, founded in 1909, interpreted the events as follows:

> One would think that the advantages for the struggle of uniting our forces would be obvious to all, but the hypnotic effect of party allegiance produces distorted interpretations, not only of theoretical constructs but of concrete facts as well. The Social-Democrats, ignoring all the facts, are trying to reduce the successes of the women's movement to the victories of the proletariat. On this occasion the premature interpretation concerned the marvellous outcome of the electoral struggle of Finnish women and it evoked an

authoritative refutation by a Finnish delegate, citizen Furuhjelm, 'Finnish women achieved their rights because they were supported by all parties, and not by democracy alone. One cannot even say that the Social-Democrats were the first to raise the question of women's equality, eight years ago. In fact the Finnish bourgeoisie had already made these demands twenty years ago'.

(Shapir, 1909: 8)

In many parts of Europe, therefore, the late nineteenth century witnessed growing claims by women for legal rights. As in Finland, the radical women's tendency formed in Germany at the end of the 1880s and led to the founding of the 'Frauenwohl' societies, which directly raised both the question of equality and of the protection of women workers. In Britain the movement began a little earlier: in 1869 single, tax-paying women were given the right to participate in municipal elections. In France the feminist movement began to develop from the middle of the nineteenth century, although no major political achievements were made before the end of the century. In Russia the end of the century also arrived without any success for the women's movement in the sphere of public law. Women who satisfied the property requirements were given the right to participate in *dvorianskii* (noble), *zemskii* (district) and municipal elections, but only via authorised male persons (male relatives or husbands). But does this mean that the credit for the struggle for women's equality should go not to the representatives of the bourgeoisie, who were present at its inception, but to Soviet power and the Bolsheviks?

BOLSHEVISM AND FEMINISM

The fanatical belief that the truth has been found and that there is no other truth makes Marxism a religion and, it would seem, our times are fated to witness the replacement of Christianity with this 'Godless' religion.

(Sipovskii, 1924: 113)

The first effect of Bolshevism was to sever the association in the minds of the Russian people of law, morality and religion. This was replaced with a crude and vulgar atheism which caused a militant lawlessness and arbitrariness among the population. The replacement of Christianity with Marxism meant that truth became only that which was in the interests of the working class, and its interests were equated with the interests of its elite – members of the party. People who did not accept these truths as expressing their interests had them beaten into them in concentration camps and in exile, and, if even this did not help, they were simply killed in order that the 'purity' of the truth of the elite be maintained.

This 'purity' of truth demanded the elimination of all opposition to the dictatorship of the proletariat, even if this opposition came from the weakest and most needy, even if it came from women. Hence, the All-Russian Women's Union – uniting thirty women's organisations – which should have been finally established in December 1917 at its congress, was not formed and the history of these thirty organisations soon came to an end. The regime did not require feminism as an oppositional force, it required obedient executors of its will. The final sentence on the feminist movement was passed by Clara Zetkin in 1920: 'feminism in essence remains non-revolutionary, and sometimes even counter-revolutionary' (Zetkin, in Milovidova, 1929: 23).

The aims of feminism were thus declared to be limited to the struggle with the privileges of men and with improving somewhat the position of women – essentially bourgeois women, without changing the nature of bourgeois society. Furthermore, the fanatical, all-embracing conviction that the root of all social conflict, including the conflict between men and women, is to be found in class contradictions, compelled the ideologues of Bolshevism to take their crusade into the realm of the private, into the ties of blood and kinship. Speaking at the united congress of the German Communist Party of independents in 1920, Clara Zetkin also said,

> We should not deceive ourselves about the fact that at the current time broad masses of working women articulate both their criticism of capitalism and their striving for communism predominantly in an emotional rather than a rational way. We must also acknowledge that the psychological characteristics of women, as well as their position, activity and sphere of interest, means that the dedication, self-sacrifice and other virtues which they show, tend to be directed towards a small number of people – their nearest and dearest. This attachment to their own flesh and blood often deprives women of the ability to be infused with a deeper feeling for their class.
>
> (*ibid.*: 300)

This 'weakness' of women led to a perceived need to emphasise the class nature of child-bearing and motherhood – indeed these could no longer exist outside the class struggle. Women ceased to be women, they ceased to be mothers, and became weapons of the class ideology of the proletariat in all its manifestations. Special institutions and organs were called for which could 'overcome all the political and social weaknesses of women', and 'teach women to see in communism not the hero of a lyrical poem but a messiah approaching, sword in hand' (*ibid.*: 300).

The living embodiment of this ideology was the figure of Liubov' Iarovaia who, by killing her White Guard husband in defence of the Revolution, became a symbol of dedication to one's revolutionary ideals for many generations of Soviet people.[2] This conflict in women between revolutionary and humanitarian principles is not unique to Russia, however. During the French Revolution many heroes, including women, emerged. They fought on both sides of the barricades, sometimes even going over from one side to the other. This is what happened to Olympe de Gouges, who proclaimed the *Declaration of the Rights of Women*. When revolution broke out, Gouges devoted herself completely to political life; her political pamphlets appeared almost daily. She gave passionate speeches at the Jacobins' club and at the meetings of the sansculottes. However, when Louis XVI was sentenced to death, Olympe de Gouges spoke in his defence in her article 'Défenseur officieux de Louis Capet au Président de la Convention Nationale' (1792). This was followed by a pamphlet in which she warned of the savage atrocities of Robespierre. Maximilian the Incorruptible was furious and the identification and arrest of the author of the pamphlet was ordered. Undeterred, de Gouges confessed to having written the pamphlet and sent Robespierre a letter in which she directly recounted the hundreds of people whom he had sent to the guillotine, and she suggested that the only honourable thing to do would be to throw himself into the Seine. For this Gouges, the daughter of a petty market-trader from Montauban, was beheaded on 4 November 1794. Her tragic death shows Robespierre in a particularly sinister and repulsive light.

God only knows how many women suffered the same fate on the guillotine of the Russian Revolution. Those who emigrated were able to oppose the ideology of Bolshevism and defend their opposing principles. But this was opposition from without – it was impossible to oppose from within. Meanwhile, the section of the Communist Academy responsible for the study of the theory and practice of the international women's movement proclaimed,

> The Soviet Union is the first state in the world where state power and the whole community consciously participates in the resolving of the women's question. If this enormous progress is to find its creative expression, millions of women must turn their convictions into deeds by their participation in socialist construction.

> (*ibid.*: 39)

Alongside the physical destruction, this kind of ideological deception led millions to believe in the righteousness of the system and, shut off from the rest of the world by the iron curtain, to consider almost all people living beyond the borders of the country to be their enemies. The press overflowed with terrible warnings, which peasants coming to the towns from the depths of the countryside, could not but believe.

> Soviet women should always remember our encirclement by capitalist forces whose secret services send spies and intelligence agents into the USSR. These enemies often choose women as their victims and try to use them to deceive and blackmail, to commit their crimes, and to damage our motherland. Spies do not stop at anything in their vile work. They pretend to be loyal friends, to be passionately in love and they often marry their victims in order to make them betray the socialist motherland.
>
> (*Zhenshchina v strane Sovetov*, 1938: 60–1)

The experience of women under Bolshevism has thus been one of the supplanting of the struggle for the rights of women by a struggle for the productivity of labour. The record targets of the five year plans had begun. The personality of the individual was dissolved into the producer. A new historical community of people was formed, the Soviet people, people without sex or flesh, possessed by the single idea of the construction of communism.

Furthermore, women's participation in socialist construction itself was not one of liberation but of co-option: the implementation of pseudo-equality. The realisation of a utopian state administered by even the most lowly kitchen assistant led to the destruction of the intelligentsia as these kitchen hands donned teachers' uniforms, doctors' coats or ministerial suits. It was only with great difficulty, and through their own supreme efforts, that women in tsarist Russia were able to gain equality in the professions with men. In 1897, in order to take up a position as a pharmacist, for example, a woman had to complete the full course of the girls' gymnasium, pass exams in Latin equivalent to the first four years of the boys' gymnasium and complete two years of vocational practice. After this she had to pass an exam to become an assistant pharmacist and, even after three years' experience as an assistant, she gained only the right to attend lectures on special courses attached to the Military Academy of Medicine. Only after attendance at these was she able to receive the title 'pharmacist'. By 1914 (17 years later) women constituted just 10 per cent of doctors (*ibid.*: 18).

In contrast, according to statistics cited in the booklet *Women in the Land of the Soviets*, published in Moscow in 1938, within the same number of years (from the Revolution to 1933), the number of women doctors rose twenty-fold. Thus by 1933 almost half of the 100,000 Soviet doctors were women (*ibid*.: 18). By anybody's reckoning this meant that doctors were being produced like blini and genuine professionalism was replaced with mass incompetence and passed off as the supreme achievement in sexual equality in the land of the Soviets. Is not this the reason why a whole new generation of medical personnel grew up who were fit for medical practice only in the Soviet Union? The same is true of the engineering profession. Before the Revolution the profession of factory engineer was relatively new and rare; there were probably no more than 12,000 such engineers in all and no more than a handful of women (Leikina-Svirskaia, 1971: 130). It was only in 1906 that the last bastion closed to women fell and new polytechnic courses for women were opened in St Petersburg. Under pressure from the women's movement, for the first time opportunities were made available to women to participate in the technical sphere. But it was only with incredible difficulty that a woman engineer was able to prove her right to receive an engineering diploma.

After the Revolution, the period of study required to qualify as an engineer was shortened and the targets for the training of engineers were sharply increased. Unqualified people, especially those who commanded the greatest trust and sympathy of the authorities, were often simply appointed to technical positions. Women were especially targeted for recruitment and by 1933 it was estimated that there were 36,000 women engineers and technicians, rising to 82,000 by 1936, a rate of 16,000 per year (*ibid*.: 18). This pseudo-achievement was demonstrated by endless comparisons with the number of women engineers in the USA – the *Women in the Land of Soviets* booklet noted that in America in 1930 there were only 113 women engineers. Even today the comparisons continue: we have more women engineers than America. What they omit to say, however, is that Soviet engineers, especially women, have long been little more than the workers' lackeys.

CONCLUSION: FROM FEMINISM TO BOLSHEVISM AND BACK AGAIN

The first and greatest difference between the pre- and post-revolutionary women's movement lies in the difference between feminism and Bolshevism. In old Russia, the women's movement was in opposition to the ruling regime and by its real, practical achievements and constant demands, it forced concessions from that regime. The struggle for access to education which characterised the pre-revolutionary women's movement was a valiant and important one. Although for us, born in the twentieth century, access to higher education seems unremarkable, for the young women at that time coming to St Petersburg or Moscow from the far reaches of Russia or from the Caucasus, it was a highly courageous step. This was especially the case for those young women from average or poor backgrounds who were supported by funds just for this purpose. Their action constituted an act of protest against ancient traditions and marked the beginning of the struggle for the recognition of their human dignity.

A second crucial difference lies in the fact that the pre-revolutionary movement never constrained itself by a single class position; it absorbed representatives from all nationalities and social strata. The legacy of Bolshevism, in contrast, is the vulgarisation of feminism, which finds its contemporary expression in the traditional and conservative consciousness which Bolshevism never rooted out. As a result, the journalistic debate about the 'woman question' today lags behind that of the last century. Today, as if this earlier polemic had never existed, the role of women as mothers and keepers of the hearth is emphasised. To some extent this is a natural reaction to the current difficulties of everyday life, to the neglect of children, and to the disintegration of the family. But natural does not mean most rational. Times have changed, and if change has bypassed us, then it is because we have lived for decades in isolation from the world and are out of touch with our own history.

Thirdly, Marxism's sole claim to truth meant the absorption of women into an all-embracing ideology. Since feminism is an international phenomenon, it was a natural victim of the closed society on which Bolshevism thrived. This is the most salient lesson for Russian women today, for they are now faced with the danger of being absorbed by a new and powerful ideology: the ideology of consumerism, which reduces women to the objects of sale. For women both these ideologies can be fought only with feminism, for it is feminism which brings the question of the dignity of women to the fore. Contemporary feminism places the human personality and individuality above all else and in so doing poses a challenge to both Bolshevism and patriarchy – for both are founded on the subordination of the individual to a hierarchy of roles.

NOTES

The translator would like to thank Dr Linda Edmondson for her invaluable assistance.

1 This notion of good deeds has been taken up again recently by the revived Lithuanian women's Catholic organisation 'Caritas'.

2 Liubov' Iarovaia is a character from a play by Trenev (1876–1945). The first performance of the play took place in 1926 and since then it has been performed regularly in all Soviet theatres. In 1941 he was awarded a State prize for his work.

REFERENCES

Ilmen, C. (1904) 'Girl's realm', *Zhenskii Vestnik*, no. 1.

Leikina-Svirskaia, V.R. (1971) *Russkaia Intelligentsiia 1900-1917*, Nauka, Moscow.

Likhacheva, E.O. (1901) *Materialy dlia Istorii Zhenskogo Obrazovaniia v Rossii*, Tipografiia, Peterburg.

Milovidova, E. (1929) *Zhenskii Vopros i Zhenskoe Dvizhenie*, Krasnii Proletarii, Moscow.

Pokrovskaia, M.I. (1917) 'Revoliutsiia i gumannost' ', *Zhenskii Vestnik*, no. 5–6.

Shapir, O. (1909) 'Pervii vserossiiskii zhenskii s'ezd', *Zhenskaia Mysl'*, no. 1.

Sipovskii, V.V. (1924) *Etapy Russkoi Mysli*, Karl Marx Publishing House, Peterburg.

Zhenshchina v Strane Sovetov (1938) Gospolitizdat, Moscow.

11 The women's movement in the USSR
A myth or a real challenge?

Valentina Konstantinova

INTRODUCTION

It is possible to conceptualise the developing independent women's movement in the USSR as a social movement of popular protest. Social movements of this type are a relatively recent phenomenon in the USSR and as yet are largely unexplored. These movements, while superficially similar to their counterparts in the west are noticeably different from them, owing to their very different economic, political, cultural and psychological roots and because of the heterogeneity of Soviet society. In this chapter I make an attempt to explain the emergence of these social movements in the *perestroika* period and the difficulties that they face after three generations of one party domination. It is only by setting the fledgling women's movement within this context that we can explain why it faces even greater difficulties organisationally and ideologically than its sister movements in the west. The chapter goes on to consider the current official structures for the representation of women, their inadequacies, and how women's issues have been left off the agenda of the new citizens' associations currently emerging in the USSR. In the light of this I go on to consider the new informal women's movement and the five discernible tendencies within it. Finally I report on the First Independent Women's Forum which was held at Dubna in April 1991 and speculate about the future of the women's movement in the USSR.

PERESTROIKA AND THE EMERGENCE OF NEW SOCIAL MOVEMENTS

There are a number of identifiable factors in the *perestroika* period contributing to the rise of new social movements. These include: distrust of the official state and social structures, Communist ideologies and socialist ideas; loss of credibility; citizens' alienation from a state which had subdued any manifestation of civil society, freedom and initiative on the part of the individual; inefficiency in both legislative and executive powers; violation of human rights; and ethnic conflict. Undoubtedly the appearance of these movements was stimulated by the 'democratisation' of society from above. Political pluralism, officially sanctioned by the leadership and accompanied by new political thinking and *glasnost'* (openness) – which provided the opportunity of discussing many issues about which there had previously been a silence – have also been crucial factors in explaining the emergence of these movements.

I want to suggest that a social movement is characterised by: free association; association of citizens supporting a common idea or pursuing similar objectives (though they may have differing views on the means of achieving their goals); a membership which is united by a common information network; and shared activities such as participation in meetings, demonstrations, gatherings, conferences, acts of civil disobedience and the formation of pressure groups and lobbies. Such movements emerged in the USSR because of changes in the moral and psychological environment: a sharp shift in values, orientations and attitudes; new standards of self-appraisal; a desire for self-realisation and a marked urge towards autonomy of the individual. Even though the 'Big Brother' and the inner censor still exist, with the *perestroika* period there came a greater candidness and honesty in speeches in the public sphere, which had the effect of stimulating a revival of morals in inter-personal relations, in politics and in the economy and an increased sense of individual freedom. Notions such as conscience and freedom of choice were reconsidered. Getting rid of the shell of false definitions has meant that people in the Soviet Union are striving to find their own position in society and are making their own contribution to reforming that society.

Nevertheless only a small part of the population is involved in these changes and one gets the impression that the majority of people, however supportive of reform, are not ready to participate actively in initiating radical economic and political reform. The objective reasons for this are linked to the specificity of the transitional period in Eastern Europe and the USSR. Totalitarian consciousness and the totalitarian state and social structures still exist, while the new democratic structures are developing slowly and with real difficulty. Among the subjective reasons for the masses' lack of involvement is inadequate political socialisation, which is partially explained by lack of information and strict censorship for the last seventy-odd years. Citizens remain relatively passive, fearing the likely changes in their society. In addition there is a lack of self-confidence and there are inconsistencies in policy amongst the country's leaders.

Reform is proceeding particularly slowly and painfully in the Soviet Union as compared to the Eastern European countries. In the latter some private sector, however small, had been retained and a nominal multi-party system existed. In contrast, in the Soviet Union three generations of Soviet people have lived under the yoke of a one-party system, a centralised and inefficient economy and a class ideology. Anything that served the interests of the liberation of the working class was deemed morally good, or, in the words of Stalin's minion Beria (in 1935), 'Our good will is a class good will. It is a good will that knows no mercy for the enemies of the working class' (Antonov-Ovseenko, 1988). Clemency, compassion, tolerance, kindness and love as human qualities were not encouraged and any manifestation of them was punishable. (In Stalin's time the colleagues of an imprisoned person were afraid openly to render financial or moral support to his or her family since they themselves could be suspected of sympathising and consequently imprisoned or sent to a concentration camp.)

Thus a psychology of intolerance, suspicion and constant enemy-hunting, both inside and outside the country, developed. The consequence for us as Soviet people was disunity and estrangement and a lack of mutual confidence; solidarity could only be manifested as a result of an order from above, from the 'boss'. Furthermore any initiative coming from an individual was punishable; all issues were resolved centrally and the individual was constantly in a state of serfdom to the state, a functionary or his or her boss.

Thus the country is now going through a difficult and contradictory period during which the mythology surrounding our conceptions about property, human rights, democracy and the market is being exposed. Public opinion polls indicate that many people are beginning to reject the old stereotypes and myths, but, at the same time, many remain in a state of confusion; the past may seem dreadful but the future is full of uncertainties. The confusion is not tempered by the fact that the myriad of democratic groupings which have emerged remain weak and unable to find a common platform.

As more and more people demonstrate this growing civil and political consciousness, the public sphere of Soviet society is becoming increasingly complex. More than twenty-five parties (including three or four large ones) have been registered in Russia, as well as nationalist movements and popular fronts. Despite acute environmental problems, the Green movement is still very weak, although in environmental 'hot spots' there are a number of well-organised democratic organisations. In addition there are a number of groups which have organised around human rights issues such as Memorial, the Moscow Helsinki Group (which was an underground group before *perestroika*, but which is now registered officially) and the Association of Victims of Political Repression. It is within this wider political context that the fledgling women's movement is also emerging.

THE EMERGENCE OF THE NEW INDEPENDENT WOMEN'S MOVEMENT

The conditions in which the new women's movement is struggling to emerge are even more difficult. The level of popular support for women's emancipation remains low – too low for there to be a positive conception of a women's movement. There remains a totalitarian way of thinking which is overlaid by a patriarchal mode of thinking and bolstered by traditional imperialist attitudes and Russian orthodox religious consciousness. In its guise of traditional Russian culture, this chauvinism permeates every level of society, from political elites, cultural workers and parliamentarians to mass levels of consciousness, and forms the stereotypes held by the majority of men and women.

After the 1917 Revolution the 'woman question' was reduced to a problem of class struggle. Women's issues were viewed solely in terms of the common struggle of the working class. The 1917 Revolution granted women equal rights with men, and enshrined them in the constitution. But because the class struggle was given primacy the Bolsheviks did not want to recognise any independent women's movement and were hostile to feminism. As Marina Malysheva has recounted, after the Revolution the independent women's movement ceased to exist, as did independent worker's movements and political parties. Even in the arts and sciences any 'dissenting' thought or movement disappeared. During the 'stagnation' years of the late Brezhnev period Soviet academic science criticised the second wave of feminism in the west as 'bourgeois'. Throughout the 1970s and the 1980s women's issues and problems were proclaimed to have been resolved, despite both evident and concealed discrimination against women in employment, including inferior and unhealthy conditions of work and night shifts, low pay and lack of promotion (Zakharova *et al.*, 1989). Outside the work-place women continued to shoulder the major responsibility for domestic tasks, endured high rates of infant and maternal mortality, increased rates of abortion, insanitary conditions in maternity departments and inadequate or non-existent medicines and contraceptives (Mamonova, 1984).

Because Russian and Soviet literature has been dominated by the 'matchless genius' of male writers it has contributed to a very odd and derogatory image of Soviet women. According to the US researcher Francine du Plessix Gray two images of women predominate in nineteenth-century Russian literature, which are based on Russian puritanical morality: (1) the idealisation of the moral virtues of women, leading to the depiction of women as morally superior to men; (2) at the same time, negative images of women's sensuality and particularly their intellect (du Plessix Gray, 1989: 118).

In the Soviet period the emancipation of women was not even an issue in the ongoing debate between Slavophile and Westerniser authors. Not even prominent advocates of democracy such as Andrei Sakharov (who, according to People's Deputy Starovoitova is the successor to such Westernisers as Radishchev, Chaadaev and Herzen) view it as an issue (Starovoitova, 1990). When the question of women is raised it is in order to encourage a return to a traditional view of women's role. In 1990 Solzhenitsyn, a Slavophile, published an article entitled 'How are we to structure Russia: feasible considerations'. In it he ties the role of women exclusively to the family: 'A normal family almost ceases to exist with us. But the sickness of the family is the backbone disease of the state. Today the family is the key to saving our future. The woman must be given a chance to return to the family to bring up children and men's pay must reflect this, though with anticipated unemployment in the initial stages it will not work successfully right away; some families would be better off if the woman continues to have a job for the time being' (Solzhenitsyn, 1990). The same sentiments are echoed by Rasputin (1990), Belov (1990), Tolstaia (1990) and Tokareva (McLaughlin, 1989). They all maintain that one of the reasons for prostitution, crime and drug abuse among teenagers and other social problems in contemporary Soviet society is the fact that women are no longer performing their 'natural', 'predestined' role in society. Russian imperialism has meant that a Russian conception of women's issues has been foisted upon the other republics and territories that make up the former Russian empire. No consideration was ever given to the national, cultural, religious and economic differences. This has actually exacerbated conditions for women in Central Asia, for instance leading to suicide by self- immolation (*Pravda*, 1988).

Religion is once more playing an increasingly important part in society. The Russian Orthodox Church is deeply conservative and patriarchal, and its repressive attitude to women has emerged unchanged by the *perestroika* reforms.

Throughout the history of the Soviet state the position of women has been determined by state-defined demographic and economic imperatives: either women must be productive workers or they must stay at home; at other times they are expected to combine the two, but never have they been able to make their own choices or to formulate the issues themselves. Currently official policy is to encourage women to return to the home and to provide some support for working mothers. Women are being reminded that they have primary responsibility for the domestic sphere, particularly child-care. What has been the response of the formal (official) and informal women's movement to the current situation?

OFFICIAL STRUCTURES AND THE REPRESENTATION OF WOMEN

Officially the women's movement in the USSR is represented by the Soviet Women's Committee, by a network of women's councils and of late by the Parliamentary Committees on Women and Family Affairs and the Protection of Maternity and Childhood of the Supreme Soviets of the USSR and the RSFSR (Russian Soviet Federal Socialist Republic). In addition the Department of Women's Affairs of the USSR Council of Ministers and the State Committee on Family and Demographic Policy of the Council of Ministers of the RSFSR all officially represent the women's movement in the Soviet Union. The Women's Councils were reconstituted in 1986 when the 'Statute on Women's Councils' was prepared and then circulated at a regional level. Written in dry bureaucratic language it is also highly ideological. Paragraph 1 says: 'Councils of women are instruments of independent public activity of the population and unite all Soviet women in the cause of Communist creative efforts.' Paragraph 2 declares: 'Councils of women engage women in social and political activity, promote their role in supervising affairs of both society and government as well as in productive life, educating them in the spirit of glorious revolutionary fighting and in the labour traditions of the Soviet people and in so doing contribute to the consolidation of the socialist way of life' (Polozhenie o Zhensovetakh, 1986).

There are 240,000 women's councils in the country, imposed from above and elected in an undemocratic way (basically the leadership of the councils was formed on orders from the management of enterprises and offices, trades unions and party committees). 'Pocket women's councils', lacking support from the grass roots and any real authority or funds, are kept busy with handling orders for food commodities in short supply and consumer goods, summer camp accommodation for children and assistance to large families.

There is a Committee on Women's Affairs, Family and Democratic Policy of the Supreme Soviet of the USSR which consists of 69 members: 39 men and 30 women, and a similar Committee of the Russian Parliament. A State Programme on the Improvement of the Position of Women, Family, Maternity and Child-care is being developed. The Institute of Socio-Economic Problems of the Population of the Academy of Sciences of the USSR was the co-ordinating organisation for working out a positional paper for this state programme. The positional paper was not accepted by the Union Parliament because its approach was deemed to be far too egalitarian by the conservative Union Parliament.

The activities of both committees are still concentrated on developing state programmes so as to satisfy the concrete needs of women and children; these needs are connected with lack of food for children, child-care, benefits for working mothers, improvement of bad working conditions, etc., rather than the development of national machinery for the achievement of equal status for men and women.

In fact the women deputies on the Committee on Women's Affairs in the Union Parliament are selected simply by a quota assigned to the Soviet Women's Committee. Women constitute about 15 per cent of People's Deputies, a fifth of them being elected from the Soviet Women's Committee. Among the deputies elected from so-called 'public' organisations women constitute 23.5 per cent (176 deputies). The same number of women deputies is elected from territorial and national territorial electoral districts.

Thus, although one may get the impression that steps are actively being taken to tackle women's issues, in fact the official women's movement remains part of the establishment, which does not have the support of the electorate and is therefore incapable of representing women's interests in a democratic way. On the other hand the unofficial women's movement, which is developing in the form of new alliances amongst women and new women's councils, is still too weak to exert any substantial pressure on existing structures from below. The result is that a vacuum is forming.

'Democracy minus women is not democracy'

This slogan of the Independent Women's Democratic Initiative formed in 1990 expresses the inseparability of democratisation and the resolution of the woman question. Democracy is vital to the emancipation of women. Democracy implies equal representation in governmental branches, but as United Nations reports make clear, only 2–3 per cent of women globally take part in decision-making procedures. Women in the USSR are very poorly represented at all levels of government, particularly in its highest echelons. Among the people's deputies of the USSR Supreme Soviet women account for only 15.7 per cent, half of whom were elected by public organisations, such as the Soviet Women's Committee, the Communist Party of the USSR, the Peace Committee and the Veterans' Committee.

In the Supreme Soviet of the USSR women constitute 18.5 per cent of the total number. Prior to *perestroika* a stable level of women's representation was maintained by the application of a quota system for women. Recently the quota system has been partially abandoned and as a result there has been a reduction in the number of women deputies in Parliament. Thus the country's policies are being shaped largely without women's participation. 'Democracy' with an evidently male face is not capable of resolving the accumulated problems of women's issues nor for that matter of the emancipation of society as a whole.

What are the benefits of *perestroika* in the USSR for women on the one hand and what is women's contribution to the restructuring process on the other? The new reality in the USSR includes more debate on the problems of women in the mass media and new research on women's issues reflecting differing views on the emancipation of women, and some active participation of women in economic and political reforms. Nevertheless the question remains as to why the majority of Soviet women have so far failed to use this opportunity of becoming actively involved in the debate or in the processes of change themselves. In drawing up a strategy for the women's movement it is vital that we try and answer this question and take account of its ideological and political context.

Firstly, the informal women's movement lacks a theoretical, philosophical and ideological foundation. For over seventy years class has been given ideological primacy in a situation which denies the very existence of women's issues as a separate and specific problem and refuses to recognise the independent women's movement. After the 'socialist revolution' the women's issue was not regarded as important and feminism – with its concept of patriarchy, male chauvinism and sisterhood – has also been resolutely refuted, even distorted, by academic scholars. Feminism is a multi-faceted phenomenon promoting women's dignity, sexual equality, and a vision of a society which has a greater concern for inter-personal relationships, more humane relationships between men and women and a more equitable and non-violent world. Perhaps it was precisely because feminism symbolises resistance to totalitarianism, orthodoxy and patriarchal structures that the Bolsheviks, Stalinists and the upholders of stagnation opposed it.

Secondly, there are political factors which determine the strategic independence of the women's movement. I would suggest that attitudes towards feminism act as a kind of litmus paper for testing the reality of political pluralism and the new political thinking. Only 6 per cent of the population express confidence in the Communist Party (Zaslavskaia, 1991: 3) and yet so far there is no appreciation within society that the new informal independent women's movement may actually facilitate democratisation and the humanisation of society as a whole. Real political pluralism is reflected not just in the existence of an independent women's movement but also a concern by other movements and parties about women's liberation.

THE STATUS OF WOMEN IN THE NEW ASSOCIATIONS IN THE USSR

If one analyses the documents of new citizens' associations the number of women active in them in comparison with men is low. It is also evident that the agenda of the new social movements, political parties, politicised associations of citizens, committees of social defence, human rights groups and independent trade unions do not concern themselves with the problem of how to achieve equality between men and women, the emancipation of women or women's rights. Only parties with so-called 'pro-socialist' or 'patriotic-democratic' orientation mention the problems of women and even then they are approached either from a traditional patriarchal angle (the importance of the role of women for strengthening the family (the Rossiiski Narodnii Front) or from a standpoint which emphasises the extension of social benefits for working mothers such as prohibition of night shifts, prolongation of parental leave and the sharing of child-care among parents (the Socialist Party).

There are no official statistics on the number of women members of parties and social movements, and besides, some of them are subject to constant changes, fusions, alliances and splits. My information is based on interviews with party leaders. Analysis of party membership indicates that women are very poorly represented as members amongst those parties which have a more formal political face. For instance, in the Democratic Party less than 1 per cent of members are women, in the Socialist Party only 2–3 per cent, in the Social Democratic Party of Russia a mere 1–2 per cent are women and in the Party of Urban and Rural Owners 10 per cent. But this should not be read as evidence of the conservatism of women, as some authors suggest it is. On the contrary I would argue that there is clear evidence of a new interpretation of the notion of 'politics' itself and of an understanding amongst women of the importance of prioritising global problems whether they be ecological, anti-nuclear or concerned with human rights. While the membership of the Green Party is not great, a third of the membership is female. In the Transnational Radical Party women account for 30 per cent of the membership and in the Blue Movement (For the Social Ecology of the Human Being) 50 per cent of the 100,000 members are women. In the Christian-Democratic Union, 50 per cent are women and in the Union of Democratic Forces (founded by Andrei Sakharov) 40–50 per cent of the members are women.

Nevertheless, even where they constitute half the membership, women are very poorly represented among the leadership of these associations. For instance in the Committee for Social Defence half of the membership is female but only 1 of the 4 leaders is a woman. The Centrist Bloc (an alliance of 23 parties which Sakharov's Union of Democratic Forces is joining), has only 2 women leaders out of 18. Nevertheless women constitute nearly half of the leaders of the Blue Movement.

Women are very active participants, and on equal terms with men, in the protest meetings in Moscow, Petersburg and other big cities. In addition women are becoming members of the Independent Trade Union, *Spravedlivost'*. In Petersburg there are 10 women out of 60 members. The threat of unemployment is probably stimulating women's membership of independent trade unions. In late 1990 and early 1991 kindergarten workers and physicians threatened to go on strike. In February 1991 secondary school teachers in Moscow went on strike. In Moscow 87 per cent of secondary school teachers are women and a third of all schools were involved in the strike action. Thus for the first time in the history of the Soviet state representatives of the predominantly female professions were either threatening strike action or were actually on strike. In the City Strike Committee women constitute a majority, but this is a professional movement; the strikers do not have formal political demands.

THE NEW INFORMAL WOMEN'S MOVEMENT

> Weak is my voice but my will power does not slacken . . .
>
> (Akhmatova, 1976: 69)

Over the past two years the informal women's movement in the USSR has been growing. In Moscow alone about fifty women's organisations have been registered. The historian U. Chafe suggests that for the formation of the women's movement the following are preconditions:

1 A society that is predisposed to reform;
2 A convincing platform around which support can be mustered; and
3 A substantial grouping of women convinced of the need to end discrimination against women (cited in Nechemias, 1991).

Whether or not these three conditions exist in the USSR currently is difficult to say. Without doubt the country is in a state of reform but it is not commonly acknowledged that women are discriminated against. Most women would concur that they shoulder a double burden and that conditions at work are deteriorating. As for the third factor only a small number of women are ready to respond to the appeal of doing away with discrimination. Possibly the probability of their losing their jobs before men may force women to recognise discrimination and the need for solidarity with other women. While the preconditions for the growth of the women's movement are similar to those for any social movement there are also specific factors, including discontent provoked by the growing discrimination against women in the work-place, at home and in public life in this period of restructuring. The burden of the transitional period in the USSR has already fallen on the shoulders of women in the form of redundancies at enterprises and offices (women with children going first), shortages in goods and services, a rising cost of living which particularly affects single mothers, widows and pensioners. These factors, combined with an aspiration for economic independence, provided some women with sufficient incentive to organise in order to create new jobs in small business ventures (for instance the associations of business women – 'Eva' and 'Geia'). Women have also organised in the creative arts (in the associations 'Creation' and 'Transfiguration').

The new women's movement is emerging during a difficult economic, political and ideological period of restructuring. Different women's alliances and associations are expressing their views on important issues in public life such as democracy, national sovereignty, pluralism, transition to the market, feminism, reform in the armed forces and religion.

In the USSR there are five discernible trends in the informal women's movement: feminist, democratic, neo-traditional, undemocratic and radical. This classification is somewhat arbitrary and it must be realised that the movement is dynamic. While these are only trends they have a definite potential which remains unrecognised in official circles by most women, and by the public at large. They all have one thing in common, a concern for the status of women. They differ, however, in their interpretation of the causes of women's subordination as well as the way of overcoming it.

The feminist movement

The feminist movement in the USSR is only just developing. The feminist wing is represented by two or three groups in Moscow and Petersburg and made up largely of social scientists and researchers, university graduates and journalists. Most of these women are already familiar with the feminist movement in the west and with the knowledge that women in their own country are discriminated against. In defending feminism, which is largely ignored by public opinion and by official channels, these groups represent a tiny oppositional intellectual minority, although they are no longer persecuted by the authorities as they used to be. In the past members of the feminist club 'Maria' in Petersburg and the authors of the 'Women in Russia' Almanac – T. Mamonova, Iu. Voznesenskaia, N. Malakhovskaia and T. Goricheva – were all compelled to emigrate in 1980. O. Lipovskaia, a Soviet feminist well known in the west, is publishing a '*samizdat*' feminist magazine, *Women's Reading*, in Petersburg. The Association SAFO (Free Association of Feminist Organisations) stands for a cultural renewal of society and for attaining the social equality of men and women. Recently members of SAFO set up groups of co-counsellors for women in Moscow. LOTOS (League for Emancipation from Stereotypes), an informal group of women researchers and advocates of egalitarian feminism, has functioned for three years. Its members use the mass media, deliver lectures and maintain contact with other feminist groups. The group challenges and defies the existing stereotypes of women and women's role in society.

The new feminist approach in academic research is being employed to investigate gender relations in all realms of social life, to construct data banks on women, women researchers in the USSR and abroad and women's organisations both native and foreign, to set up research centres and to develop an information network for the new women's movement. These are some of the objectives of the Centre for Gender Studies of the Institute on Socio-Economic Problems of the USSR.

Currently, it seems, we are witnessing the beginning of the dissemination of feminist thinking beyond the sector of middle-class intellectual women who laid the social groundwork of a feminist wing. For instance, women employed at the KAMAZ autoplant decided to set up a Committee on Equal Opportunity after attending a presentation by the British scholar Liz Bargh.

Undemocratic and democratic wings

I want to suggest that organisations within this tendency are characterised by a fairly traditional view of politics and political activity. One
can distinguish between democratic and undemocratic wings on a
number of criteria, not only on their attitude to democracy, to
perestroika, pluralism, national sovereignty, the shift to the market
economy, but also on the interpretation of the causes of women's
subordination.

Representatives of the democratic alignments believe that the
resolution of the 'woman question' is dependent on the achievement
of democratic structures, the unification of women and their fight for
equal rights as well as their participation in the administration of
society. One of the democrats' demands is that there should be an
adequate representation of women at all levels of decision-making. The
democratic wing includes various organisations that differ in their
strategies. The Committee of Soldiers' Mothers (in Russia) and
identical organisations in other republics are the most active women's
alignments, and seek the enactment of a bill to create an alternative civil
service, a similar bill on deserters and the elimination of construction
battalions in the army. Other organisations include the Inter-Regional
Political Club in the city of Zhukovskii (near Moscow) and embryonic
women's parties have appeared in Petersburg and Tomsk. The political
strategy of the women's political party in Petersburg is only just
becoming evident and there is a suspicion that it is ready to use
undemocratic methods in practice. In addition there is a Committee on
Equal Opportunities in the city of Naberezhnie Chelny and a new type of
non-hierarchical socio-political women's organisation called the Association of Independent Women's Democratic Initiative. The motto of this
Association is 'Democracy minus women is not democracy'. The
association amalgamates various women's alignments that support
democratic objectives and supports the demand that women should be
represented in all echelons of government, challenging patriarchy as the
rule of men and calling for the economic independence of women.

The undemocratic or conservative wing of the women's movement is
represented by the nomenclature or state machinery personnel and
many (although not all) of the leaders of the women's councils at the
republican, city and district levels. In the Baltic republics these
nomenclature women who participate in the official structures come
from both the native and immigrant populations, including a certain
group of Russian speaking women who, having become aware of the
discrimination against them as an ethnic minority, put the blame on

perestroika. In 1990 in Kuibyshev an All-Russian Conference, 'For a Socialist Future for our Children', took place; 50 people participated, most of whom were representatives of the Russian-speaking population of the Baltic republics and women from the RSFSR. The conference called for a hunger strike in the event of a transition to the market economy being announced, denounced *perestroika*, democracy, pluralism and defended the Communist Party of the Soviet Union as the only force capable of saving socialist achievements. Hackneyed declarations such as 'those not with us are against us' were voiced and there were reports of a new women's organisation called 'Nike', which opposes the emancipation of women. The undemocratic wing expresses anti-restructuring sentiments, as its members fear that they will lose both power and privilege and are prepared to sabotage reforms. In the republics these sentiments are exacerbated by inter-national conflict.

The radical trend in the new women's movement has so far not gained its proper shape. Radical feminism as it exists in the west has not as yet emerged in the Soviet Union. In Moscow a club for lesbians and gay men operates quite openly. In September 1990 prostitutes blocked traffic at one of the city's hotels, demanding legalisation of prostitution. E. Debrianskaia, a representative of the Libertarian Party that upholds the rights of sexual minorities including women, distributed contraceptives during the demonstration.

The neo-traditional trend is represented by women's clubs and associations for women with shared interests (such as fitness) and by professional organisations such as the International Association of Women Cinematographers and the Moscow Club of Women Journalists. Nevertheless the neo-traditional trend has also gone through changes; associations for business women and professional advancement are also being set up.

THE FIRST INDEPENDENT WOMEN'S FORUM, DUBNA, 1991

The fledgling informal women's movement is not as yet a political force presenting a real challenge and capable of effectively influencing socio-political life. None the less, it already has definite potential, as evidenced by the First Independent Women's Forum held on 29–31 March 1991 in the town of Dubna in the Moscow region. It was attended by 180 people representing 48 women's organisations from 25 Soviet cities and towns. In contrast to the events being organised under the auspices of the Soviet Women's Committee this was an open forum: it was advertised in several newspapers and on the radio. The forum's programme was put together by researchers and representatives of several informal women's groups: the Centre for Gender Studies (at the Institute of Socio-Economic Problems of the Population, Academy of Sciences of the USSR), the group SAFO (Free Association of Feminist Organisations) and journalists from Petersburg. At the plenary sessions the following speeches were delivered: 'Women as the object and subject of social change'; 'The women's movement: a view from within'; 'The convention on the abolition of all forms of discrimination against women: the fate of the document in the USSR'; 'Women as objects of consumption'; 'Women and market relations'; 'Democracy and women'; 'Why it is difficult to fight discrimination against women: imaginary and real reasons'; 'The image of women in the media' and 'The participation of women in democratic movements 1988–91'. After the plenary sessions, the forum continued its work in four pre-planned sections: (1) women and market relations and the enterprise; (2) women and politics and the problems of the independent women's movement; (3) problems of women's artistic creativity; and (4) discrimination against women in patriarchal culture. There was also an unplanned section on violence against women.

The discussion which took place in the section on women and politics clearly reflected the polarisation of political forces in Soviet society (although the overwhelming majority of participants at the forum were supporters of democratic change). Opinions were divided on the following questions: the preservation of the Union, the role of the Communist Party in society and the consolidation of women's organisations. The majority of participants in the sections thought that it was still too early to talk about the consolidation of the women's movement and for this reason it was decided to create an independent women's information network, that is, horizontal information links. The forum decided to issue a concluding statement. In the section 'Women and market relations and enterprise' the participants outlined a number of desired measures: the creation of a bank of commercial information for women entrepreneurs; the creation of a support fund for women's enterprises; the development of constant contacts with the media; the creation of alternative forms of finding work for women who have lost their jobs; and the development of programmes of training, psychological adaptation and testing aimed at various socio-professional groups of women.

In the unplanned section, 'Violence against women', the question of violence against women – rape, sexual harassment at work and battering – was raised for the first time publicly. Until then discussion of such issues had been a taboo subject in Soviet society.

The majority of participants were independent, democratically thinking women and this made the forum both interesting and challenging. Judging by the preliminary results of a survey conducted among the forum's participants, women flagged up three basic tasks for the women's movement to tackle:

1 the overcoming of existing stereotypes, feminist education and mass conciousness-raising among women;
2 the achievement of genuine equality and the realisation of our rights; and
3 the preparation of women candidates for office.

Other tasks of the women's movement mentioned included: mutual aid, the uniting of women, the revival of spirituality in society, ecology and charity. Women who gathered at the forum expressed their desire for freedom, a worthy life and mutual respect between people.

The forum was attended by 26 foreign guests (from the UK, the USA, Sweden, Germany, Canada, Austria, France and India). At a round table on the problems of the feminist movement there was a lively discussion of feminism in these countries.

Lack of information makes it difficult as yet to discuss a 'post-forum effect'. On the basis of the information we do have, however, we can say that three tendencies have become evident. Firstly, a new, although small, independent women's movement has been created. Secondly, women's organisations – mainly of the democratic and feminist trends – have developed contacts and, in some cases, united. Thirdly, already existing women's organisations and politicised citizens' associations have united.

For example, following the Dubna forum the Voters' Clubs (who supported the democratic forces in the local elections) and women's organisations in the city of Perm united. At the all-union level, the Independent Women's Democratic Organisation has begun co-operating with the All-Union Peace Society (a coalition pacifist organisation) on issues such as the introduction of an alternative military service.

Nevertheless the women's movement, as we have seen, is still a fledgling movement lacking its own ideology, tasks and methods of struggle. There is a danger therefore that the 'woman question' will once again be dissolved into the general political arena and the women's movement manipulated by other movements and parties which are in fact not concerned with the real issues for women. The CPSU actively publicises the problems of the women's movement and has organised departments in the Central Committee of the CPSU, the Russian

Communist Party and at regional party committee level. The central party organisation of Moscow and Petersburg are publishing women's newspapers and the first independent women's forum was given a positive evaluation in the Communist press (thus indirectly rehabilitating feminism). In such a context it is likely that non-feminist women leaders will be put forward. For instance at the Congress of the United Women's Party in Petersburg one of the members of the party declared that feminism is being planted in the USSR by the CIA and the CPSU! In addition we should not anticipate any prioritisation of the problems relating to the emancipation of women in the USSR as a result of alliances between existing independent women's organisations and political citizens' associations; the most we can expect is that they will ensure that these problems are put on the agenda.

CONCLUSION

Thus the women's movement in the USSR as a new, independent, autonomous movement has a humanitarian potential addressed to the individual and his or her dignity, and an emphasis on equal opportunities for men and women and interpersonal relations as well as a higher quality of everyday life. Hopefully its resistance to orthodoxy will facilitate the democratisation of society and the formation of a national consensus so necessary for the stability in the country and the world. It is not something that will happen overnight and there is a hard road ahead, but the new movement acts as a light at the end of the tunnel.

REFERENCES

Akhmatova, A. (1976) *Poems*, Moscow, Raduga.
Antonov-Ovseenko, A. (1988) 'Karera Palacha', *Zvezda*, no. 9.
Belov, I. (1990) 'Vse vperedi', *Nash Sovremennik*, no. 3.
Mamanova, T. (ed.) (1984) *Women and Russia*, Beacon Press.
McLaughlin, S. (1989) 'In interview with Viktoria Tokareva', *Canadian Women's Studies*, Winter, no. 4: 75–6.
Nechemias, A. (1991) 'The prospects for a Soviet women's movement: opportunities and obstacles', in J. Butterfield and J. Sedaitis (eds) *Perestroika from Below: Social Movements in the Soviet Union*, Westview Press.
du Plessix Gray, F. (1990) *Soviet Women: Walking the Tightrope*, Doubleday.
Polozhenie o Zhensovetakh, 1986.
Rasputin, V. (1990) 'Cherchez la femme', *Nash Sovremennik*, no. 3: 169–72.
Solzhenitsyn, A. (1990) 'Kak nam obustroit Rossiiu', *Literaturnaia Gazeta*, 18 September 1990: 3–6.
Starovoitova, G. (1990) Speech at the opening session of the Founding Conference of the Helsinki Citizen's Assembly, Prague, 19–21 October 1990.

Tolstaia, T. (1990) 'Notes from underground', *New York Review of Books*, vol. 37, no. 9: 3–7.
Zakharova, N., Posadskaia, A. and Rimashevskaia, N. (1989) 'Kak my reshaem zhenskii vopros', *Kommunist*, March, no. 4.
Zaslavskaia, J. (1991) 'Kogda zabluzhdaetsa vlast', *Moskovskie Novosti*, no. 13.

Name index

Subject index